The Scarlet Mile

The Scarlet Mile

A SOCIAL HISTORY OF PROSTITUTION IN KALGOORLIE, 1894–2004

Elaine McKewon

UNIVERSITY OF WESTERN AUSTRALIA PRESS

First published in 2005 by
University of Western Australia Press
Crawley, Western Australia 6009
www.uwapress.uwa.edu.au

National Library of Australia
Cataloguing-in-Publication entry:

McKewon, Elaine, 1966–   .
    The scarlet mile: a social history of prostitution in Kalgoorlie, 1894–2004.

    Bibliography.
    Includes index.
    ISBN 1 920694 22 6.

    1. Prostitutes—Western Australia—Kalgoorlie.   2. Prostitution—Western Australia—Kalgoorlie.   3. Gold mines and mining—Social aspects—Western Australia.   4. Women—Western Australia—Social conditions.   5. Western Australia—Social conditions—20th century.
    I. Title.

306.742099416

Cover image: Girls writing on blackboard outside Hay Street brothel, © Ainslie and Garwood 2005

Produced by Benchmark Publications Pty Ltd, Melbourne
Consultant editor Amanda Curtin, Curtin Communications, Perth
Designed by Sandra Nobes, Tou-Can Design, Melbourne
Typeset in 11pt Bembo by Lasertype, Perth
Printed by BPA Print Group

For my mother, Theresa, and my brother Mark,
whose love and encouragement
have enabled my every achievement

Foreword

Prostitutes, police, politicians, popularity, platitudes, as well as hypocrisy and history—it is all here. In its evocation of life in the Hay Street brothels of Kalgoorlie, *The Scarlet Mile* allows us to look into the soul of a country town and also into our own hearts to consider our behaviour, views and values.

You will cry at the plight of the abandoned wives and single women driven into the brothels for an income and a life for themselves and sometimes their children and other family members.

You will laugh at the hypocrisy of the media, churches, police and people who judge and condemn these 'fallen women' as the source of ills and troubles in society.

You will be amazed at the strength and skills of the women in dealing with their work and low status while supporting themselves and their children—and giving generously to the town of Kalgoorlie when times were hard.

You will be impressed by the resilience of the women and their ability to support each other while building strong and cohesive workplaces, yet finding time for some fun and entertainment.

You will be happy to read that many of the women retire into a comfortable old age, and find pleasure reminiscing with their children and grandchildren about their time as one of the Hay Street 'girls'.

You will applaud the ability of the women to negotiate within a hostile town culture and develop their business, while dealing with an ever-changing 'legal' framework.

You will enjoy the story of the brothels becoming part of the recreational life of Kalgoorlie, as on warm evenings and weekends local people strolled down Hay Street to have a look, with some sneaking back at night to become customers.

You will perhaps become part of the tourist scene of Kalgoorlie, where people come from far and wide to experience the infamous red-light district.

You will gain an understanding of the attending injustices as you read of how the police, local council and state government of the time perceived the need to control the brothels and the women—and how the police have controlled them through implementing the Containment Policy, a policy that was never passed through state legislature and into law.

You will ponder the hypocrisy of the social mores, then and now, that see women being prosecuted for giving men pleasure and men not being pursued legally.

This history is an indictment of Australian society's treatment of women—women who should have union coverage and be protected as workers with decent working conditions, instead of being designated 'fallen angels' on whom an oppressive, patriarchal and hypocritical society dumps blame, guilt and anger.

I hope that the experience of reading this book will lead you to become a voice for the abandonment of the illegal Containment Policy, the decriminalisation of prostitution and the legitimisation through Parliament and the union movement of sex workers' rights—be they women, men, gays or transsexuals.

Enjoy!

JANN MCFARLANE
Former Federal Member for Stirling

Contents

Abbreviations and conversions

ABC   Australian Broadcasting Commission (now Australian Broadcasting Corporation)
ATO   Australian Taxation Office
CIB   Criminal Investigation Branch
DLI   Department of Land Information
SIERA   Support, Information, Education and Referral Association
STD   sexually transmitted disease
WEL   Women's Electoral Lobby

1 mile	1.61 kilometres
1 foot	30.5 centimetres
1 inch	25.4 millimetres

Australian currency changed from pounds, shillings and pence to dollars and cents in 1966. Because of variations in currency values over time, actual conversions are difficult. At the time of the currency changeover, the following conversions applied:

1 penny (1d)	1 cent
1 shilling (1s)	10 cents
1 pound (£1)	2 dollars

Acknowledgments

I would like to give special thanks to the people of Kalgoorlie-Boulder who agreed to be interviewed for *The Scarlet Mile*, including local residents and authorities, and in particular the women who worked as Hay Street madams and workers during the 1960s to the 1990s. Their candour and commitment to sharing their stories have helped to create a valuable historical record.

A number of people and organisations provided historical documents and photographs to be used in this history, and I am especially grateful to those who allowed their images to be used gratis: Professor Raelene Frances, the Museum of the Goldfields, the Department of Land Information, 'Judy', Leigh Varis-Beswick, Elma, Carmel Migro, Irene, Mary-Anne Kenworthy and the City of Kalgoorlie-Boulder. I would also like to thank Lynne Smith of *The West Australian* and Adrian Kenyon of Phoenix Communications, who substantially reduced their organisations' usual fees for reproducing copyright images in this educational volume.

I would like to express my great appreciation to all staff at the J. S. Battye Library in Perth for their tireless commitment to training and assisting researchers to access the mountain of information on public record. Over the course of my research, some people have also gone above and beyond the call of duty to assist me, and I would like to thank Eddie Piper, former treasurer of the City of Kalgoorlie-Boulder (now the city's director, Corporate Services), for taking the time to contact me to arrange my first regional radio interview to reach the people of the goldfields; Andy Biliczka, former administrative officer at the City of Kalgoorlie-Boulder, for always cheerfully expediting my research into the council's historical records; Ray Delbridge, former councillor of the City of Kalgoorlie-Boulder and

Manufacturing Workers Union official, for introducing me to some of the goldfields' more resilient characters, who certainly added a special texture and perspective to this history; and Nigel Tapp, former chief of staff at *The Kalgoorlie Miner*, for his early news coverage of my research, and for the generous hospitality I enjoyed as a guest in his home whenever I visited Kalgoorlie on 'official business'.

I am enormously thankful to those people who directly supported me in researching and writing *The Scarlet Mile*: Mary-Anne Kenworthy, for conceiving the idea of this history book and then seeking me out and offering preliminary funding to get the project off the ground, which provided a lifeline for me to continue researching the sex industry in Western Australia; Professor Raelene Frances of the University of New South Wales, for her ground-breaking research on prostitution in Western Australia during the years 1895–1939, and for her constructive comments on the first drafts of the manuscript; goldfields historian Norma King, for recording a power of information about the lives of women pioneers; and Professor John Selwood of the University of Winnipeg, for his enduring friendship and support, and for his helpful comments on the first drafts of the chapters. I also owe a great debt of gratitude to my editor, Amanda Curtin, for her highly skilled and thorough work on the manuscript, which helped to further strengthen *The Scarlet Mile*.

I have also had the benefit of friends who helped take the sting out of having to work full time while writing *The Scarlet Mile*, and for this I would like to thank Jann McFarlane, Vivienne and Millan, Robert Tait, Pieta McCarthy, Craig Anderton, Digby Saunders, Paul 'Paolo' Ruffini, and Peter 'Blackus' King, whom I'll always remember as quite a character in his own right, and for his stoic support for *The Scarlet Mile*. I must also thank the staff at the Queens Tavern in Mount Lawley, who often furnished me with lovely pints of Guinness and warm hospitality as I wrote and edited the manuscript in the evenings and on weekends.

I am fortunate to have had the encouragement of my family in New Orleans, especially Aunts Camille and Mary, Linda and David, Charles and Dawn, Joan and Yves, Johnny and Gail, Glenn and Lorré, and Mark (Sr and Jr) and Cindy. With respect to my life in Australia, I owe my greatest debt of gratitude to my husband, Ian Grant, for his compassionate and fiercely intellectual nature, for providing a tower of support whenever I found myself 'under siege', and for his insightful and constructive reviews of this manuscript and all my scribblings over the past decade.

ELAINE McKEWON
January 2005

Introduction

To millions of people in Australia and around the world, Kalgoorlie is famous for two things: goldmining and brothels. The Hay Street brothels in Kalgoorlie have operated openly for a hundred years, unofficially regulated and approved by police authorities and the local council. No other town in Australia has had such a stable and open red-light district. At the same time, and despite the historical social significance of the Hay Street brothels in Kalgoorlie, prostitution has hardly rated a mention in most history books.

The Scarlet Mile charts the history of prostitution in Kalgoorlie during the years 1894–2004. Researching this 'hidden history' presented a constant challenge, since prostitution has been so sparsely documented in the official and public records of Western Australia.

Prostitution itself is not illegal in Western Australia, although most prostitution-related activities, such as soliciting and keeping premises for the purpose of prostitution, are criminal offences under the state's *Police Act 1892*. Yet in a significant departure from this official policy of prohibition, police authorities in Kalgoorlie have never seriously sought to eradicate brothels; they have instead granted criminal immunity to a limited number of brothels, in order to 'contain' the activity and enforce unofficial restrictions on the businesses and the work force. This informal policy of selective policing came to be known as the Containment Policy.

Meanwhile, the powerful social stigma associated with prostitution has strongly discouraged sex workers from speaking openly about their work. In the absence of open dialogue, popular misconceptions have obscured the history and even the nature of the sex industry. Often what people think they know about prostitution is actually based on conjecture, prejudices and myths that have been handed down unchallenged from one generation to the next.

1

The Scarlet Mile aims to give 'scarlet women' a voice that they have been denied historically, while offering general readers and scholars a rare insight into the lives of prostitutes in Kalgoorlie. Although the book has been carefully researched and referenced for academic use, it is intended to be as entertaining as it is enlightening. Apart from humanity's deep and abiding interest in all matters sexual, many people would be fascinated to learn 'what really goes on' behind the bright lights of Hay Street, and why brothels have always been such a prominent social institution in Kalgoorlie.

Historical research for *The Scarlet Mile* involved mostly primary sources. The early history was pieced together using information gathered from Kalgoorlie Municipal Council and Kalgoorlie Roads Board minute books, historical maps of the early town site, archived oral histories and personal diaries, old newspapers, property title searches, history books written on Kalgoorlie, previous academic research, and my interviews with long-term Kalgoorlie-Boulder residents, whose recollections date as far back as the early 1920s. I would especially like to acknowledge the ground-breaking research of Raelene Frances (formerly Davidson), whose Masters thesis provided a wealth of information and analysis regarding prostitution in Western Australia during the years 1895–1939.

The more recent history focuses on interviews with women who worked as sex workers and madams in the Hay Street brothels during the 1960s to the 1990s. These women spoke candidly about their lives, their work, their reasons for entering the sex industry, their living conditions under the now infamous Containment Policy and their aspirations for the future. The book also records the response of the people of Kalgoorlie-Boulder to changes in the Containment Policy in 1995, including the heated media and council debates, workers' experiences after the changes, and interviews with the mayor, police authorities, health-care providers, local residents and Hay Street clients.

The most prominent theme articulated in *The Scarlet Mile* is that of women determined to break the cycle of poverty. Faced with the confronting reality of immediate economic crisis and long-term poverty, these women have rejected the prescribed ideal of 'virginal' femininity to provide a finan-cially secure future for themselves and their children. Given Kalgoorlie's relatively remote location, there also remains a distinctive pioneering spirit among Hay Street women.

The history and character of Kalgoorlie have forged another endur-ing motif in the book: that of an isolated, independent mining town with a fierce determination to self-govern. This is borne out by the fact that Kalgoorlie has maintained its own prostitution policy and red-light dis-trict uninterrupted for nearly a hundred years. In fact, the Containment

Policy originated in Kalgoorlie, and was later introduced in Perth during the 1920s. Despite major interruptions to Containment in Perth, including police crackdowns and 'tougher' state legislation outlawing brothels, the Hay Street brothels in Kalgoorlie always remained unaffected and business continued as usual.

The book also highlights a notable paradox in that, while local residents have generally long regarded prostitution as an essential service or a 'fact of life' in Kalgoorlie, the brothels and the work force have been shunned by people in the town—apart from on their occasional evening drives down Hay Street to ogle the women. The sex trade appears to have been accepted—even feted—on the proviso that the brothels and the work force remain in Hay Street. Local residents vocally reconfirmed this preference during the public debate surrounding the relaxation of local Containment in 1995.

As *The Scarlet Mile* goes to press, the Gallop Labor government in Western Australia continues to promise to introduce equitable prostitution law reform; perhaps this history will serve to inform the law reform process. With the sex industry and its participants remaining so woefully misunderstood, I am also hopeful that the book will help to foster a greater understanding of prostitution in our collective social memory.

CHAPTER I

Scarlet women on the early goldfields

It comes as a surprise to most 'outsiders' to learn that the Hay Street red-light district has co-existed on the same street as the local police station in Kalgoorlie since 1902. No other town in Australia is known to have so openly supported the presence of prostitution within its jurisdiction. Equally intriguing is the fact that police have historically sanctioned the Hay Street brothels, despite their official prohibition under Western Australian law. This unofficial policy of regulation (now known as 'Containment') continues to enjoy the approval of the local community in Kalgoorlie, where the red-light district is now a popular tourist attraction.

The origins of this unconventional approach can be traced directly to the overwhelmingly male-dominated culture and economic prosperity of the early goldfields. Thus, in order to better understand the origins of prostitution in Kalgoorlie and the experience of the first prostitutes on the goldfields, it is important to appreciate the social, economic, political and physical conditions of life on the frontier. These conditions, along with the relative geographic isolation of Kalgoorlie, have also strongly influenced the town's sense of character and independence, including its policy of regulating brothels.

News of prospector Paddy Hannan's discovery of gold in 1893 summoned men 'from all parts of the world' to seek their fortunes at Hannans

Find in Western Australia. Wealthy prospectors tracked major investment opportunities, while poor prospectors tried their luck at alluvial mining. Scores of men from Australia and overseas also migrated to sell their labour in the mines or to take on other forms of manual work in the expanding goldfields settlements. As anecdotes of great successes at Hannans Find gained momentum, so did the flow of migrants. In November 1895 journalist Julius Price of *The Illustrated London News* gave this description of the goldfields in Western Australia:

> from all parts of the world crowds of eager fortune-hunters are daily making their way to the Goldfields. All the nations of the earth are represented in the motley throng—Germans, Frenchmen, Russians, Turks, Italians, Spaniards, Americans, Englishmen—all rub shoulders as they press forward towards the new Eldorado...from the rich prospector on the look-out for good investments...to the broken-down clerk or poverty stricken labouring man, who has managed to gather enough to pay his way somehow to the 'fields'.[1]

This gold rush can be seen in the context of a broader series of major gold discoveries during the nineteenth century, which galvanised a peculiar 'breed' of humanity to traverse the globe in search of their own El Dorado. As a result, major goldfields developed in California (1849), New Zealand (1861), South Africa (1886), the Pilbara/Kimberley region in Western Australia (1880s), the Eastern Goldfields of Western Australia (1893) and the Klondike (1897).[2]

The town site of Hannans Find—later named Kalgoorlie (see Figure 1)— bore all the hallmarks of an archetypal gold-rush settlement. Hessian tents provided the standard accommodation for pioneers, who could take little comfort in the punishing conditions awaiting them. Nurse Ann Stafford Garnsey, one of the first nurses on the Eastern Goldfields of Western Australia, wrote in her memoirs that the heat and the dust were as inescapable as they were insufferable:

> The loosely-woven hessian gave us very little protection from the dust-storms, and the heat inside those camps was at times so suffocating that it was no unusual thing to throw the mattresses open over our heads as a slight protection against the dust and sand, and a bottle of water and sponge beside us to mop our hot, dusty faces.[3]

At the same time, chronic water shortages severely restricted the water consumption and washing habits of the pioneers. Only brackish water could be obtained from underground reservoirs, and this water was purified by being heated over a wood fire and the steam being condensed. Condensed

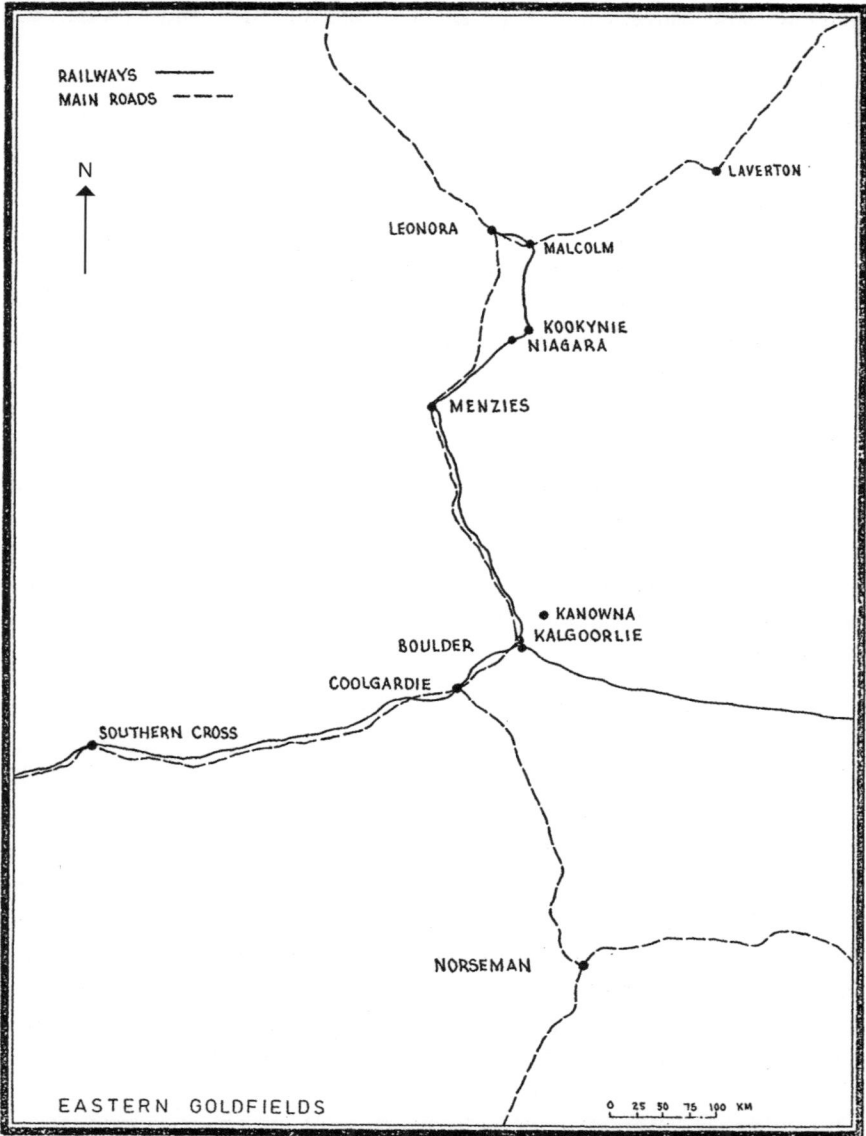

Figure 1 *Map of the Eastern Goldfields, showing major centres of the nineteenth-century mining boom.* Courtesy Dr Raelene Frances (formerly Davidson), University of New South Wales

water was also scarce, which kept its price relatively high, and so water was always consumed sparingly.[4] Floy Matthew of Kalgoorlie explained how early residents managed this precious commodity:

> You'd buy your water from condensers near Cassidy Street. Then they started delivering the water in a large metal tank on the top of a horse drawn dray. Occasionally it might be three days from the time my Grandmother ordered it till it was delivered. It was 2/6d a gallon. By the time it got to her place it was evening and the water would still be hot (especially in the summer). So she'd leave her family wash to do until then while the water was not out of the tank. They'd reserve a little bit for making tea and drinking; then the bodies would be washed; then the clothes; then the floor; and the last little bit would be put on the geranium growing in a cut down kerosene tin at the back door.[5]

The wood required to run the water condensers came from clear-felling the natural bush barrier that surrounded the town site. This left Kalgoorlie unprotected from frequent dust storms that deposited a thick layer of red dust on every object left exposed. Even the early hospital wards could not provide adequate sanctuary. After touring Kalgoorlie Hospital's tent wards during the late 1890s, Sister O'Brien openly lamented the dusty condition of the patients:

> [The patients were]...the dirtiest looking objects imaginable, covered in dust and sand indescribable...tents and more tents, men everywhere, old singlets and trousers were the order of their dress. The hopeless look of everything would have discouraged the stoutest heart.[6]

Working practices also reflected the scarcity of water on the early goldfields. Conventional gold-prospecting methods involving rockers, sluice boxes and considerable amounts of water proved impractical in the searing, dry desert heat, and so a process known as 'dryblowing' was used.[7] Water shortages also affected the operation of the cash-strapped Kalgoorlie Hospital, which struggled to cope with repeated epidemics of typhoid fever while trying to maintain limited basic supplies of water and medicines for patients. The mounting number of typhoid deaths forced the Progress Committee and Warden (chief administrator of mining towns under the *Goldfields Act 1886*) to send a telegram to the Premier of the Swan River Colony, requesting immediate gazettal of Kalgoorlie as a municipality so the powers of the *Public Health Act 1886* could be used to contain the crisis:

> Health of the town most unsatisfactory. Fever spreading, deaths daily and business threatened. No sanitary measures enforced or enforceable. Progress

Committee having no legal powers. Townspeople desire to avoid...panic... Municipality immediately necessary...and full powers required. Will you gazette...immediately and meanwhile give Warden any powers possible to enforce necessary sanitary arrangements.[8]

In a letter to his parents in South Australia in March 1896, prospector Charles Deland indicated that adequate standards of sanitation and public health had not yet been achieved in Kalgoorlie; he also noted that the clearing of bush around the town had served to eliminate most of the insects and other wildlife that had once been part of the territory:

Of course sanitary arrangements need a lot of attention and we use a great deal of Condys fluid and Carbolic acid. The rubbish tip is about 2½ miles from the town and they say the flies there are that thick that you can hear a roar all the time and everything looks quite black...

We are remarkably free from insect pests, there are few if any ants in the town but out in the bush you really cannot find a place to sit down during the day. Mosquitoes and fleas there are none whatever, also snakes. There of course are no kangaroos or in fact any living creatures native to this country...[9]

Another basic health service sorely lacking in early Kalgoorlie was dental care. Often a complaint to the doctor about an aching tooth led to painfully disappointing results. In a letter to his fiancée, Mary, in 1896, goldfields solicitor Felix Cowles described an occasion when he assisted the local doctor in 'removing' a patient's tooth:

Last Friday night I assisted the Doctor to draw a tooth by holding the victim's head—only he did not draw the tooth. He had about eight shots at it but fell back beaten and in disorder every time—vowing he would have that tooth or die for it. I was more concerned about the patient's chances of dying and administered medical comforts from time to time between the acts. After about an hour we called in the chemist. He wrestled violently but only succeeded in bringing away the top. As the stump was then un-get-at-able, the operation was postponed till the sufferer gets back to civilisation and proper dental appliances.[10]

Offsetting these primitive and often hazardous conditions was a pervasive sense of camaraderie in the mix of pioneers and prospectors. Theft of possessions left in unguarded tents was rare, as was violent crime, apart from the occasional drunken brawl. This was arguably a predictable feature of frontier life and one that the pioneers apparently took in their stride; in another letter to Mary in 1896, Felix Cowles related the following ringside account:

Just as I had got into my pyjamas I heard unmistakable sounds of a fight...I nipped out barefooted as I was, and found the scene of conflict. Only about twenty people were there, but it was a good fight while it lasted and a vivid moon lit the scene like an arc light.[11]

Despite the diversity of their backgrounds, most of the men shared a common lament: their extreme isolation from women. Although a small number of women had travelled to the goldfields in support of their menfolk, the conditions of frontier life were generally considered prohibitive for women. In addition to the harsh physical conditions, there were few social amenities to attract and sustain a female population. In her memoirs, Mrs Mary Cowles (having married Felix) wrote that her mother feared the worst for her daughter as Mary set out for the goldfields to live with her new husband:

> Mother was anything but happy at the prospect of letting her only daughter risk what appeared to be certain death: there were no proper houses, certainly nothing that a gentlewoman could live in, no servants, no water, no food except out of tins, from which those who survived the inevitable typhoid fever died of ptomaine poisoning—no eggs, no vegetables, nothing apparently but flies, dust and intolerable heat. That I would have no friends because no lady would be able to endure the life.[12]

At the same time, other women migrated independently to the goldfields in search of employment—the main groups being nurses, barmaids and prostitutes. While the nurses' skills would no doubt have travelled well to any new population (regardless of its location or demographic composition), it is safe to suggest that the abundance of lucrative employment opportunities for barmaids and prostitutes owed much to the dearth of women on the goldfields.

In her memoirs, Nurse Garnsey recalled the immense popularity of 'musical' barmaids, arguably the predecessors of 'skimpy' barmaids who still work in many pubs on the goldfields. During the gold rush, musical barmaids were renowned for their beauty, good cheer and the soothing effect they had on the lonely men, who enjoyed their piano playing and sing-alongs. A rather startled Nurse Garnsey first learned of the musical barmaids on her train journey from Bridgetown to Coolgardie in the late 1890s, when Irish-born publican Mrs McInerney (a fellow passenger) offered the young nurse a change of career:

> She said I was far too young and fresh to spend my time nursing. The work was too heavy, and that hard grind and poor pay would soon knock me out. If I would only go to her hotel, outback at Leonora, she would give me ten

pounds a week, and there would be tips, too. Musical barmaids always got lots and lots of tips—sometimes they were large nuggets.

I asked what was really meant by 'musical barmaid'. She thought I was relenting, and told me: 'Well, you play to the boys every night, and they sing. I have a pianner; it cost a heap to get it up to Leonora, too. When the boys stand round singin', you see, it keeps them peaceful and happy, and they'd like the looks of you'.[13]

Musical barmaids appear to have generated substantial profits for the publicans who employed them, at least enough to justify what must have indeed been a considerable expense for Mrs McInerney to transport her 'pianner' from Perth to Leonora. In a further testament to the barmaids' charm and popularity, Nurse Garnsey observed that

Men spoke of them with great respect—almost with reverence. Many a man was cheered and helped by the good advice given to him by a barmaid.

It was natural that the men wanted women to talk to—there were so few girls on the 'fields'. They were easily less than half of one per cent of the population. The streets were always crowded with men, and, when a solitary girl tried to steer her way through them, there were many inquisitive looks and sotto voce remarks, 'Who is that?' and 'Where has she come from?' Yes, there were decidedly too many men for our peace of mind![14]

Of course, this extreme gender imbalance was a well-known feature of life on goldfields all over the world. In Robin May's history of the great nineteenth-century gold rushes, two stories recorded on the Californian goldfields highlight the obvious effect that 'female deprivation' had on the isolated men:

And then there were the women, not many of them, but a growing band, even though in 1850 less than 8% of Californians were female. All-male dances were only too frequent in the early days as the lonely miners let off some of their high spirits, and the appearance of a woman, however homely, tended to attract a crowd of respectful, awed onlookers. When Mrs Galloway arrived at Downieville, the miners—who had been totally without female company—rushed out to greet her and carried her and her mule into town.

When Herman Reinhart reached Humbug City in northern California in 1852 he found a saloon kept by a man named Nobles, whose 'Fancy Woman' was a fine-looking German girl who sold drinks at 50 cents. Many miners paid the 50 cents just to see her, and some said they had not seen a woman for five years.[15]

If they chanced to encounter a young woman in Kalgoorlie, married men sometimes committed not only adultery but also bigamy to sustain sexual relationships.[16] A few tales of 'married men behaving badly' in Kalgoorlie found their way into letters written by Charles Deland in 1896 to his fiancée Effie in South Australia:

> Of those [men] who are here it is very hard to say who is single and who is not. It surprises me the number of men who have wives in the other colonies that pose as unmarried men and flirt with every barmaid in the town.
>
> It often makes me feel peculiar having to talk nice to girls who I know to be the lowest of the low, but who buy the finest and pay the best for their clothing. It is nothing unusual for a girl to order a £7.7 dress or pay 10/6 for a pair of silk gloves or hose.[17]

Like the men, women in the paid labour market had migrated in response to lucrative employment opportunities associated with the strip of major goldmines that soon became known as the 'Golden Mile'. During the 1890s, prostitutes collectively formed the largest occupationally identifiable group of women on the goldfields. Generally speaking, those who were English, Irish or Australian–born had independently made their way to the goldfields. On the other hand, another contingent of women had arrived under rather more sinister circumstances. French and Japanese syndicates brought hundreds of women into the country to work in brothels during the 1890s using deceitful tactics and abduction. These women were not allowed to leave the brothels and were not paid for the work they performed. This has correctly been referred to as 'sex slavery' or (less accurately) as the 'white slave trade'.

At the same time, independent women who worked in brothels were also often exploited by their employers; however, because of their illegal status under the *Police Act 1892* (WA), they could not approach authorities for assistance. Prostitutes were also politically and socially excluded from the great labour movements and reforms of the period, such as the *Workers Compensation Act 1902* (WA). Historian Kay Daniels has argued that the illegal status of the sex industry and the lack of industrial identity among prostitutes are the product of male-dominated societal attitudes that perceive sex as the opposite of work and the prostitute as the antithesis of traditional femininity. Daniels maintains that these prejudices are manifest in popular myths that distort the role, sexuality and identity of women who work as prostitutes.[18]

The Police Act assumed an 'abolitionist'[19] approach to prostitution, which precluded any form of official regulation. Prostitution itself was not made illegal; however, criminal offences were created for prostitution–related activities such as keeping a brothel, soliciting and living off the earnings of prostitution. Thus, while the Act allowed police to target more organised and visible forms of prostitution (often the subject of complaints to local police and councils), it excluded private prostitution involving wealthy men and their mistresses.

In contrast to the official prohibition, local police never seriously sought to eradicate brothels on the early goldfields. Instead, they tended to 'turn a blind eye' to these premises and their occupants, as long as there were no accompanying criminal offences, such as behaving in a drunken or disorderly manner or associating with known criminals.[20] Nevertheless, there is some evidence that prostitutes who operated alone from their own homes in Kalgoorlie were at least occasionally targeted by police following complaints from neighbouring residents. In the 1900 case of *Moore v. Guidotti*, a woman admitted to using her home for the purposes of prostitution, but the judge ruled that the house was not a brothel because it was used by only one prostitute.[21]

As Kalgoorlie became a more family-oriented town, there was a steady increase in the number of brothel-related complaints to police and local government authorities. In response to residents' complaints that the police did not or could not take action against certain brothels, the Kalgoorlie Roads Board and the Kalgoorlie Municipal Council enacted their own local by-laws prohibiting brothels. On 30 September 1898 the Kalgoorlie Roads Board passed a by-law (minuted in its entirety) that provided for any brothel complaint signed by three or more 'respectable' ratepayers to result in the board requesting a list of names, ages, sexes and occupations of all the 'inmates' of the premises. In cases of non-compliance, or 'if upon consideration the Board consider[ed] the house to be a brothel or house of ill-fame', the board would then declare the premises to be a nuisance, and give notice in writing for the nuisance to be abated within forty-eight hours, or the proprietor, management and occupiers might face conviction and a fine of £20 each.[22] Two and a half years later, in April 1901, the Kalgoorlie Municipal Council enacted By-law No. 77 (also minuted in its entirety) for 'the suppression and restraint of brothels, disorderly houses, houses of ill-fame and places used for habitual prostitution'.[23]

It is significant that both the Kalgoorlie Roads Board and the Kalgoorlie Municipal Council took the trouble to record these rather lengthy by-laws in their entirety in the official minute books. Certainly, this level of attention had never been paid to any other by-law. At the same time, there is no evidence that either the roads board or the municipal council actually used its own by-laws to pursue the closure of any brothels in the town. Instead, all letters of complaint received were minuted and referred directly to the police, who were already empowered to close brothels under the Police Act. Perhaps the local authorities needed to be *seen* to be taking some form of additional action in the face of increasing complaints from 'respectable' residents.

Meanwhile, the local media recognised the value of popular fascination with 'scarlet women' and newspaper reports featuring the 'scandalous harlots' provided titillating entertainment for Kalgoorlie's 'respectable' readers. During the late 1890s and early 1900s, *The Sun* and *The Sunday Times* ran two long-running series entitled (respectively) 'The scarlet stain' and 'Voices of Babylon'.[24] These reports loudly disapproved of the illicit sex trade, while offering a conservative yet curious readership a glimpse of the decadent underworld of Kalgoorlie. The headlines alone in one 1898 edition of *The Sun* perhaps best summarise Victorian social attitudes towards prostitutes, as well as the overtures that newspapers made to those attitudes:

> THE SCARLET STAIN
> The Pariah Sisterhood of Shame
> Shameless Flaunting of Vice will not be Tolerated
> Our Streets Must be Purged of their Shameful Harlotry
> Town Council Stamping Out Dens of Infamy[25]

Yet while these headlines appear to support a policy of extreme intolerance, the report acknowledged that it was impractical to attempt to eradicate the sex trade in Kalgoorlie, and that any such attempt might cause prostitutes to 'invade' residential areas:

> The social evil as it exists on the gold fields is a frightful open sore, gross and palpable to every man, woman, and child who walks our streets—an offence to public decency, a danger to the moral sense of the community, a source of hideous disease...a shame and a reproach to our local governments. The evil is here. It is useless to blink it...all without exception are convinced of the absolute futility of attempting to completely root out the evil of prostitution...All are agreed that these evils can be greatly lessened...None, with the exception of the Rev. Mr. Gordon-Savile, seem to be very hopeful of any considerable amelioration of existing conditions as a result of the apparently far-reaching by-law just passed by the Town Council of Kalgoorlie and about to be passed by the Roads Board. Expulsion of prostitutes from the town, if practicable, would probably mean an invasion of the residence areas...[26]

Perhaps not surprisingly, popular verse that appeared in newspapers around the turn of the century tended to trivialise or vilify prostitutes. One notable example is the poem entitled 'Hire and sale', penned by Dryblower Murphy in 1903:

HIRE AND SALE
Delilah sits alone among
The smart and smug dress circle crowd.
At her the scornful glance is flung.
To her no graceful head is bowed:
The stalls upon her look askance,
The unwashed in the gall'ry grin,
The boxes view with scornful glance,
Her livery of shame and sin.
For her there shines no Light Divine,
Her soul is in the moral mire,
Writ plain upon her is the sign, 'For Hire'[27]

Generally speaking, the popular press seems to have vacillated in its portrayal of harlots, presenting them as passive objects of depravity at one end of the scale and aggressive forces of evil at the other. The latter view was dramatically expressed in a fire-and-brimstone passage entitled 'A book of chronicles' in the Coolgardie newspaper *The T'othersider* in 1897:

Now it came to pass that a terrible scourge overspread the Cities of the Desert—a scourge that is more deadly than the Black Death . . . such a shocking and disgusting character is this visitation that men discuss it with bated breath, and mention it not in the presence of their womenkind. And the scribes of the Daily Recorders are fearful to mention in any guise but that of a jest.

Now this plague hath a history in the Cities of the Desert, and hath passed through many phases. The first to introduce it were a Nation called the Japanese . . . these Japanese are men of small stature, and wiry, and industrious. They are admirable from all points—at a distance of seven thousand leagues.

Then it happened that so great a noise was spread abroad by the lucrative traffic in vice which could be carried on in the Cities of the Desert, that whole hordes of immoral women descended upon our shores. The first to land were the females from the great Republic called France . . . They have rounded arms and beautiful tresses of dyed hair. And they paint their faces, and pencil their eyebrows, and blacken their lips, so that they look more like unto angels than the wicked sirens that they are. And their flowing tresses hang down the bareness of their backs and over their shoulders . . . And they sit on stools sideways in the doors of their tents, lounge about in groups on couches in their window frames. And they use all their vicious beauty and accursed arts to cause men to gaze upon them, and to stir up evil passions within their breasts.

And the name of the plague is Immorality. And the Japanese women over-ran the Cities of the Plain, and built houses with doors and windows painted green and yellow; and provided their windows with shutters of wood, so that none might gaze upon their filthy practices.[28]

And so it came to pass that early goldfields newspapers indulged their Victorian audience and perhaps their own commercial interests with character assassinations of scarlet women. Meanwhile, the women who battled hostile physical and social conditions to pioneer the sex trade on the goldfields were made more than welcome by thousands of grateful men, and so the trade flourished.

Despite the official prohibition on brothels under the Police Act, local police continued their unofficial policy of selective policing and turned a blind eye to brothels where no other offences were being committed. In the years that followed, the Kalgoorlie Municipal Council and the local police authorities would cooperate discreetly to develop an unofficial policy of 'Containment', to gain some measure of control over the town's well-patronised scarlet women.

CHAPTER 2

Of vice and men: Foreign devils and Japanese flowers

Kalgoorlie continued to grow and change rapidly during the years after the gold rush. Greater numbers of women joined their menfolk in towns on the goldfields once there was basic infrastructure—railroads, sealed roads, street lighting, tramlines, footpaths and electricity supply to new homes—as well as schools, hospitals and houses of worship. To the great relief of the entire goldfields population, running water also arrived in 1903, having travelled through 352 miles of pipeline from the Helena River at Mundaring Weir in Perth—thanks to the genius of the state's Chief Engineer, C.Y. O'Connor, who conceived and designed this ambitious scheme.

Meanwhile, police in Kalgoorlie continued to selectively enforce the anti-prostitution laws, generally 'tolerating' prostitutes who did not associate with known criminals, operate 'sly-grog' (unlicensed liquor) shops or behave in a 'disorderly' manner in public. Newspapers continued to exploit popular fascination with Kalgoorlie's 'Scarlet Stain' by publishing a new series of sensationalist articles that pitied the women, especially migrant women who had been forced into the trade by male-owned and operated international syndicates.

At the turn of the century, prostitution in Kalgoorlie existed on several levels of organisation and disorganisation. At the more organised end of the scale, male-dominated French and Japanese syndicates transported women from overseas, often against their will, to work in brothels under the syndicates' 'protection'. At the opposite end of the scale, women from British, Celtic and Australian backgrounds who worked in the local female-owned and operated brothels in Kalgoorlie enjoyed a much higher degree of independence. There were also reports of prostitutes soliciting in the streets and pubs around the town, often with a male 'protection agent' in tow.[1]

Yet brothels continued as the most popular venue for prostitutes to attract and provide services to clients; the more discreet 'houses of ill-fame' were disguised as legal businesses such as laundries, tobacconists and dressmakers.[2] Enterprising landlords often charged prostitutes vastly inflated rents for their premises, sometimes 500 per cent higher than the rent charged to other tenants.[3]

It is not surprising that brothel-keepers were among the first owners of properties in Hay Street following its gazettal in June 1902.[4] On the other hand, it seems surprising (at first) that most of the women who owned Hay Street brothels were married.[5] But in the days before divorce was widely available to the general population, marriages often ended when the husband simply walked out on the family. Women who had been raising families generally did not have the skills to take advantage of the limited paid work opportunities available, and thus many abandoned wives would have been driven to work as prostitutes to survive, and in many cases to support their children as well.

Title searches also reveal that, while men and 'respectable' women were registered on their land titles according to occupation[6], those women who owned, and lived in, the Hay Street brothels were generally registered on the titles simply as 'Spinsters', 'Married Women', 'Widows' and (later) 'Divorcees'.

Apart from Hay Street, the locations of choice for prostitutes in Kalgoorlie at the turn of the century appeared to be Hannan and Maritana streets, although brothels also operated along Brookman, Egan and Wilson streets. It was reported in *The Sun* in 1900 that English and Australian prostitutes tended to concentrate in Egan Street, while prostitutes of other nationalities favoured Brookman Street.[7]

Women from Japan and France formed the predominant group of prostitutes in Kalgoorlie, and their brothels clearly outnumbered the others, according to a report in *The West Australian* in 1900:

> Only a little time ago there were not half-a-dozen of these shops in the notorious Boulevard [Brookman]. Now there are 14 or 15 French houses, with an average of two wantons to each house. There are three houses kept by English women, two by Italians (in with the syndicates), one by an Austrian (also a member of the 'club'), and nearly a dozen Japanese. Between Wilson and Lane

Streets there is not a respectable private residence—they are all devoted to the Babylonian Venus and the shrine of lust. The revolting reality is there for anyone to see whether he wishes or not.[8]

Marked differences in behaviour reportedly distinguished prostitutes by nationality, and the postures and mannerisms of the French and Japanese prostitutes came under scrutiny in one report on the 'social evil' in *The Sunday Times* in 1900:

> The French girls and the Japs flourish as the proverbial green bay tree, and for the reason that she does not parade the streets and is seldom seen without her little den, the almond-eyed maiden is left religiously alone [by the police]. Not so the French girl. She reclines in more or less graceful and enticing attitudes in her doorway, and as a consequence the police fire her in ... The French girls made themselves too conspicuous, and as a consequence of complaints made by the neighbors, were brought before the magistrate on Thursday. They have got to move and seek other premises, but the Japs are allowed to remain because, as one of the policemen put it, 'they are so well behaved'.[9]

While the Japanese prostitutes were regarded as well-behaved or 'ideal' prostitutes, the English prostitutes in Kalgoorlie were berated for their relative lack of professionalism:

> In the English brothels in Egan Street, and some of the 'shops' even of the main street of Kalgoorlie, the vice itself is gross and has nearly every other grossness added ... The French prostitute ... does not drink, she does not as a rule use bad language, and on the slightest symptom of venereal malady, she generally ... declines to take custom. As much, if not more, may be said for the Japanese ... But the English harlots on the fields ... have an utter contempt for cleanliness, either of person or speech ... Their dens are known to the police as sly-grog shops and the rendezvous of thieves and desperate characters. Some of the women are hardly ever sober, and as a consequence become dangerously diseased.[10]

One Egan Street prostitute (presumably English) appeared to have abandoned all sense of discretion, when she solicited one of three uniformed police constables on the footpath in front of her house. Police Constable Whelan's court deposition on 2 May 1898 detailed their remarkable encounter with Delia:

> About 8.00 p.m. on the night of the 22nd April, in company with Police Constable Robinson and McFarley, I visited a home in Egan Street where the accused lived. She was sitting on a chair in the centre of the footpath. She said 'Goodnight' and caught Police Constable Robinson by the arm and said, 'Come inside and have a short time. I'll take my clothes off for 7/6'.[11]

The hapless Delia was fined £2 for accosting the police constable for the purpose of prostitution.

Consumption of alcohol greatly increased a prostitute's chances of being arrested, and brothels known as sly-grog shops were very unpopular with police. Not only did the police consider drunken prostitutes a nuisance 'of the worst kind', they knew that sly-grog shops attracted the custom of criminals. Another reason these establishments fell out of favour with local authorities was their serving of alcohol mixed with boot polish or methylated spirits: these concoctions were directly responsible for many cases of delirium tremens (DTs) on the goldfields.[12]

Most of the brothels in Boulder's red-light district, Richardson Street, also doubled as sly-grog shops. The first attempt to drive prostitutes out of Boulder was conducted in the late 1890s[13], a move protested in one prostitute's letter to the editor of *The Kalgoorlie Miner*. This rather articulate protest was labelled 'pathetic' by the editor of *The Sunday Times* when it reprinted the letter:

THE BITTER CRY OF OUTCAST WOMAN

The editor of the 'Kalgoorlie Miner' has recently given publicity to a pathetic letter from one of the 'unfortunate class' at Boulder City. The writer in her letter says:-

Through the medium of your widely-read paper, allow me to protest against the persecution to which the unfortunate women of Richardson-street are being subjected. There is a certain ring of influential men in the Boulder who will be satisfied with nothing less than a complete exodus of our class, and the question is staring us in the face, Where are we to go? We cannot get a shop or house for love or money in the Boulder, and they are about to take the same measures in Hannans. If they persist in hunting us down, and drive us out of the town altogether, it will not be safe for respectable women to walk the streets at all. In the present state of society we are needed and it is nothing short of madness to attempt to put us down altogether. We are social outcasts, every man's hand against us and every woman's too; but, fathers and brothers, remember our sin makes your daughters and your sisters purer, our vice makes their virtue surer. We cannot go and take situations, for who would employ us, and even so, the life we have led does not fit us for it. It is the leading publicans who are against us, and speaking for myself I can say, when serving behind a bar I first started my career. And what have they against us? We do not stand at our doors and accost men, we are not foreigners, that they should oppress us, and I would like to know if they will find us lodgings when we are obliged to leave here (in the police station I suppose). I hope some abler pen than mine will take this up, and thanking you in anticipation,—I am, etc.,

'ONE OF THEM.'[14]

A second campaign by police in 1903 seems to have succeeded in permanently closing down all the Richardson Street brothels in Boulder, amid rumours that a group of influential local publicans had been instrumental in forcing the closures. In one court case reported in *The Kalgoorlie Miner*, Sergeant Moore made clear the police position that prostitution and alcohol did not mix:

> I know the accused keeps a house in Richardson-street. In consequence of a complaint I went to the house to get a girl out. I found the girl there. The accused was there at the time and another woman. The accused was very drunk at the time. The house is a brothel of the worst kind.[15]

Following this successful purge of the Boulder brothels, the prostitutes apparently moved their businesses to Kalgoorlie.[16]

One prostitute repeatedly defied the police and operated sly-grog shops all over the goldfields. Pansy Arlington, who had been born Margaret Rita Willmot in Kentucky in 1865, first arrived on the goldfields in 1895. Pansy was an attractive, well-educated, worldly woman who could spin a good yarn or two. She had a penchant for potent and cheap whisky, and usually occupied the most popular hessian dwelling wherever she travelled. One contemporary writer who called himself 'Tempora Mutantur' described her hessian establishment in Laverton as 'Pansy Arlington's Palace of Pleasure'.[17]

Pansy always attracted her share of police attention during her travels on the goldfields; her brothels were regularly raided and her liquor confiscated on several occasions. And then there is the bold and beautiful Pansy's legendary facility with her revolver. Following one police raid, Pansy appeared in the Coolgardie Quarter Sessions on 18 December 1899 charged with conspiring to murder Police Constable Hoy in Laverton. After a two-day trial, she was found not guilty.

Following her extensive tour of the goldfields, Pansy returned to Kalgoorlie in 1904 to manage a brothel in Hay Street. She continued to have the occasional brush with the law, and in 1905 she was arrested for stealing jewellery from two other prostitutes and for using obscene language. A year later, Pansy was again arrested for using obscenities.

As Pansy's drinking habits grew steadily worse, her health deteriorated. In 1906 she received treatment from Dr Leger Erson for 'alcoholic excess'. Fearing the horrors of sobering up, a melancholic Pansy swallowed a solution of wax matches. When she confided this to her long-time friend Thomas Williams a few days later, she begged him not to call the doctor, as she feared he would tell the police, who would give her 'six months hard'. However, her condition rapidly deteriorated, and Williams left her in the care of three neighbours—Annie Quinn, Emily Scarlett and Mrs Smith—to telephone Dr Erson.

The doctor immediately recognised the smell of garlic in Pansy's room as a sign of phosphorus poisoning. Unable to persuade Pansy to go into hospital, he prescribed medicine to be administered by Annie Quinn. Although the medication alleviated her pain and vomiting, Pansy took a bad turn during the night. At 5.30 next morning, after an all-night vigil at Pansy's side, Williams phoned Dr Erson again; however, 'while the doctor was tying up his horse at the telephone post, she breathed her last'. The coronial inquiry confirmed that the cause of Pansy's death was 'heart failure caused by phosphorus poisoning, self-administered'.[18]

Life for Hay Street women was not always doomed, nor even gloomy. Marcia Verne, a prostitute known locally as the 'Brazen Brunette', organised the first social event for prostitutes in Kalgoorlie in July 1903.[19] She hosted the occasion at her Hay Street brothel, and her guests included a popular woman known as the 'Indian Queen', as well as several French and Japanese prostitutes. While a German band played throughout the evening to the gathering of women on Marcia's lawn, the brothel's surrounding fence and roof were reportedly 'swarmed with Japanese spectators', most likely local Japanese laundrymen.

One of the lasting mysteries surrounding the Kalgoorlie brothels is their use of brothel tokens (see Figures 2 and 3). The actual function of the tokens and the extent to which they were used remain unclear. Two brothel tokens, excavated in 1990 at Kanowna and Broad Arrow by local 'hobby archaeologists' Robert Money and Michael Doyle, are now on display at the Museum of the Goldfields in Kalgoorlie. Manufactured by Cartaux, Paris, circa 1900, the face of one of the hollow, pressed metal tokens shows the finely etched features of a woman's facial profile, crowned by the lettering 'Russian Princess'. The other side of the token is imprinted simply 'Martha, 140 Brookmann [sic] Street'.

Speculation abounds as to how the token system worked. Former museum curator Pamela Moore suggested that the token could have been given to a client by a prostitute or madam called Martha, at a brothel called the Russian Princess.[20] Alternatively, the tokens could have been issued through businesses such as tobacconists and used instead of money at brothels.

It is also possible that a client purchased the token at the brothel, and then 'paid' it to the prostitute of his choice, instead of giving her money. A system whereby prostitutes cashed in their tokens at the end of the shift would have reduced the chances of workers 'holding out' on earnings from their bosses, and avoided disputes over workers' pay at the end of the shift.

Figure 2 *Brookman Street brothel token, c. 1900 (front). Manufactured by Cartaux, Paris, it is believed that such tokens (hollow coins with metallic exteriors) served as 'business cards' for some brothels in Kalgoorlie during the early 1900s.*
Courtesy Western Australian Museum (Museum of the Goldfields).
Photograph by Gary Blinko, copyright WA Museum

Figure 3 *Brookman Street brothel token, c. 1900 (back).* Courtesy Western Australian Museum (Museum of the Goldfields). Photograph by Gary Blinko, copyright WA Museum

Historians Casey and Mayman offer perhaps the most plausible explanation: that the tokens were used as business cards for brothels, especially when business began to decline in the years following Kalgoorlie's economic 'boom' of the 1890s. Customers would be given the medallions in the hope that this would encourage a return visit; alternatively, the token might be passed on to another potential customer. Casey and Mayman add that a number of these tokens may have found their way into the foundation stone of the Kalgoorlie Town Hall:

> Each displayed a female figure, a Brookman Street address, and some encouraging and enticing legend such as 'The Russian Princess', 'The Girl from Paris', 'The Hula-Hula Girl', or even more direct hints at exotic delights…Many of these medallions went into circulation, and among other things they offered a scandalous opportunity when the foundation stone of the Kalgoorlie Town Hall was laid. At the ceremony, citizens were invited to throw coins into the soft mortar before the second stone was lowered to seal them there for ever. This some did, but it is still hard to look at the dignified front of the Town Hall without giving a passing thought to what the others tossed into the soft mortar for the building to stand on.[21]

While brothel prostitution was still the most common mode of operation in the sex trade, some prostitutes were famously mobile. One prostitute named Lizzy Dupont was immortalised in *The Sun* for her

> somewhat frisky exhibition of skirt dancing in Brookman Street, winding up with a fine exhibition of high kicking…Two policemen who were standing close by at last interfered, reluctantly, but firmly. You bet they didn't hurry to end the exhibition as the young woman was fair and her lingerie choice…[22]

According to E. Cam Deland (brother of Charles), one of the first bakers on the goldfields, a fair number of residents would also have been momentarily mesmerised by the early goldfields version of Lady Godiva, a woman known as 'The Great Boulder', who took a fancy to breezing down the Boulder Road perched atop a bicycle and 'dressed only in a blouse and knickers'.[23] It seems clear that various states of dress and undress helped prostitutes to distinguish themselves from other women in the town, which was particularly useful in attracting custom in the early days before the trade was confined to one area. Prostitutes are known to have 'dressed in loose gowns, or short chemisettes, with bare arms, bright stockings and painted faces'.[24]

This contrasted sharply with the classic Victorian uniform for women, which ensured that no inch of flesh went unnecessarily exposed. The 'kit' consisted of a long skirt and jacket, pale cotton stockings, a cotton or muslin blouse that concealed the arms and the neck, a petticoat and that famous instrument of torture known as the corset.

Hotels provided another outlet for soliciting by prostitutes, and the pubs in Kalgoorlie's West End continued to host the trade:

> In the 'skirt room' of most of the West End hotels up to a dozen men and women may be found carousing together any night of the week. The men libertines and bludgers, the women harlots without exception...Outside the pub's pavement nymphs from sixteen to sixty wait to accost the chance wayfarer.[25]

Nevertheless, most prostitution in Kalgoorlie was conducted in the French and Japanese brothels. Predictably, the media of the day made the most of the sensational rumours surrounding the 'white slave trade', including reports that false pretences and violence were used to force the young women into prostitution.[26] While the small number of substantiated cases might indicate that foul play was rare, it seems more likely that most cases of forced servitude were never reported to police. The women feared their bosses and the police, and often could not speak English proficiently. *The Sun* reported in 1904 that one Spanish prostitute named Nina Delacourte had been assaulted in Kalgoorlie but had not reported the incident to police, because 'we never go to the police in Spain'.[27]

While it is impossible to say how many women were lured under false pretences or coerced to work as prostitutes on the goldfields, *The Sun* certainly took a novel approach in probing the mystery. In 1900 the paper published a passionate appeal, in both English and French:

> Sisters with a sullied name and a soiled career. 'Still for all slips' of your part of humanity—We make an appeal to you in the interest of your future fate and happiness, to stir yourselves for freedom. Rouse! make all the efforts of your womanhood to escape the clutches of those vampires for whom you are slaves. If you really desire to break your fetters and to live the life of a true woman by escaping your present misfortunes, The Sun—the editor and the proprietors of this paper—will help you by every legitimate means in its power. If you need help or advice will you kindly write to us—in French or English—or call upon us by appointment, and we will see that you procure all the benefits of the protecting laws of England, and such other relief and assistance as is at our command. We think you are women, and not monsters; and if our help can assist you to verify that opinion you are more than welcome to it. Write to 'The Editor of The Sun, Kalgoorlie,' and set to work for your liberty and honour.[28]

The Sun's reporter added that he would not hold his breath for a flood of responses, and this is perhaps just as well. The paper received no correspondence from the young 'captives', apart from one letter written by an 18-year-old former prostitute who told the extraordinary story of her own captivity in a French syndicate. Her letter to *The Sun* led to the conviction of several of the men involved.

This young woman, Natalina Appendino, had been working at a registry office in Marseilles when she was approached by 'Mr and Mrs Lance' to work as a shop assistant in Western Australia.[29] When she arrived in 1898, she was informed that she would be earning her living as a prostitute. She immediately feigned illness and was sent to Kalgoorlie Hospital, only to be collected a week later by another madam, Mrs Gaillard, who informed Natalina that she had been sold to another pimp for the sum of £15.

Mrs Gaillard had bought the young woman and her debts from the pimp for £65, but soon sold her unwilling recruit for £35 to Paul Loubens, who ran the Peerless Tobacco Shop in Brookman Street. While working for Loubens, Natalina gave him £39 of her earnings to keep in a trust for her. Yet when she decided to leave his employ to work as a domestic servant for a 'respectable' local couple, he refused to return her money to her.

Two years later, Natalina read the French translation of *The Sun*'s appeal and asked for the paper's assistance in getting her £39 earnings returned to her. Indeed, *The Sun*'s involvement set the full force of the law on Paul Loubens and six other pimps. During Loubens's trial, it emerged that his prostitutes paid him half their earnings, averaging £10–15 on a good night, plus £3 per week for room and board. Unable to produce alternative proof of his material means of support, he was convicted of vagrancy and sentenced to three months' imprisonment.

One 'Mr Lance' was also charged with vagrancy and was advised that he could well be facing more serious charges of procurement and abduction. Having been released on bail, he caught the first train to Kanowna to collect money from a woman who ran a brothel under his 'protection'. Suspecting that another young recruit named Josephine had alerted the police to his operations, he cut her throat before shooting himself. Josephine survived.

Another case that highlighted the pimps' deceptive and coercive tactics was reported in *The Sunday Times* on 17 March 1901. After leaving home in Paris, a young woman named Lizette had met a charming Frenchman on one of his recruiting tours for Western Australia. Unaware of his modus operandi, she fell in love with him and agreed to accompany him to the goldfields. However, on her arrival in Kalgoorlie, Lizette immediately found herself 'imprisoned' in a brothel.

She was eventually assisted to freedom by a young client, a miner from Kanowna, who gave her enough money to travel to Perth. Lizette's pimp soon caught up with her and tried to persuade her to return to Kalgoorlie. Furious at her refusal, he assaulted her and was later charged in the Police

Court. It is not known whether Lizette ever made her way back to her homeland; at last report, she had been interned at the Callan Park Asylum for Lunatics in New South Wales.

At the opposite end of the spectrum, at least one French prostitute is known to have met with a much happier fate upon retiring in Kalgoorlie. Violette Adrienne Lisere had worked as a prostitute in Brookman Street before operating a brothel with Big Blanche D'Arville in Hay Street. Marriage was one means of escape from the rigours of the trade, and Violette accepted her Afghan lover's marriage proposal while Big Blanche was away on holidays, simply leaving this brief message in her hasty departure:

> I am tired of this life—so tired. Glad I will be to start a new life. He I am to marry is black-skinned, but he has a white heart, and a good heart. Farewell, it must be—I go. Farewell![30]

On 31 March 1907 *The Sunday Times* published what seems to have been a rather mean-spirited announcement of the nuptials of Violette Lisere (simply identified as a 'Brookman Street woman') to Gool Mahomet, a wealthy 52-year-old native of Afghanistan who had arrived in Western Australia in 1888 and had earned 'more than the average man's share of this world's goods' through his camel contracting business. The report was headlined 'A mixed marriage—Afghan and Aspasia—a pair of undesirables married at Coolgardie'.

Such unflattering references to Aspasia of Miletus were common in early twentieth-century books about Ancient Greek history, and these would have influenced the thinking of classically educated men working as journalists. As a foreign-born Athenian, Aspasia was not allowed to marry in Athens, and so all her sexual liaisons were considered 'suspect', even though her long-term relationship with the statesman Pericles produced a son. A fiercely independent woman to whom Socrates brought his students for philosophy lectures and discussions, Aspasia would long be reviled in the literature as a concubine, a *hetaira* (prostitute) and a madam.[31]

In Coolgardie in 1907, madam Violette converted to Islam so that she could marry Gool, and they were married 'under Mahometan religion...in the Mahometan Church, Coolgardie'. Then the newlyweds were almost immediately declared unmarried, having been wed by Dowd Khan, who did not possess the required licence (for this, he was fined £10). The bridegroom paid the fine without hesitation, and the couple were married by another local who was legally qualified to perform the ceremony.[32] It is not known whether Violette accompanied Gool when he left Australia permanently in 1928, presumably to ensure that he passed away in his homeland (a common practice of Muslim migrants at that time).[33]

One Frenchwoman seems to have fared exceptionally well from her years as a brothel owner in Kalgoorlie and Perth. Marie Louise Monnier, known as Madame Josie de Bray (see Figure 4), owned several brothels in Brookman Street in Kalgoorlie during the gold-rush years, and then later negotiated a virtual monopoly on Roe Street brothels with police authorities in Perth during the 1920s. In the late 1930s she returned to France to live in St Nazaire, where she was reportedly 'trapped' during World War II. Upon her return to Western Australia in 1949, *The Mirror* publicly welcomed her back and crowned her 'the undisputed leader of the ancient and sordid profession out of which she made so much money'. Josie obviously tended to give as good as she got, hitting back at one reporter, 'You know, son, working on a newspaper is a dirty way of making a living!'[34]

Despite returning to quite a fortune in Perth, from years of accumulated rent for her Roe Street brothels, Madame Josie allowed these premises to deteriorate to such a state that in 1951 they were all condemned by the Perth City Council as unfit for human habitation.[35] In contrast to these obviously poor living and working environments, Josie herself preferred to live in a 'big house in Mount Lawley'[36], a relatively wealthy inner-city suburb of Perth. With respect to the early days of her business in Kalgoorlie during the gold rush, it is not known whether Josie had connections to French syndicates or standover men when she established her brothels and work force.

Whether or not they had been forced into the trade, the French and Japanese prostitutes were generally regarded as a most unfortunate class of young women, who were more 'sinned against than sinning'. The men known as their pimps or 'macros' were loathed by the townsfolk because they profited from the captivity and misery of young women. In a letter to the editor of *The Sunday Times*, one local who called himself 'The Aberdeenian' could scarcely conceal his contempt for the well-to-do 'bludgers' who he said lived the 'high life' at the young women's expense:

> In the local Police Court and in the Press we very frequently come across cases of prosecutions of women for 'soliciting' and for keeping disorderly houses. These cases may be proper and ones that should be brought on, but, Mr Editor, what about the men who are the causes of the women seeking the streets for a living? Some [of the men] work a few days a week, or perhaps not at all, yet they are dressed in the latest fashion, smoke cigars and drink the best English ale and nothing but the choicest spirits. These gentry look down upon a hard working, honest man who can only afford colonial beer and perhaps has not got the latest cut in pagets.[37]

Figure 4 *Madam Josie de Bray (Marie Louise Monnier), who owned brothels in Brookman Street, Kalgoorlie, during the early 1900s.* Courtesy Battye Library (from *The Mirror*, 1949)

Occasionally, popular hatred of the pimps meant that the prostitutes themselves suffered the brunt of angry mob behaviour. Dennis O'Callaghan recalled one incident when the living quarters of the Japanese prostitutes were attacked by an angry mob:

> Towards the end of May, 1898, a rough mob of undesirables came to the different mining towns. Some of them blew into Kanowna and wrecked a portion of the Japanese women's quarters (women of easy virtue). They smashed windows and fired revolver shots through the galvanised iron walls of the houses. They may have had some provocation, or perhaps did not like the idea of well-dressed Frenchmen (belonging to a syndicate) walking around Kanowna, Kalgoorlie and Coolgardie, in the busy mining centres, with their walking-sticks and gloves, and bludgeoning on poor unfortunate French and Japanese women.[38]

Instead of being protected by them, prostitutes were often exploited by their pimps. Nurse Garnsey wrote in her memoirs that pimps frequently had to bring their workers into hospital for treatment, as the women suffered the ravages of disease or exhaustion:

> One little pet of a Japanese—Oyoni—said to me: 'I not want get better, nurse. I want go sleep and no more wake up.' In Perth I chanced to meet one day the man she called her 'boss.' I asked him about Oyoni, and he hesitated; then told me that she was dying in Perth Hospital. I hurried along to see her. Poor little Oyoni! So wasted and so sad—just a faded flower. She recognised me and held my hand, and tried to say 'My nurse.' The nurses in this hospital did not know anything about her. To them she was just 'one of those Japs from the houses,' who had to be screened off away from other decent patients. But I knew her, and to me she was a pitiful sacrifice. I was overwhelmed with bitter thoughts and feelings.[39]

Indeed, there did not seem to be much public outcry over the plight of the Japanese prostitutes. Then again, all Japanese migrants endured flagrant anti-Asian sentiment in Western Australia. The Japanese prostitutes also took great pains to trade discreetly, and thus seldom attracted the attention of the police, the media or the community. Of course, there were a few exceptions to this uneasy peace. One resident complained in a letter to the editor of *The Kalgoorlie Miner*:

> Sir—Having the misfortune to reside within a stone's throw of the Japanese settlement in Kalgoorlie, I read with considerable interest the letters on the above subject which appeared in your journal last week. Every statement made by your correspondents was strictly correct. One by one all the respectable inhabitants are leaving the locality, and the number of brothels is increasing every week. It is not my intention to deal with the subject from a social purity standpoint, but I would draw your attention to the matter from a purely business aspect. There cannot be the slightest doubt that the value of property in the neighbourhood of these brothels is being steadily reduced...there are a number of residence area [property] holders living south of the spot who are compelled to give that part of Hannan-street a wide berth, especially if they are accompanied by any womenfolk...[40]

The broader Japanese community moved quickly to distance itself from the Japanese brothels, and organised a formal request that the brothels be closed. Their collective motivation may well have been primed by the strong anti-Asian sentiment of the day and fears of a backlash from the white population if they were seen to tolerate Japanese brothels. These fears would have been well founded, as an 1898 report in *The West Australian* demonstrates:

Of late there has been an immense amount of correspondence in the Press, and talk among citizens, about the prevalence of Japanese in the town [of Kanowna], the chief objection to their presence being the modus operandi of most of them in regard to obtaining a living. In a word, most of the houses of ill-fame in the town have been and are run by 'Japs', and hence their existence here has been hailed as a curse.[41]

Thus, the Japanese community on the goldfields found itself alienated from all sides of the broader community, and the Japanese prostitutes took special care to operate discreetly. Like other houses of 'ill-fame' in Kalgoorlie, Japanese brothels were often disguised as laundries or tobacconists in the 1890s, a practice highlighted in the following poem published in *The Sun*:

VIRGINIBUS PUERISQUE
There's a little tawny damsel, who grins behind her fan,
She's a dealer in commodities exclusively Japan;
He'd find her stock almost scanty,
If the landlord took a list
Yet she does a thriving business, does this gay tobacconist.[42]

The tobacco connection also found its way into court evidence given by Mr H. W. Ellis, a chemist, who testified in a May 1904 libel case that one 'Dr Matsuo' managed a Japanese brothel operation that spanned the state of Western Australia:

I asked Matsuo what business he was carrying on there in the adjoining shop. He answered 'chinta', an Asiatic expression which means brothel. I asked him if it was a good business, and he said no . . . The stock in the shop consisted of a little grocery, a little tobacco and cigars. If they sold the whole of that stock at 10 per cent profit it would not bring in the rent. I have seen people going into the shop. They were mostly men. In Broome and Perth I have seen hundreds of Japanese brothels. These shops were of that stamp.[43]

Matsuo apparently paid an inflated rent of £3 7s 6d to the building's estate agent, a fee exceeding that paid by white tenants by £1 8s 6d. Despite what seemed like overwhelming criminal evidence against Dr Matsuo in this libel case, there is no record of him ever being charged by police for involvement in prostitution.

While Japanese prostitution in itself attracted remarkably little attention from the police, there were rare incidents that required thorough police investigation and quick intervention. One case involved a young Japanese prostitute in Kanowna named Matsuo Otana and her lover Mukai Soyo-kichi, a cook in a Kalgoorlie restaurant.[44] On the evening of 30 August 1898, Soyokichi arrived from Kalgoorlie on the last train to spend the night with Otana, as he often did. The following morning, the two had a cordial breakfast with Osugo Enowna, a Japanese prostitute who shared the house and worked with Otana. Shortly after breakfast, Otana approached Enowna to ask her consent to return to Kalgoorlie with Soyokichi. Enowna had no objection, but reminded Otana that she still owed her share of £35 for the construction of the house from which they worked.

The West Australian reported that Otana had returned to her bedroom after breakfast to pack her clothes, when the first shot rang out. Enowna rushed to the door of the room to find Soyokichi with a revolver trained on Otana, who was kneeling on the floor next to a clothes trunk. Enowna called out to Soyokichi, who dropped the revolver on the bed and shut the door. Another three shots came from the bedroom, and Enowna fled the house to raise the alarm.

The scene of the crime was soon overrun by a small army of law enforcement officers and medical and religious authorities. Otana and Soyokichi were transferred to the hospital grounds; within half an hour of his arrival at the hospital, Soyokichi joined Otana in the morgue. The coronial inquiry found that Otana had been murdered by Soyokichi, who had then committed suicide.

Another tragic case involved a young Japanese prostitute named Sono Samamoto and her husband, Chomatsu Yabu, a laundryman.[45] There was apparently some doubt as to the validity of their marriage, but it was known that they had had a child together, who had died. By 1902 their four-year relationship was showing signs of strain, and in November of that year, Samamoto called the police after Yabu ransacked their house and furniture. Soon after this incident, Yabu bought a revolver from ironmongers McKenzie & Co., only to exchange it the following day for one he could carry in his pocket. He purchased fifty cartridges and signed the docket 'Chomatsu'.

Two weeks later, Samamoto left Yabu in Kalgoorlie to live with a kindly older Japanese laundryman in Kanowna named Jinarto Yano. Yabu sent a series of telegrams to Samamoto, demanding that she return. She ignored the telegrams, and Yabu soon boarded a train to Kanowna.

Shortly after his arrival, two neighbours heard gunshots fired inside Yano's house. As they rushed to investigate, they saw another Japanese man leaving the house, carrying a revolver. When he disappeared, the two men—Bates and Carey—entered the house and found the bodies of Jinarto Yano and Sono Samamoto, felled by gunshot wounds.

Bates and Carey described the gunman to police, who warned their colleagues in Kalgoorlie to be on the lookout for Yabu at the train station, but the evening darkness worked to the advantage of the killer. The Kalgoorlie police then proceeded to make inquiries at the Japanese brothels in Hay Street, where one Japanese woman admitted that she knew Yabu and said that she now feared for her life. The Japanese women were moved to a safer location for the night, and Police Constable Brown waited in the shadows behind the brothel for the wanted man to appear.

Around midnight Yabu appeared at the back gate of the brothel, revolver in hand; as he opened the gate, he was confronted by Constable Brown. Turning to flee, Yabu fired two shots that narrowly missed the constable. At the same time, the sound of gunshots and the shrill alarm of Constable Brown's whistle brought police reinforcements charging to the scene. Another police constable fired two shots, one grazing Yabu's scalp and the other entering his shoulder, enabling police to take him into custody. Yabu was sentenced to death for the wilful murder of Jinarto Yano and Sono Samamoto, but the sentence was later commuted to twenty years' imprisonment.

The number of Japanese prostitutes working on the goldfields steadily declined following the passage of the Commonwealth *Immigration Restriction Act 1901*, but those Japanese prostitutes who had arrived prior to this would have had perhaps thirty working years left on the goldfields, provided they did not fall victim to hazards such as disease or murder. Inevitably, the number of Japanese brothels also gradually declined during the following decades.

Meanwhile, the number of prostitutes had begun to decline overall, in tandem with the number of unmarried miners on the goldfields. Thousands of men who had worked independently as prospectors began to bid the 'fields farewell in the early 1900s, as gold fever subsided and large mining companies worked deeper mines and assumed control of the gold industry in Kalgoorlie. At the same time, many men who laboured in the goldmines had brought their wives and families to settle in Kalgoorlie.

Even though prostitution was beginning to decline, the number of brothel complaints to the local council would soon increase, owing mainly to the rising number of 'respectable' women and children settling in the town. The council would struggle to respond to these complaints effectively, and would eventually identify an alternative to the prohibitionist approach, which had proved most ineffective in dealing with the 'social evil' of prostitution in the town.

CHAPTER 3

Containing the 'social evil' in Kalgoorlie

During the first decade of the twentieth century, the Kalgoorlie Municipal Council apparently reached the consensus that the only thing worse than regulating the 'social evil' was not regulating it. As Kalgoorlie increasingly sought to define itself as a stable, middle-class, family-friendly town, the growing population and its changing social composition placed yet more pressure on the council to come to terms with the local sex trade.

State and local laws had failed to have any significant impact on the number and location of brothels in the town, and the embarrassing problem of open soliciting by prostitutes on the streets and in the pubs continued. At the same time, sexually transmitted diseases (STDs) were becoming an urgent public health concern on the goldfields. Nurse Ann Garnsey wrote in her memoirs that a special hospital ward at Coolgardie was always filled with patients suffering from venereal diseases.[1] These public health concerns and local planning issues would soon combine to lay the foundation for the unofficial 'Containment Policy' in Kalgoorlie.

The first proposal to create a red-light district was presented in a report tabled by the Social Evil Committee at a council meeting held on 28 October 1901. The committee recommended that brothels be confined to 'one street in West Kalgoorlie', and the relevant motion succeeded after a protracted council debate and the first of many divisions over the issue.

Councillors who opposed the creation of a red-light district cited the lack of legal endorsement from the Western Australian Government, and put forward their own (unsuccessful) motion that council write to the state government to request that Parliament

> immediately bring in a Bill to regulate prostitution and that a certain portion of each town be appointed to prostitutes to reside in, with the consent of the Municipal Council concerned, and that every prostitute be licensed and under medical supervision.[2]

It would thus appear that councillors on both sides of the debate actually supported the idea of a red-light district in Kalgoorlie, but one side refused to adopt the plan without the state government's endorsement. Although the above motion was not passed, it did document the public health and planning imperatives driving the council's pursuit of a regulation policy, and foreshadowed the very conditions that would soon form the basis of the local Containment Policy.

It did not take long for local resident groups to rise in opposition to the council's proposal to create a red-light district: deputations from the Clerical Association and the West Kalgoorlie Ratepayers Association addressed the next council meeting on 11 November 1901.[3] These deputations were heard, thanked and dismissed, with no further action indicated. Similarly, most letters received from local residents complaining about brothels were minuted with instructions that no further action be taken.

Any hopes that the state government might offer direction and support in regulating brothels were dashed with the passage of the *Police Act Amendment Act 1902*, which gave police greater powers to prosecute keepers, occupiers and landlords of any premises used for the purposes of prostitution. This legislation was nevertheless useful to Kalgoorlie police in targeting women who had previously operated independently from their own homes. First-time offenders convicted of 'keeping a premises for the purpose of prostitution' faced a fine of £20 or six months' imprisonment (with or without hard labour). Thus, despite the absence of any provision for official regulation, the Act was indispensable to local police in Kalgoorlie: prostitutes could now effectively be concentrated into brothel employment, and brothels could be concentrated into a designated zone of containment.

In what appears to have been its first step in creating a containment zone for prostitution, the Kalgoorlie Municipal Council implemented one notable change: the block of Brookman Street west of Lane Street was renamed Hay Street and gazetted on 27 June 1902[4]; this is precisely the area where the Hay Street red-light district later developed. It seems safe to suggest that the council had discreetly 'earmarked' this area for the purpose of containing Kalgoorlie's red-light district. A map of the Kalgoorlie town site dated 16 July 1897 (see Figure 5) shows that the area bounded by Forrest, Lane, Egan and Lionel streets had not been allocated individual lots, while the rest of the town site had been divided into private town lots.[5] Above all, there is little doubt that Brookman Street's partial name change on 27 June 1902 (see Figure 6) served to distract from the fact that the red-light district, the police station and the local courthouse all co-existed on the same street in Kalgoorlie.

Kalgoorlie's growing 'respectable' (read middle-class) population, possessed of little tolerance for the trade conducted by prostitutes, intensified the flow of complaints about brothels to the council during the following years. This eventually forced the issue into its final great debate at the council meeting held on 22 May 1905, when Councillor Erson put forward the following motion, which was lost after a marathon debate and several divisions:

> that in the interest of public morality as well as in the interests of the city generally it is desirable that all brothels east of Wilson Street should be removed and that steps be taken by this Council to secure reform in the direction indicated.[6]

In the years that followed, the council's 'rule of thumb' seems to have been to direct brothel-related complaints to the local police with the request that they take immediate action. The only exception was a letter received from the West Kalgoorlie Progress Association, which complained that the number of brothels in the municipality had increased and requested that the council take action to close them. Since this letter contained no specific locational details regarding the brothels, the council simply forwarded the letter to police.

The council thus seems to have adopted the policy that police would only be asked to take action when details were provided for them to act on. All letters of complaint that included the *location* of the alleged brothel were forwarded to police, requesting that they take immediate action—even those letters complaining of brothels located in Hay Street. It is noteworthy that local residents continued to refer to Hay Street as 'Brookman Street' in numerous deputations and letters to the council—obviously unaware that 'Hay Street' existed. As late as 1907, the council minutes do not include any corrections to several residents' references to 'Brookman Street between Lane and Lionel Streets', despite the 1902 gazettal of Hay Street.[7] It appears that the council's creation of Hay Street, and the reasons behind its gazettal, remained a closely guarded secret for some time.

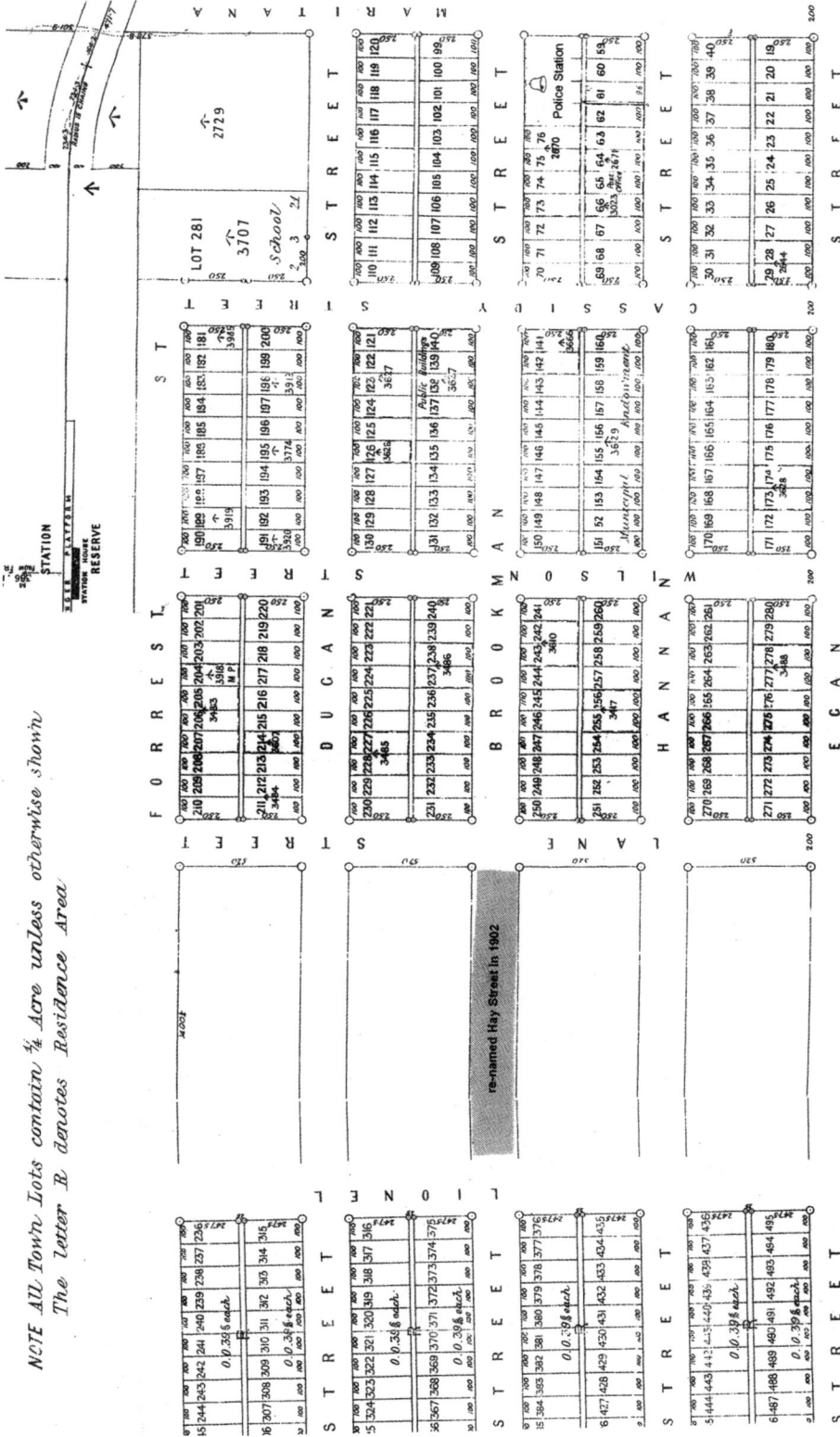

Figure 5 Map of Kalgoorlie town site, showing Hay Street and the local police station (at the corner of Brookman and Maritana streets), 16 July 1897, produced by the Western Australian Commissioner of Crown Lands. Courtesy Battye Library (35/7/KALG/1987)

ST.

HAY

BROOKMAN Co. 27-6-02. Co. 36/02

326

325

LIONEL

817 82 250

a 0 7 b

817 93 P

RIGHT OF HAY

100

ST.

— Scale 100 an to an Inch —
EXTD.

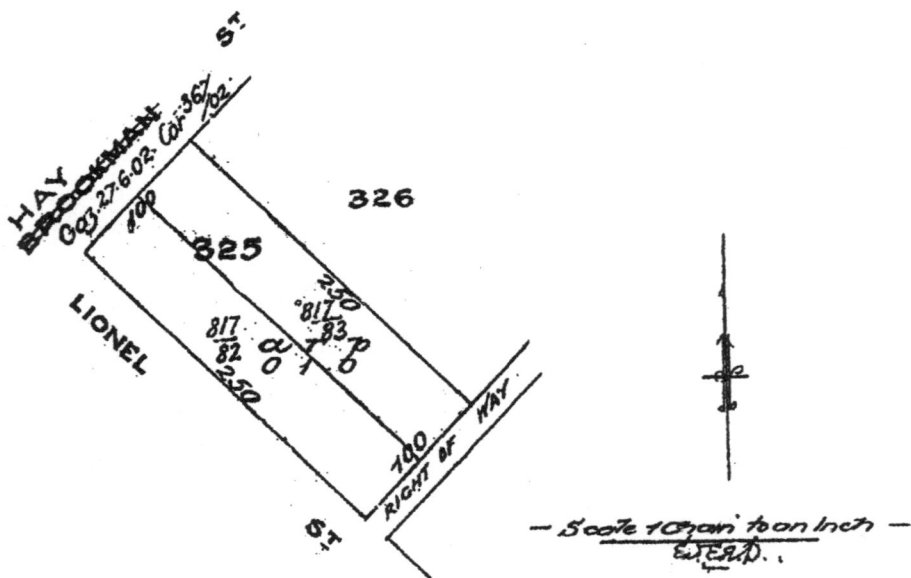

Figure 6 *Certificate of Title for the property at 181 Hay Street, showing Brookman Street crossed out and replaced with Hay Street, gazetted on 27 June 1902.*
Courtesy Department of Land Information, P380

At its meeting held on 16 July 1906, the council accepted 'a petition signed by Messrs Paterson and Co. and ten other ratepayers, asking that steps be taken to have the brothels in Brookman Street between Wilson and Lionel Streets suppressed'. The council referred the petition to local police with the request 'that immediate steps be taken to abate the evil'.[8] In his letter of response to the council, the inspector of police explained that 'steps were being taken to suppress, as far as possible, brothels in Brookman Street'. The council minuted the letter, with no further action indicated.[9] By that stage, it seems that the unofficial Containment Policy was well and truly up and running.

Two later brothel-related council minutes are also worth noting. In his December 1906 letter to the council, local resident Mr F. Rickarly respect-fully requested that council take immediate action 'to prevent the Police removing certain women from Brookman Street on 25 December 1906'. The reason for Mr Rickarly's request is not recorded in the council's min-utes, which only note that the council's letter of response to Mr Rickarly simply quoted the relevant local by-law that prohibited brothels.[10] Then in December 1907 an extraordinary piece of correspondence was received from the Under-Secretary of Western Australia, advising the council 'that the police have succeeded in having had all the brothels in Kalgoorlie closed, and the women compelled to leave the town'.[11] The council briefly recorded the letter and its remarkable claim with thanks. There being no further mention of brothels in the minute books until several decades later, it appears that the council quietly handed the matter over to the police soon after creating the Hay Street red-light district in 1902, thereby setting two central features of the policy that would come to be known as Containment: police regulation and a designated zone of 'tolerance' for the brothels.

While the Hay Street red-light district had more or less settled the planning issues for the council and the police, there were growing public health concerns relating to the spread of venereal diseases, especially syphilis, which was often fatal. These concerns were influential in creating a need for the health component of the developing Containment Policy. Prostitution-related public health concerns became the domain of law enforcement, and police soon began to enforce an unofficial policy of compulsory medical examinations for prostitutes. While many of the women had been voluntarily undergoing fortnightly medical examinations since the late 1890s[12], it seems unlikely that their clients had been taking similar precautions, nor is there any indication that the men were encouraged to do so by the authorities.

The precedent for compulsory health examinations for prostitutes had been provided in the British *Contagious Diseases Acts 1864–69*, which aimed to provide disease-free prostitutes for English soldiers in garrison towns. *The Sunday Times* joined in the push for a similar system to be implemented locally, and one editorial in 1909 argued:

> A CD Act is wanted in Western Australia for several reasons. It is wanted in the interests of morality and public decency; it is wanted for the protection of the prostitutes themselves; it is wanted because syphilis is becoming dangerously prevalent and because the only effective means of checking it is to put the women of the town under some restraint.[13]

In the state House of Representatives, W. J. George (Member for Murray) supported this view and argued that the Contagious Diseases Acts in Britain had been 'remarkably beneficial for the men'.[14] However, religious and feminist groups managed to defeat moves to include venereal diseases on the list of notifiable diseases under the Western Australian *Health Act 1911*, arguing that this would constitute a local version of the British Contagious Diseases Acts, which regulated and thus condoned the 'white slave trade'.

The absence of enabling legislation did not impede law enforcement in Western Australia; police routinely forced prostitutes to undergo disease screening when they were arrested. If a woman was found to be infected, the usual outcome was her conviction as an idle and disorderly person or as a vagrant under the Police Act, with six months' imprisonment in Fremantle Gaol.[15]

Women who worked as prostitutes also, predictably, assumed full responsibility for unwanted pregnancies that resulted from sex with their clients. Historian Raelene Davidson confirms that abortionists were very common in Western Australia at the turn of the century, and counted prostitutes among their clients. One backyard abortionist known as Robert Bruce even 'used a notorious brothel in Kalgoorlie as his base'.[16]

Brothels became more concentrated in Hay Street as brothel owners and prostitutes attempted to avoid arrest, although Japanese brothels are known to have operated in east Brookman Street in Kalgoorlie and on Richardson Street in Boulder until at least the 1930s. Kalgoorlie resident Lorna Mitchell recalled that, during the 1920s and 1930s, a row of Japanese brothels stood on Brookman Street in Kalgoorlie near the corner of Maritana Street, where the law courts stand today.[17] Remarkably, this location would have put these brothels directly across the street from the Kalgoorlie police station. Boulder resident Olga Dawes remembered well the Japanese brothels that operated on Richardson Street in Boulder during the 1920s and 1930s, which used laundries as a front for their businesses.[18]

Boulder resident Joy Kenneally chuckled as she related a celebrated family story from the early 1920s about her Irish father-in-law's furious reaction to the news that there were Japanese brothels on Richardson Street. When Conrad Kenneally learned that his family's new home would be facing directly on to a row of Japanese brothels, he swore that it would not. A devout Catholic and proud family man, Mr Kenneally had well-defined views on the matter, and used every means available to maximise the distance between his family and the Japanese 'dens of infamy':

> The Japanese brothels were on the corner of Richardson and Brookman Streets, and the Kenneally house was on the opposite corner facing the brothels. And no way was Con, that's my father-in-law, going to have their house facing the brothels. So he had it jinkered away, to the very other end of the block, and so it faced Brookman Street, not Richardson Street. When my husband was little, and they were going to school, they were forbidden to walk home past that part of the street. They had to walk on the other side of the street.[19]

Mary Lardi, Conrad Kenneally's daughter, recalled that as a child she was fascinated by the Japanese lanterns that graced the simple weatherboard dwellings on Richardson Street. She also spoke with respect about the women who lived in the controversial houses across the street:

I know my mother used to say they were lovely people. I was only a little child at the time. You wouldn't have known them from any other house, because it was so well run and everything. It was a beautiful place, very well kept, and they had a high fence. And we didn't know [it was a brothel] because we were only kids.

I can still see the hallway with the Japanese lanterns. I remember that, because when you're a child, these things fascinate you. I wouldn't have known anyway, because in those days, life was just...well, you weren't told anything.

And it was your father who decided that the family home would not face the Japanese brothel?
Well, I mean they were Irish! Irish—and we were Roman Catholic, so you know that wasn't on. He came out from Ireland, and I think he bought the house and put it on the block.

You mentioned you could see the hallways of the brothel—the Japanese would leave their front door open?
Yes, looking for business I suppose! I think her name was Mrs Kurazaki— I think she lived on the corner, and Mrs Kurazaki also had a market garden.

Did your parents lodge any complaints to the town council, or the police, about the brothel?
Well, I don't think so, because I think in those days, from what I gathered from my mother, it was a quiet and select sort of thing—it wasn't so open as they have them today. I mean, the ones in Brookman Street [in Kalgoorlie] when I was going to the dances in Kalgoorlie, that was quite a known thing and everybody knew that the brothels were down there. But this was sort of select.

Did the women sit in the doorways of the brothel?
Oh, yes. I can't remember her name, but this lady was very kind, and she'd give you lollies if she ever saw you going past. Oh, yes—they were very generous, and they also had a big vegetable garden. I can remember they used to give Mum vegetables.

What did the women wear?
Well, one lady used to wear the grey frock with the Chinese...very high collar. Now if you went down Hay Street [today], you see them out there now and they've got next to nothing on. But these ladies were sort of...modest ladies...or modest ladies for brothels! *[Laughter]*

How did you find out they were brothels?
My mother told me as I grew older that that's what it was. She said it was a 'bad house where bad men went'. Probably some of the good men in Boulder

went there too! Of course, that's the way my mother was brought up in Ireland, and that's the way she brought us up here.[20]

While the *Immigration Restriction Act 1901* stemmed the flow of Japanese prostitutes into Australia, a small number of Japanese women who had already entered the country continued to work in brothels in Kalgoorlie and Boulder. Local police allowed Japanese brothels to operate outside the Hay Street red-light district, a practice perhaps influenced by strong anti-Asian sentiment on the goldfields (which made Asians vulnerable to hostility and assaults) and the quiet mannerisms of the Japanese women. Then the outbreak of World War II would have effectively closed any remaining Japanese brothels. The Emperor had ordered all his subjects to return to Japan before the war, and many obeyed—including Karayuki San, or Japanese prostitutes. Japanese people who chose to remain in Australia were interned in concentration camps during the war.

Meanwhile, during the 1930s and 1940s, Kalgoorlie's Containment Policy had helped to make Hay Street a legendary feature of life in Kalgoorlie. The brothels represented an important social institution for the local men who patronised them, while offering a constant source of amusement and gossip for 'respectable' townsfolk. There was also the excitement of the occasional 'legitimate' contact with the women, should a young man's work bring him to Hay Street. Goldfields resident 'Spud' recalled his first experiences with the Hay Street brothels while delivering newspapers and recycling bottles as a youngster in the 1930s:

> Well, I used to deliver papers there, and I'd pick up the cool drink bottles, and the plonk bottles and the beer bottles. For the beer bottles, we used to get a ha'penny each. Bloody good money. One girl might say, 'In the passage way there are some beer bottles and plonk bottles'. Another girl there might say to you, 'Can you put these in your cart, and take them back?' A cart, on a pushbike, was like the grocer's thing—the box in the front—and a second one behind. You might get thruppence [3d] for a haul.
>
> Then I'd go down to the laundry, and back again to Hay Street. Now for champagne bottles, we used to get thruppence each, especially if they still had the 'alley' in them. In the old days, when they made the champagne bottles, they used to put a little glass vot in the bottom of them, so that when it filled up, and the air ratio got it...it would hit the ceiling. That stopped the gas from getting out.

> *At that time, did you know what Hay Street was all about?*
> No, not actually. I found that out when I was about 10. I'd been doing the rounds for a few years by then, and that was when my mother found out where

I was getting this money from, to help support the rest of the family. And then I copped a razor strap.

I had been doing some extra work for one of the girls, I can't remember what now, and she gave me a 10s note. Well, I was pleased as punch, and I slipped Mum the 10s note for my younger sister. She'd just started school, and I can't remember what she needed...new shoes, I think. Mum asked, 'Where'd you get that from?' I said, 'The lady I've been working for gave it to me'. She said, 'You take me and show me'. So I took her out there. Mum seen the place...and I copped it—razor strap all over my back and face. Couldn't go to school for two days, I was just black and blue. Mum kept saying, 'You've been with one of those hussies!'

So later, did you and your friends tend to walk past the brothels often?
Bloody oath! Well, what were they there for? And sometimes the madam would come out yelling, 'You bloody bastards! The police will be right out!' All of a sudden, old Sergeant Carmody would come riding down on his motorbike. And good old Sergeant Carmody, when you copped a kick in the arse, matey, you knew it. They wouldn't book ya, they'd just give you a smack. Then they'd take you home to your mother and father, and you'd cop another one. They were good, though, they wouldn't charge you or nothin'.

Sometimes they wouldn't tell Mum or Dad for a few days, and then old Sergeant Carmody would have a quiet word to them. And I remember once I was sitting in the bath, and Mum came in first, razor sharp, and smacked me—whoomf! 'You've been down there again, haven't you?' Whoomf! 'No, Ma, no! I haven't!' 'You're a liar!' Whoomf! I copped another one.[21]

Another local lad who found a good source of casual income by way of the Hay Street brothels was 'Johnno', who worked for a wood yard in nearby Dugan Street during the 1930s and 1940s:

I first became involved with the girls on Hay Street when I was delivering the wood. There were about twelve to fourteen houses there in those days, and their main means of heating was fire. I've never known of any other brothels to be located outside of Lane and Lionel streets. There would have been four on the north side, and about eight or nine on the south side.

Because that road [Hay Street] was our main thoroughfare from the wood yard—which was two blocks down from the girls, in Dugan Street. Quite a bit of our work was going up the street past the girls, and at times if they wanted to order wood, they'd hail you or sing out to you, and tell you they're out of wood or nearly out of wood. They nearly always used to get a half a ton of wood weekly, which in them days was worth 14s. All their cooking and all their heating was done by the fire. So they would have had an open fire in the lounge room, I presume. Of course, their kitchen was their main usage of the wood, in the old wooden fire stoves.

Where did the girls signal from?
Well, in those days it was very strict…they were not allowed to be out on the footpaths, they were not allowed to come outside their doorway. As well as working down that end of town, I also lived down that end of town. So if I was with a group of people who were going uptown, whether I was on me own or with a couple of mates, we always used to find it necessary to walk up Hay Street and have a look at the girls.

Even the madams were very strict in those days. If they saw us young fellas, standing out star-gazing out front, quite often the madam would come out and tell you to get on your way, and send you up the street.

But I delivered the wood there, and quite often the madam would say, 'I'm right out of wood now, and the yardman won't be in until this afternoon—have you got time to split a few bits of wood for me?' And I'd say, 'Yeah, that's OK'. So I'd grab the axe and I'd just split up three or four blocks of wood. I'd just throw it in a wheelbarrow there, and wheel it up as far as the back door, and for that the madam would give me 2s. Sometimes she might give me 2s 6d. And at that time I was only earning £2 12s 6d a week. And if that happened two or three times, from a couple of the houses, well, I used to make a bit of spending money like that.[22]

On other occasions, Johnno earned extra money by running errands for the brothel madams and workers:

One or two of the girls there might want you to post a letter. Or I remember taking shoes into town to get them repaired. The girls would say 'Can you take them up today, and pick them up tomorrow, and pay them and let me know how much?' On the wood cart I used to drop around and do a few little extra jobs for the girls, and take them back and tell them how much it was, and she used to give me that and a few shillings extra. Several times they'd just sing out while I was going along the street and say, 'Will you post these for me?' And I'd hop off, and then post the letters for them, and they'd give you a shilling. When I was only earning £2 12s 6d, I'd always remember the extra money, which used to come in handy.

What would it have cost to have sex with one of the girls?
I think it was about 7s 6d to go with one of the girls back then. From what I can remember they were all around the 20–25 age group.

Can you share any particularly memorable experiences?
On occasion, particularly on a cold winter's day—I always remember it—if I delivered a load of wood to the back garden, sometimes the madam would

say, 'Would you like a cup of coffee or tea?' or 'Would you like a piece of toast?' And quite often then I used to go into the kitchen, and sit there and have my cup of tea or sometimes a bowl of soup. And I know many a time I've had a cup of soup in the house there, and then got on my way.

And one particular incident I remember, I had to deliver a load of wood there to a house. I opened the back gate, went into the backyard, and turned the horse around to unload the wood onto their wood heap. And there was a girl lying out in the sunshine with nothing on, reading a book! And I went on about my job, unloading my load of wood. Then I got my order book and started to trot off to the back of the house to get the money or the docket signed...this one house was running an account with the yard. And as I started to walk up to the house, this lass sung out, 'Hey, come over here. There's no one up there. I'll sign the book'. And I turned back around and walked over to her and she just politely placed the book down and covered herself up, sat up and signed the book. I think that would have been the first time that I had seen a completely nude woman, just relaxing in the sunshine and taking it as another day in her life as a working girl.[23]

Given the young local male population's unshakeable fancy for gazing upon the Hay Street women, it is perhaps not surprising that the brothels resembled makeshift corrugated 'fortresses', with their tall fences and security gates. Frank Stevens, born in Kalgoorlie in 1930, recalled that the Hay Street brothels' distinctive appearance featured high corrugated iron fences that visually sealed off each of the premises, apart from narrow 'runways' where the women sat well inside:

You could tell by the fencing and that...what they were. You know, they had high corrugated iron fences in those days...and usually with the cyclone wire access gate. Some of them even had security from the verandah to the front fence, which wasn't very far—probably 5 or 6 foot. The fences were still up in the 50s.[24]

While there is no evidence to suggest that the local council demanded these fences, it is significant that in 1951 the Perth City Council ordered that the owners of all the Roe Street brothels construct similar enclosures[25] to 'prevent occupants from exposing themselves to the public'[26]; these took the form of tall timber fences along the frontages (see Figure 7).[27]

There is strong anecdotal evidence that Hay Street experienced something of an economic 'boom' during World War II. Mr Stevens recalled that, while serving his motor mechanic apprenticeship near Hay Street in 1944, there were from twelve to fourteen brothels in Hay Street, which often had long queues extending along the footpath.[28]

Figure 7 *Roe Street brothels, Perth, c. 1958. These high timber fences, ordered by the Perth City Council in 1951, were similar to those that encased the Hay Street brothels during the same period.* Courtesy The West Australian

This seems likely to have been related to the deployment of hundreds of American servicemen stationed on the goldfields during World War II. Australia's vulnerable position in the South Pacific had prompted the Commonwealth Government to forge strong military ties with the United States. As a result, hundreds of thousands of American troops arrived for deployment at strategic military bases throughout Australia[29], including the Royal Australian Air Force base near Kalgoorlie.[30]

While many Australians embraced the new arrivals and drew comfort from images of American power and chivalry (as seen in Hollywood movies), there was also a powerful backlash against the United States presence from Australians who feared the permanent 'Americanisation' of their culture. A number of developments might well have helped to fuel this fear: Australian cinemas took to beginning each movie session by playing 'The Star Spangled Banner' instead of 'God Save the King', while some popular Australian radio stations played the American national anthem daily.[31]

At the same time, every American serviceman of every rank earned around twice as much as his Australian counterpart, while also enjoying a highly favourable monetary exchange rate in Australia. A common catchphrase was that the 'Yanks' were 'overpaid, oversexed and over here'.

The Americans used their spending power with customary abandon, and quickly cornered the market in every black-market item worth having in Australia during the war—including Australian beer, following the Commonwealth Government's order that its production be cut by one-third.[32] Across the country, Australian men also resented the 'Yankee big-spenders' because of their somewhat 'hyped' popularity with Australian women[33], and because many young women ended up marrying their American beaus and moving to the United States.

Fifty years later, there was still evidence of anti-American sentiment on the goldfields. One afternoon during the mid-1990s, I sat chatting with local residents in a Boulder pub, recording their stories about the Hay Street brothels. One long-time goldfields resident had declined to be interviewed and sat at the bar; when he heard of my American origins, he sat himself across from me at the table and unleashed a tirade of bitterness about 'all those arrogant, cock-sucking, mother-fucking Yanks who threw their goddamned money all around Kalgoorlie and Boulder, and then pissed off back to the States with the young women'. As luck would have it, this prickly pear soon settled and ended up sharing a story or two that helped to inform and enliven *The Scarlet Mile*.

The rather more diplomatic 'Red Dean', a former goldfields union official, recalled an enterprising wartime scheme hatched by a number of local lads to cash in on the big-spending Yanks and their penchant for preferential treatment:

> Down on Hay Street, some of the young local fellas made a few pounds, because there'd be a queue outside the brothels, and they'd get in the queue, and when they got up the front, some Yank'd come along, and they'd say, 'I'll sell you my spot'. So the young fella took the money off the Yank, maybe two or three quid, and went to the back of the queue.[34]

Certainly, Hay Street had been well established as the only domain in Kalgoorlie where brothels and prostitutes were permitted to exist. Under the Containment Policy, women were forced to live in the brothels and remain there at all times, apart from visits to the doctor or the hairdresser, which were allowed on the proviso that they travelled only by taxi.

Former Boulder resident Shirley worked as a hairdresser at the Erik Salon in Hannan Street during the early 1950s, and remembered that there were about five Hay Street women who visited the salon on a weekly basis. They always arrived and left by taxi, and usually enjoyed a few laughs with their hairdressers, although Hay Street business was never discussed. Another Hay Street woman sent her hairpiece to and from the salon by taxi, on its own, for its weekly shampoo and styling.

Shirley and her husband Norm remembered well one striking young Hay Street woman who attracted considerable attention during the mid-1950s. With her fondness for racing around the town during the day in her (American) red Kaiser Vagabond car, while stepping out in fashionable and revealing shorts, she became known by locals as the 'Vagabond'. The refractory young woman managed to defy the local Containment rules for a month or so before she vanished from the scene. It is not known whether the police forced her to leave Kalgoorlie or she continued to work on Hay Street, perhaps on the proviso that she would make use of the local taxi service to conduct any further business about town.

Shirley's mother had encountered some interesting characters while working as a barmaid; one of her regular customers in Boulder was a former Hay Street woman named Bonnie, who lived nearby with her young daughter. Shirley recalled that Bonnie travelled mostly by bicycle around Kalgoorlie-Boulder, and always 'wore her hair like a man'. Shirley also said that, while her parents did not like the idea of their teenage daughter getting too friendly with the 'scarlet-stained' woman, she always enjoyed chatting with Bonnie whenever she encountered her at the hotel: 'Bonnie was just a normal person, to me. She spoke most respectfully to me. She was just another lady, like any other lady that I knew'.[35]

While prostitutes continued to endure a powerful social stigma associated with their trade, many 'respectable' local residents and visitors to Kalgoorlie were nevertheless fascinated by the Hay Street women. Curious townsfolk began to stray into the red-light district for a titillating glimpse of Kalgoorlie's 'other world'. In the decades that followed, Hay Street would become a focus of intense popular fascination for local residents and a 'must-see' attraction for tourists visiting Kalgoorlie.

CHAPTER 4

Hay Street and the long arm of the law

In the collective social memory of Kalgoorlie, the 1960s and 1970s might well be remembered as the golden age of traditional Containment, as the Hay Street brothels settled in to a period of relative stability under the unofficial Containment Policy. Removed from the sort of political 'meddling' that had resulted in the closure of Perth's Roe Street brothels in 1958, the Hay Street brothels would be defended time and again against 'outsider' influences.

Half a century after the French and Japanese 'sex slave' syndicates had abandoned the post-boom goldfields, Kalgoorlie's local Containment Policy had created a unique set of discriminatory working conditions for Hay Street women that continued to set them apart from the rest of Kalgoorlie (if not the twentieth century). Stability under the Containment Policy was achieved with some considerable sacrifice on the part of the Hay Street women: in order for Containment to be accepted by Kalgoorlie's 'respectable' residents, prostitutes had to accept their place firmly outside the local community.

Meanwhile, the brothels had begun to appeal to the curiosity of Kalgoorlie's 'respectable' residents and visitors, and this interest intensified during the rather more colourful 'swinging' 1960s. Hay Street was also fast becoming the town's most popular tourist attraction, second only to the Golden Mile.

Because the Containment Policy has never been written down, it is nearly impossible to determine when or why each Containment rule was introduced in Kalgoorlie. While certain Containment conditions clearly originated with Kalgoorlie police authorities—the locational restrictions on brothels, police registration and compulsory health examinations for staff—a number of former Hay Street workers have claimed that some Containment rules (such as the restrictions on workers' movements in town) originated with the Hay Street madams. In any case, police authorities have confirmed that local police in Kalgoorlie enforced the following Containment rules at least as early as the 1960s:

- Brothels had to be located on Hay Street, between Lane and Lionel streets.
- Brothels, madams and workers had to be registered with the local police.
- Brothels had to be owned and managed by women only.
- Workers had to be at least 21 years of age.
- Workers had to have weekly medical examinations.
- Workers had to reside on brothel premises.
- Workers were comprehensively banned from visiting Kalgoorlie's town centre—including hotels, cinemas or the public swimming pool.[1]

Despite the extreme personal restrictions imposed on them while working in Kalgoorlie, the women made the most of life on Hay Street. Former workers Val, 'Judy' and 'Rita' and former madam Irene shared their stories of life on Hay Street—filled with spirit and humour, despite their often unfortunate circumstances.

A portly and eloquent woman of 60 years, Val said she arrived from Perth to work on Hay Street in 1962, the year after her taxi-driver husband of thirteen years walked out on her and their six children. Unable to make ends meet on her welfare payments, she began working in the Hay Street brothels, leaving the children with a female relative during her weeks away from Perth. Val lost custody of her children while working in Hay Street, when her occupation was revealed during divorce proceedings; her children were then placed in the care of various foster parents:

> I now feel guilty about losing the kids...I didn't know...where do you go? Where does a woman...When he left me in 1961, the welfare kept me and they gave me less than £10 a week to feed myself and six kids. I paid £5 out of that for rent, to get a house big enough for us, and I used to go out at two o'clock in the morning, and go out and pinch somebody's milk and bread...until one morning it was raining and my two sons came in with their raincoats on, they were 12 and 13, and they said, 'We'll go out and get the

bread today, Mum'. And then I realised they knew I was stealing, and I had to stop it.[2]

Years later, she managed to restore contact with four of her six children. Speaking philosophically and freely in her living room, in the company of her young adult granddaughter, Val told how she retired from the sex industry in 1968 to live with her future husband in the state's South West. Now separated, she lives alone in a small unit in the outer suburbs of Perth.

Former Hay Street workers Judy and Rita, both from Sydney, also worked in Hay Street during the 1960s. Judy (see Figure 8) described a lively atmosphere in Sydney at that time, when she first ventured 'on the game':

> I done the nursing aide's course at Prince Henry hospital in Sydney, and I was there for four years. During the last year, that was during the Vietnam War...and at the Wayside Chapel in Kings Cross, we used to go down there for cups of tea. It was a little church, and they used to have a theatre sort of thing there, and all the young people, they used to have debates and everything.

Figure 8 'Judy', who worked in the Hay Street brothels during the late 1960s.
Courtesy Judy, private collection of photographs

It was really great fun. We used to have our own little debate team, and it was nearly always about the Vietnam War. Then the Americans used to come for a week or two of R and R. So we got into the swing of them! We just made friends with them, because all of them used to go up to the Wayside Chapel.

Oh, they felt terrible about the war. Sometimes they'd ring up and say they wanted a girl or something like that. And many of them...all they really wanted to do was talk to somebody. So that was the time I left nursing and I got a flat in Kings Cross. There were about four or five girls working with me.[3]

Following a series of brushes with corrupt policemen in Kings Cross, Judy moved to Perth and then to Kalgoorlie in early 1969, where she began working in Hay Street. Months later, she left Kalgoorlie to travel with her future husband to the Northern Territory and Queensland. Now divorced, she lives in Kalgoorlie with her teenage daughter.

While teaching as a driving instructor in Sydney, Rita met a number of sex workers for the first time:

The reason I decided to work [in the sex industry] was because I got a job at the East Sydney Driving School, as a driving instructor. And I decided that the guy I was working for was such a crook, and this is how I heard about it. Because many of the girls who were getting their licences there were workers from down in Palmer Street, East Sydney. And of course I got talking to them and I thought, Oh well, I can always fall back on this, if I ever need to. You know, it sounded pretty good.

Then I worked out how much it would cost to get a car fitted out, and I thought I might get my own driving school, and that's when I decided to start doing it. I just worked by myself. I used to have a few select customers because the clubs I used to work in Wollongong, a lot of guys used to put it to me, so to speak. And I would just pick out one here and one there that seemed OK, who could manage what I was asking. I had a flat in Wollongong, I used to live out in the suburbs myself, and once a week I used to see these five guys. And I just put it all in the bank, whatever I made. I didn't use it, because I was living on me wages. And I couldn't take them home, because I was living with me brother. But I started, and then I didn't like it, and so I didn't carry on with it. Probably four years later I took my next customer. So there was a big gap there.[4]

In Sydney, Rita befriended future Hay Street madam Irene, who persuaded her to try her luck in Kalgoorlie in 1969. After a few years' working in Kalgoorlie, Rita went on to manage a number of Hay Street brothels until the mid-1980s, when she retired from 'the life' to get married. She still lives happily in Boulder with her husband.

During the early 1960s, five brothels are known to have operated on Hay Street—four on the south side and one on the north. Then in 1966 Kalgoorlie entered a period of enhanced prosperity, when nickel deposits were discovered at Kambalda. In response to the increase in the local male work force, the number of brothels operating on Hay Street increased to seven. Rita said the brothels looked much like the rest of Kalgoorlie's houses:

> Oh, Kalgoorlie houses—they were made of tin, with tin walls, and fibro, weatherboard—just real Kalgoorlie houses. There were no bricks...
>
> When I first came here there was another house between 181 and Stella's [143 Hay Street], another little shanty sort of a house, and at the time it was not operating, but they pushed it down. It had been operating...but it was condemned. It was just a little shanty, but apparently someone had been operating in it before.[5]

Former Hay Street madam Irene (see Figure 9) was taken aback by the stark 'tinniness' of Kalgoorlie when she first arrived in 1969. As the plane circled Kalgoorlie in preparation for landing, Irene's bird's-eye view of the housing stock prompted this observation:

> If you had a can opener, you could open the whole town! [Laughter] I'll never forget that, when the plane came down. I said, 'Gee, all you need here is a can opener'. It was all tin![6]

Most of the custom-built corrugated iron brothels accommodated four to eight workers in individual bedrooms, with separate lounge and dining areas. Val and Judy said that it had been a long-standing Hay Street tradition for each brothel to employ a cook to prepare the workers' meals, and a housemaid to clean the premises daily. While Judy recalled that many of the workers did not always eat three meals a day, the madams generally insisted that all workers 'knock off' the evening meal of 'meat-and-two-veg' when it was placed on the table, perhaps with a view to maintaining workers' general health and sustaining their energy throughout the working evening.

> We had all our meals taken care of...[the madam] had a cook there. Oh, we were waited on hand and foot. We had our washing done, our dinners cooked, our rooms cleaned. The rooms were lovely.[7]

One former Hay Street cook, long-term Boulder resident Elma, chatted brightly about her days cooking and cleaning in the Hay Street brothels during the 1960s. Yet when she initially responded to the newspaper advertisement for a casual cleaner, she hesitated to take the job because it would take her into the infamous Hay Street brothels. It is perhaps a testament

Figure 9 *Madam Irene, who managed and owned brothels in Hay Street during the years 1969–89.* Courtesy Leigh Varis-Beswick, private collection of photographs

to Kalgoorlie-Boulder's fairly laid-back attitude towards the brothels that neither Elma nor her husband found the job proposal objectionable, after they had discussed the matter:

> I read the paper one morning and [the advertisement] said they wanted a casual cleaner. It said apply...it was a taxi driver's number. So, anyway, I rang up. And he said the place was at...the brothels. I said, 'Oh, just hang on'. I went back to talk to my husband in his workshed...and I said to him, 'What do you think, if I put in there and got the job?' He said, 'Oh, their money's as good as anybody else's. You don't have to participate in anything that goes on in the house'. He said, 'You're there to work and that's it'. So that's how I came to start work there.[8]

During her last few years working in Hay Street, Elma even ended up taking over the reins of management for brief periods for a few of her employers. She remembered well the customary briefing by the local Criminal Investigation Branch (CIB), including stern instructions that the women were not allowed to step off the verandahs of the brothels, which were set back 2–3 metres from the Hay Street footpath:

I looked after Nancy Taylor's place. She went over to Sydney for two weeks. I had to go see the head detective up there...He said, 'There's two things I want to tell you. Working hours, those girls step off the verandah, they're gone. And I want you, if there's anybody cruising down the street in their car, I want the car number'. You ever try to sit on the verandah and take number plates! [Laughter][9]

Workers' bedrooms were arranged alongside each other in a row facing on to Hay Street. Each bedroom had two doors: the back door accessed the rest of the house, while the other doorway connected to a small outdoor corridor, which led to an opening on the Hay Street footpath. Val said that all workers were expected to be 'on the door' by 5.30 every evening, and they usually worked through until at least the early morning hours. Val described her view from the door, through which there was 'no exit' under the strictly enforced Containment Policy:

> You had to sit back—you had your chair and your table, and you had your doorway, and you had your little sort of runway down to it. And they'd [clients] often come in and stand there. And you weren't even allowed to get up and stand at the door...the chief bloke [detective] had a thing about it. He used to even sit in his car opposite us, to see we weren't plying our trade outside the door. You weren't allowed to stick your nose outside the door, and speak to the men.
>
> We all had lights over us, darling, all pretty lights over us.[10]

Sitting framed inside their doorways, Hay Street's 'ladies under the lights' projected an enchanting image, not just for visiting clients but also for the slow but steady stream of curious onlookers who orbited the brothels nightly in their cars and tour buses.

Former Kalgoorlie resident 'Rose' grew up on Hannan Street during the 1950s and 1960s, with 'only a back alley separating us from the Hay Street brothel backyards'. While Hay Street remained shrouded in mystery for Rose and her young friends, she recalled that late-night activities around the brothels occasionally provided a bit of light entertainment and gossip for neighbours:

> In Hannan Street near Lane, there used to be a wine saloon...closing times at night at this wine saloon and Hannan's Hotel, just down the road, would be fun for all the neighbours to watch. All the drunks would get kicked out and they usually headed to the Hay Street brothels around the corner on foot, yelling and swearing and banging on people's fences along the way—which set off all the neighbourhood dogs into a barking frenzy until they passed. The Hay Street ladies were maybe the only ones that would put up with them, and Kalgoorlie had a lot of lonely single men living there.

Lots of drunken men staggering past, or sober ones going to their cars parked away from the Hay Street area, often parked in such a manner to block our driveway. . .we even recognised some of them as people we knew, sneaking in to visit the girls of Hay Street. There was no television in Kalgoorlie back then, [so] all these activities in the street kept us well entertained.[11]

As curious as it may seem, the colourful lights and ladies of Hay Street provided 'family entertainment' for more than just neighbouring residents in Kalgoorlie. Local resident Leslie moved to Kalgoorlie with her husband and children in 1965. Having found little amusement in the town to help keep her restless progeny occupied, her accidental 'car tour' down Hay Street one evening proved to be quite a hit with her young brood:

It was mainly the three older ones. Their ages were 2, 4 and 6, and then I had the baby. And in the evenings they used to say, 'Mum, can you take us down past. . .to see the ladies and all the pretty lights?' I think it became as Australian for them as taking the kids into town to see the Christmas lights. Because that's all it was to them, 'the ladies' and 'the pretty lights'.[12]

Of course, the women of Hay Street did not always attract such unobtrusive attention from local thrill-seekers, and the brothels remained an irresistible target for young male pranksters. At the same time, Hay Street women occasionally managed to 'give as good as they got', as local Australian Broadcasting Commission (ABC) journalist John Bowler remembered learning as a young lad:

Well. . .I was in high school, and we had just got our driver's licences. . .and we had a chook pen in the backyard. And this chook died, and I thought, Oh well, we'll go down and throw it down at the crackers [brothels], you know? So I got my mate to drive Dad's car. . .it was this old little four-cylinder. . .and it wasn't the best getaway car in the world. I said to my mate, 'Now you drive, and keep the revs up because it bloody stalls'. We pulled up and I rushed up to the front door with this dead chook and sort of swung it around, and threw it down the aisle. And I rushed back out and jumped into the car, and my mate tramped it—and it stalled the car. We were laughing and giggling that much—he couldn't start the bloody car!

And the madam had enough time to pick the bloody chook up, rushed back out, opened the door and flung the chook back into the car! *[Laughter]* And we're sitting there with feathers flying everywhere, crying laughing, you know, tears running down our faces.[13]

Unfortunately, such ungracious antics saw tears flowing within the brothels as well. Val said that during her six-year Hay Street 'tour of duty', she endured an oppressive volume of abuse while sitting passively in her doorway, and often helped to dispose of dead animals that had been hurled at other women. At the extreme end of the scale, harassment of the women got dangerously out of hand:

> We even had a few bombs thrown on the roof. My friend was very, very lucky, because she had just gone out to get some water, and she had just walked into her bedroom, through a door off the lounge room. And a bomb hit the roof—and there were pieces of tin about that long [10 centimetres] sticking in the door. If she had been in there, she would have been...
>
> And you had the roughies that'd come down, you know, you had the ones driving past in cars and yelling out obscenities. And Mona was such a placid person...what did they used to yell out...'Mona Lisa, Mona Lisa—If we grease ya, will it ease ya?' *[Laughter]* Yes, there was a lot of humour about the place, as well as everything else.[14]

Former goldfields policeman Peter Blyth recalled in his memoirs that he and a partner were once called to the Hay Street brothels to investigate a rather dangerous series of pranks on the women:

> Some idiots had been throwing firecrackers through the wire at the girls in the brothels, and one [woman] had been burned, so a mate and I were sent there in plain clothes and a private car to sweat off on the offenders. It took a couple of nights, but eventually they came back and we nabbed them.
>
> The madam was so pleased that she took us down the back yard and told us we could have a duck each. No, there was nothing wrong with our hearing, she had a big yard full of ducks and told us to take one apiece. We were a bit reluctant at first, as that sort of thing could put us on a spot, but she assured us it was a gesture of gratitude on her part and she would be offended if we refused.
>
> Well we caught the ducks and took them back to the lock-up, where a trusty prisoner plucked and cleaned them for us in return for some tobacco.[15]

The grateful, duck-bearing madam in Mr Blyth's story would appear to be madam 'Lulu', a Greek migrant, described here by Rose:

> Lulu kept lots of ducks in the backyard of her brothel and she had a magnificent German shepherd guard dog by the name of Zita. Every day Lulu would take Zita for a walk around the neighbourhood and, being the friendly lady she was, always stopped and had a chat to all the neighbours. Everybody loved Lulu as she was always so friendly and kindly.
>
> Occasionally, Lulu's ducks would escape from her backyard when somebody would forget to lock the gate or they would fly over her fence and end up wandering all over the neighbourhood. One afternoon after school, I was waiting to be served in Mr Les Laming's shop in Hannan Street, when a

pair of low-flying ducks flew into the shop, causing us to scatter in all direc-
tions in fright, including Mr Laming. These ducks were crashing into shelves,
knocking groceries off the displays and creating such havoc, squawking and
quacking, until they were caught by Mr Laming and taken back to Lulu, who
was horrified and paid for all the damage done.[16]

Rose also said that the Hay Street brothels substantially increased the
amount of vehicular traffic in the neighbourhood:

> Every night, carloads of young louts, supposedly having nothing better to do,
> would do laps of the block in their cars, giving cheek to all the girls sitting
> outside on verandahs. . .sometimes yelling out obscenities and tooting their car
> horns or driving really slowly so they can check out all the girls. This would
> go on nearly all night long and one just got used to all this noise as being part
> of normal life in the neighbourhood.
>
> Tourist buses, packed with gawking tourists, also used to cruise past at
> night, really slowly, making lots of noise, slowing down and trying to let
> tourists snap photos of girls in scanty attire. Taxi cabs were always coming
> and going at all hours, picking up and dropping off men. Police vans were
> always patrolling the block, especially in the back alley, and would be shining
> powerful spotlights into everybody else's backyards at all hours of the night,
> every night, looking for prowlers or stopping to question men walking down
> the back alley.[17]

Of course, Hay Street meant much more to those men who explored
the 'Scarlet Mile' with a greater sense of purpose. Val recalled that most
clients were young Australian miners, although there were also a significant
number of migrants:

> There were a lot of Italians and Yugoslavs, because they didn't talk much
> English, and apparently the girls 'outside' [Hay Street] wouldn't. . .tolerate
> them. We also had a lot of passing trade, from when the old train used to come
> through from the eastern states in the morning, and it would stop there for an
> hour, and there would be a bit of a rush hour.[18]

Judy confirmed Val's ethnic grouping of Hay Street clients, and said that
historical anti-Asian sentiments on the goldfields had remained particularly
fierce in Kalgoorlie for many years:

> [Clients were] nearly all Australians—you'd get the odd Yugoslav or Italian. It
> wasn't like it is now, all multicultures. You'd never see an Oriental person. They
> weren't allowed in the town. That was still on in the sixties.[19]

In his memoirs, Peter Blyth recalled another occasion when he was
called to investigate a disturbance on Hay Street. This time the brothels

were having a particularly hectic week because of the firemen's convention in town, and emotions were apparently running high:

> A Sergeant and I were doing van patrol on afternoon shift, when we were called to a disturbance at the Hay Street brothels. This bloke had been giving one of the madams a bit of a stir, so we tossed him in the back of the van. We were about to head off when one of the madams from another house came running to tell us that a girl had gone crazy and was threatening to kill a customer.
>
> The Sergeant sent me to have a look, and when I got there the girl had this bloke pinned against the wall with a big carving knife held against his belly button. Both were naked and she was screaming about what she was going to cut off first, while he had his hands above his head in surrender.
>
> I hadn't read about this one in the Police Manual, and I didn't have it with me so I improvised. I signalled to the bloke not to let on that he'd seen me, then I walked up behind the girl and let fly with a good open handed slap across her bare bum. She dropped the knife alright, and that's not all she dropped.
>
> By this time the Sarge had arrived and he took the bloke aside and told me to get the girl dressed. I tried to persuade her to put her clothes on, but she refused to co-operate, although she did make me one offer which I didn't find hard to refuse.
>
> I tried to wrap a blanket around her, but she kept throwing it off, so I said 'Bugger it' and frog marched her out into the street and put her into the van. The other prisoner in the van fairly came alive then. He said, 'Jesus, me bloody luck's changed.'
>
> The Fire Brigade teams from around the State were in town that weekend for the annual competition, and there were quite a few of them lined up along the footpath. When they saw me bring the girl out, a loud cheer went up, but one bloke complained it wasn't fair that they had to queue up and wait, while I could just walk in and help myself. As we headed to the lock-up, I rode in the back of the van to act as chaperon between the frustrated felon and the haywire harlot...[20]

Notwithstanding the occasional troubles on Hay Street, these peak times in business were no doubt welcome because of the increase in income they brought. During the quieter times, it helped to have a regular clientele to maintain reasonable levels of earnings, and Rita observed that older workers generally demonstrated a greater awareness of this aspect of the business:

> The idea on Hay Street was that you'd get yourself a regular clientele, so you could tell your regulars to come in on the quiet nights. So they'd come in, and that way you've got a steady trade all the week through.

You got all ages, [but] the young ones weren't really much chop. There were only a few girls who had a bit of ambition—to get in, make some money, and get out of the business. Out of all the young girls under thirty...they might have looked nice but they didn't have much personality. And a lot of guys would go with them because they were so pretty, but they would never come back. And without a regular clientele, their money wouldn't pan out, you see.[21]

Fees and services were similar in all the Hay Street brothels, and the standard arrangement between workers and management was a fifty-fifty split of workers' earnings. Clients were quoted basic fees and services at the door, and workers tried to negotiate additional time or services in the rooms.

During the late 1960s the basic short-time (ten minutes) service was quoted as 'six and ten', or $6 for straight sex (sexual intercourse) and $10 for a strip (sex in the nude). Thirty dollars entitled the client to stay thirty to forty minutes, and an hour booking cost between $50 and $60. Overnight clients were charged between $100 and $150.

Rita found Hay Street's fee structure and earning potential so abysmally disappointing compared to her standard fees in Sydney that she decided to set a minimum fee of $10 per customer for herself:

> Well, when I first came to Kalgoorlie, it was six and ten. But I wouldn't work for six and ten...and you've got to give three dollars of it away. My cheapest job over east I was getting was $25. I didn't travel all these miles to work for three dollars.
>
> There were lots of overnighters. We used to start it from about 12.30, sometimes if they paid extra they'd start at eleven, but you'd try to keep 11 o'clock till 12 free, 'cause the pubs started closing at 11 o'clock, see? But if they wanted to pay the extra hour, on top of their all-night charge...a lot of guys did.
>
> After the split, if you had $150 [at the end of the shift], you were doing exceptionally well. On a bad night, you wouldn't crack it.[22]

Many workers deeply resented giving madams 50 per cent of their earnings, and often did not share the money they earned as tips or through negotiating extra services. There was also plenty of opportunity for conflicting interpretations of what constituted 'earnings':

> *Judy:* In the nickel boom days, they used to tip, but the madam wanted half. Of course, we considered our tips extra money and didn't want to declare it. Well, why should we? The madam didn't deserve any of that.[23]
>
> *Val:* Now if a boy got to be a regular customer, and decided to bring you a present, [Mona] wanted half the price of it, 'cause it was something you were

earning in the house. And I can remember once this bloke bought me this beautiful nightie and negligee, and she said, 'I'll have that, so I can take it down the street'. And she used to go to a shop and value it! So I thought, 'Well if you want half of it, you can have half of it'. So I cut it in half, and I gave her her half. She would never come at me again after that.[24]

If the occasional conflict over earnings caused a sense of distrust, the situation was not helped by the fact that workers were forbidden by police to leave the brothels and go into town to deposit their earnings. Judy remembered that Hay Street women tended to use less conventional (and apparently less secure) methods of banking:

> I think everyone just kept their money in their rooms. And sometimes we'd give it to Mona to look after. And she would put it in the bank for us. We trusted her. Everyone had their own bank account, but at the madam's bank.
>
> And Mona used to sleep with all her money in her bed. Oh, she had heaps—thousands and thousands and thousands.[25]

Despite the extra income offered by the provision of 'extra' services, many Hay Street women (and apparently a high number of Perth sex workers) strongly resisted the introduction of oral sex into the service structure during the late 1960s. Management of this issue tended to differ between Perth and Kalgoorlie, and apparently workers in the Hay Street brothels felt less pressure to agree to the practice:

> *Rita:* You had house prices. . .there wasn't a lot of oral sex around at the time, but there were a few girls doing it. I never did that. I think they used to charge an extra $15, in the early part, and everything was shared with the madam.[26]

> *Judy:* I got sacked [in Perth] because they were doing all sorts of different things, you know? They were doing fellatio and the whole bloomin' works! And I didn't do that—I was just doing straight sex. And they kept asking me to do all that, and I didn't want to. It was $20 for sucking their cock. Ten dollars for a root, and $5 for massaging their cock. *[Laughter]*[27]

Workers always bathed between clients and turned away men they suspected might have an STD.[28] But as not all clients carrying STDs had begun to show signs of infection, and workers in Western Australia were not allowed to enforce compulsory use of condoms, workers were sometimes infected, as were other clients. The women continued to travel in groups to the doctor's surgery every week, to be screened for STDs and to have their 'doctor's books' validated. These documents were kept by the madam and produced for local police in the event of a brothel inspection. Judy outlined the basic structure of Hay Street's unofficial 'health policy':

We used to all go together [to the doctor]. We'd get a taxi, and we would all have our appointment there at the same time with old Dr Watson. He was an old doctor. He was good.

We used to wash the clients and check them. And if you weren't sure, two girls had to check. Some of them would have rashes and things on them. And so we'd tell them they had to go, but not before putting a drop of tincture of iodine on them, in case they tried to go anywhere else.

If there was anything wrong with you, you weren't allowed to work. Every few weeks one or two workers would test positive. Gonorrhoea was most common in those days. After a course of antibiotics, which took the whole week, you could go back to work.

Now in Sydney, we never had sex without a condom. And I got a bloomin' shock when I came over here. And the madams wouldn't have condoms in Kalgoorlie or Perth. It was because the men didn't like them, and that was it.[29]

Of course, condoms would have been equally useful to the women in preventing pregnancies before oral contraception became widely available. As a result of clients' and madams' resistance to condom use in Western Australia, work-related pregnancies were not uncommon in Hay Street. Judy recalled that some women resorted to 'home abortions', using knitting needles and catheters, while others sought the services of 'backyard' abortionists operating in Kalgoorlie and Perth.[30]

Throughout the 1960s, the weekly trip to the doctor for STD screening was the only outing from the brothels for most Hay Street women. Banned from the town's restaurants, hotels, shops, the public swimming pool and even the local cinema, Hay Street women found themselves virtually imprisoned in the brothels, as former taxi driver Johnno recalled:

Well, quite often a couple of the girls would have the afternoon off, but they were not supposed to go into any of the hotels. . . On numerous occasions I've taken two or three of them down to the Coolgardie Hotel, and very discreetly just gone into the lounge there, and sat there and had a couple of drinks with them. They'd have their little afternoon out, maybe for an hour or a couple of hours. Then I'd return them home, back to their house.

As long as you were back by about half past four, no later than five o'clock. Because the girls had to have their tea, and be what they call 'on the door' by half past five, six o'clock.[31]

Val fondly remembered many a lively Sunday spent with other Hay Street women in nearby Bulla-Bulling, where Italian-born publican Mario and his wife Rosa welcomed the women with generous hospitality and feasts of Italian food. Mario also delighted in serenading the women with his favourite operas, sometimes until dawn.[32] Rita said she often enjoyed taking Sunday dinner at Bulla-Bulling with Mona and her workers, and she continues to sing the praises of Mario and Rosa, for their good-natured hospitality towards the Hay Street women:

> When I was at Mona's I used to take them up to Bulla-Bulling every Sunday for lunch at the hotel up there. It's just a roadhouse. . .and like a garage. Mario and Rosa used to make the best spaghetti every Sunday. He used to play opera, and we used to go up there and have lunch, and have a nice bottle of wine. Mona used to love going up there, and even when she was a bit crook I used to take her up there, even when I wasn't working for her.[33]

A few goldfields publicans outside Kalgoorlie obviously saw the potential value in attracting the custom of locally barred Hay Street women. Yet given local Containment's strict rules, some discretion was obviously recommended. One evening the publican of the Kambalda Hotel quietly made his way to a brothel Rita was managing, to extend his welcome to the women. Unfortunately, his somewhat 'coded' message was met with Rita's total confusion:

> When they shifted Kambalda. . .and rebuilt the town, the guy came down. It was funny this night because the CIB were sitting in the dining room at 129 [Hay Street], and he came down on the door and he said, 'I just wanted to let you know. . .that you're not barred from the Kambalda Hotel'. And I said, 'Why would I be barred? I've never been in the place!' And he said, 'Oh, no. I'm the manager of the Kambalda Hotel, and I'm letting you know you're not barred'. And I said, 'Why would I be barred? You're going to bar me from the hotel?' And he said, 'Well, I thought that was the CIB rule. I'm just letting you know it doesn't matter what the CIB say, you're not barred'. And the CIB are sitting in the dining room listening to all this! I cracked up laughing, and said, 'OK, no worries, mate'.[34]

Workers were also banned by police from socialising with women who worked in the other Hay Street brothels. Such socialising, and the inevitable comparing of conditions, could have encouraged more frequent 'defections' of workers to rival brothels, and this was apparently a sore point for the Hay Street madams at a time when they were prohibited from advertising for staff. Some Hay Street madams took their insecurities (and perhaps animosity) to extreme lengths, according to Rita:

> Irene came up. . .it was her birthday. It was during my three days off, because I wouldn't work when I was menstruating, and 'Maria' wouldn't open the gate to let Irene in. She was jealous of Irene.
>
> Irene had been in Perth, and was just passing through [Kalgoorlie], and I had said to Irene, 'Well, come here and camp for the night, and you can take

off early in the morning'. And we could have a chat, because we hadn't seen each other for six months. And Maria wouldn't let her in. So I just put a coat on and told her to go around to a friend of mine's in town, and I'd meet her around there. And of course, I just had the biggest blue with Maria, because I just walked out. Well, if I was working, I'd understand, but I wasn't working anyway, so it wouldn't have hurt to have let her in the back gate.

I stayed out until about 3.00 am, and when I got back to Maria's of course there was hell to pay, but never mind, I got over that. Then I decided that I had had enough of it. I packed up a few things and took off. I locked up me room, and said that I'd be back in a few weeks. You couldn't jump house at that time, you had to [leave town] for three weeks. That didn't bother me at the time, because I had planned to go away anyway.[35]

Rita's account highlights another Containment rule that prohibited workers from 'jumping house': workers could not leave one Hay Street brothel to work in another without first leaving town for three weeks. This condition was enforced by the police, but would seem to have mainly benefited the madams, in that it deterred workers from leaving their employ. During her years managing a number of Hay Street brothels, Rita attempted to ease these employment transitions, where possible, by communicating with other Hay Street madams, so that the workers were not forced to leave town:

If the madams were in agreement, then you could go up to CIB and check it out up there. So what I'd do in the meantime, I'd go and speak to Stella and tell her that this girl has been to see me and if she's got any qualms about the girl coming and working up at my house.

You know, because I didn't want to...start making it look like I'm asking the girl to come work for me. Occasionally one would come back and say, 'Well, I've seen Stella, and it's cool. Can you ring up the CIB for me?' And I'd ring up and they'd say, 'No worries, Rita'. And in the meantime, Stella would be getting the shits, or something, you know? Because the girl hadn't confronted her at all about it. So I made it a point...I did it for all of them in the end, because I thought it would be the easiest way. There wouldn't be any friction in the street, any animosity.[36]

Given that the madams' agreement was enough to lift the restriction on women who wanted to change employers, it seems clear that the local CIB had no particular interest in this rule, but had historically enforced it at the behest of the Hay Street madams.

While Kalgoorlie's Containment Policy imposed a number of personal restrictions on sex workers that did not exist in any other jurisdiction in Australia, Judy found the 'truce' with police in Kalgoorlie preferable to her brushes with the law in Sydney's Kings Cross. She, like others, believes that many of the extreme limitations on the workers originated with Hay Street madams, and not the police. Judy also said she believes that Hay Street madams paid police to enforce these rules during the 1960s and 1970s.*

Elma became highly suspicious of police graft while working as a cook for Hay Street madam 'Ingrid'. Elma said she could not understand why Ingrid felt compelled to make payments to local police, given that 'everyone in town' knew about the Containment Policy:

> The fridge was on that side of the passage. . .and I had to go and put something in the fridge. And Ingrid was letting the two detectives out, and I saw one gesture. . .with his hand held out. I asked what was going on, and she said, 'Oh it's a bright idea [one of the Hay Street madams] thought up, and it's to do with our protection'. I said, 'But you've got the protection. You shouldn't have to pay them'.[37]

Generally, madams and workers obeyed Containment rules in order to avoid arrest and to maximise their incomes. But Val reported that it was not always that straightforward; curiously, she was arrested twice during police raids in the mid-1960s, in episodes she described as farcical:

> Oh, yes, we all knew they were coming, because [madam] Mona knew everything. And then at 5.00 am—bash, bash, bash at the door. Of course we were all up and dressed, ready. And then up to the police station, then they'd book you, and get you to go to the court for 9 o'clock, and half past 9 you were told, 'Oh you'd better get back and earn the money to pay your fine now'. And that was it. It was quite hilarious.
>
> When we got raided, the girls weren't allowed to mix even then. There was one house sitting here, and one house sitting there, you know, and we weren't allowed to talk to each other. It was so hilarious and so. . .stupid.[38]

While women working in different Hay Street brothels found it nearly impossible to socialise with each other in Kalgoorlie, there were a few madams who generously accommodated the women's desire to maintain their friendships while working in separate brothels. Val recalled that such a madam was the charmingly irreverent Nancy, who owned 143 Hay Street from 1963 to 1968.[39] Val spoke with respect and affection for Nancy, who

---

* It must be noted that, while there is no known direct evidence of police corruption in Kalgoorlie, any system of selective law enforcement gives rise to suspicions of corruption. A number of people interviewed for *The Scarlet Mile* related hearsay evidence of corruption, and while it is difficult to confirm how much of this is based on speculation and how much is based on actual knowledge, this evidence has been recorded as reported.

seems to have offered a much more light-hearted working environment than most Hay Street madams:

> I had a friend who worked over in Mona's, while I was working at Nancy's. At Christmas time, Mona was away, and about 1 o'clock in the morning, Nancy came in and she said (to me and one other girl), 'Come on, you two, here's a dozen bottles of beer. Go out the back way and go over and have a party with so-and-so. I'll ring you up when you've got to come home'. So we stayed over there for a couple of days! Mona would have died if she had known what was going on.
>
> And Nancy was a bloody old piss pot! But she always wore these lurex frocks, and they were the 'Grouse Gear'. She'd be that damned drunk by the end of the night, I'd often have to pull her off the bucket where she'd squatted, and put her to bed. And then she'd sit there sometimes, and you'd have a customer in, and she'd be sitting there patting him on the bum. She was absolutely gorgeous.
>
> When a bloke would come in and say, 'Look, I've got a dollar here, what can I get for a dollar?' And you'd say, 'Oh, Nance, there's a rich bloke up here, and what can he get for a dollar?' She'd be saying, 'A dollar, darling. A whole dollar?' Then some would say, 'Haven't you got anything young in there, Nance?' And she'd say, 'No, they're at such-and-such, down the other end of Brookman Street'—which of course was the police station. *[Laughter]*[40]

In 1967 Nancy purchased the premises at 181 Hay Street, then sold her brothel at 143 Hay Street to madam Stella Strong the following year.[41] Nancy owned the 181 Hay Street property for another fifteen years, although she generally leased out the premises to be operated as a brothel, rather than managing the business herself. Elma also remembered that Nancy had acquired shares early in the mid-1960s Kambalda nickel boom, which perhaps enabled her retirement:

> That was at the time of the nickel boom. I know Nancy had a lot of shares...bought a lot of shares in nickel. Nancy had bought 181, but the police stopped her and wouldn't let her operate it as a brothel. So she went down there and got a lot of renovations done...she had to put a big iron fence right across the front of the two houses. I don't know, she must have pulled a few strings, because next thing you know, down come the iron fences, and that's when Ingrid took it over.[42]

Elma proudly recalled that during her years working in Hay Street, she formed close friendships with madam Ingrid and a worker, 'Pat' (see Figures 10 and 11), whom she considered to be special people. On one occasion, Ingrid insisted on paying Elma for the full three weeks she had taken off

Figure 10 *Madam 'Ingrid', who owned brothels in Hay Street during the 1960s.*
Courtesy Elma, private collection of photographs

Figure 11 *'Pat', who worked in the Hay Street brothels during the 1960s.*
Courtesy Elma, private collection of photographs

work to nurse a wrist she had broken while off duty. Unlike her first Hay Street employer, madam Mona Maxwell, Elma had always found Ingrid to be a most trusting and generous employer:

When I started with Mona, I cooked, I cleaned, I washed laundry, I ironed. You know how much a week I'd get? Ten pounds. Ingrid paid me £60 a week. I had my 60th birthday there. I was 74 when I finished up there.[43]

Elma described Pat as a spirited and independent woman who 'liked her Jim Beam'. Apparently, Pat also had a fiercely protective streak, especially with Elma's youngest daughter:

Pat used to come out to my place. And somebody said to me, 'Don't you happen to know she was out *there* [on Hay Street]?' I said, 'Look. You shut up. If I want to stuff my joint full of them, it's not your business'.

Pat took a fancy to my youngest daughter. She *loved* her. She bought her maternity smocks and she bought all these baby clothes, nappies and singlets and little nighties.

My daughter's husband. . .he'd gone out, then came back to my place. . .and Pat was staying at my place. So we were all sitting in the lounge room this Sunday night, and he was getting grisly with my daughter, and she said, 'Oh, I think I'll go on home, Mum, get him to bed'. And she was pregnant, and trying to pick up the baby. And he was making out he couldn't hear. And Pat said, 'Put that little one down!' And she shook my son-in-law and said, 'Get up! Pick up that child and walk out that door! Here she is ready to drop the other one, and you pretend you're not hearing me'. She told me later, 'He came that close to getting punched out'. But she was a defender.[44]

Pat left Kalgoorlie, but Elma said they remained friends long after both women had ceased to work on Hay Street, until Pat's untimely death:

Pat went to Melbourne, and came back and got a house in South Perth, and she used to look after prostitutes' children. And she was really strict with them. When she was washing up. . .the boy had to wipe up the dishes, and the girl saw to all the spoons and forks. She wasn't allowed to touch the knives.

I had to go down to Perth for a check-up. I was just waiting outside the hotel to get a taxi up to the hospital, and I thought, 'Oh, I'll give Pat a ring'. She said, 'Where are you?' I said, 'Outside the Melbourne Hotel, in Wellington Street'. And she said, 'Have you got your cases there?' I said, 'Yes'. Then she said, 'I'll be there—only you can't stop there. As soon as I get there, that back door's going to be open!' [Laughter] She had a beautiful home.

And then the next thing I heard. . .I was in K-Mart and one of the girls working in Hay Street said, 'Did you know Pat died?' I said, 'No, I didn't'. She said, 'Yeah, she. . .she passed away. . .'[45]

Another famously affable Hay Street madam was former Perth madam Mary Scrimgeour (see Figure 12). Mary purchased the property at 129 Hay Street from the Public Trustee in September 1961, following the death of former owner Angelina Trancy. Having owned the property for forty years, Angelina died intestate on 23 May 1957. On 3 October 1957 the Public Trustee filed an 'Election to Administer' her estate in the Supreme Court and sold the property (in due course) to Mary.[46]

Elma had heard from a number of madams that the 1958 abatement of Containment in Perth had caused a migration of madams and workers from Perth to Kalgoorlie. For reasons that are not known, the police in Kalgoorlie had not previously allowed women from Perth to work in the Hay Street brothels:

> They were not allowed to employ girls from Perth until Roe Street closed. So the girls came from Sydney or Melbourne, before the coppers closed down Roe Street.[47]

Mary Scrimgeour had no doubt transferred her business interests to Kalgoorlie in 1961 to escape the chronic threat of prosecution in Perth. Although she purchased 129 Hay Street in Kalgoorlie in 1961, it is not

Figure 12 *Mary Scrimgeour, who owned the brothel at 129 Hay Street during the years 1961–78.* Courtesy Battye Library (from *Claremont-Nedlands Post*, 1993)

known whether Mary operated a brothel on the property during most of the 1960s. However, Rita recalled that one day in the spring of 1969 a modest transportable dwelling slowly wound its way to the corner of Hay and Lane streets and settled quietly into its new base: Mary Scrimgeour had arrived.[48] Judy worked briefly for Mary, and described her as a generous, kindly woman:

> I went to visit her one day. She collected dolls, and I was looking after these little twins, and I had them with me—two little Aboriginal kids. And she gave them a doll each. It was lovely. Oh, she was a nice lady. She used to drive me down to the airport, every time I went back to Perth. She and I really clicked. Everybody was nice back then.[49]

George Williams, a Perth-based journalist, came to know Mary during the 1970s and recalled with amusement her vast collection of dolls. He also said she was a person who thrived on her flamboyant, eccentric image.[50] Over the years, she had gained a reputation for hosting loud gatherings that echoed laughter and singing from her flat in The Avenue in Nedlands, an affluent suburb of Perth. In Perth she also owned the Happy Haven, a Containment brothel in Maylands. Yet Noleine Scrimgeour liked to keep her life as a madam as far removed as possible from her personal life, as she once explained with respect to her working names, 'Mary' and 'Dulcie': 'They're my pinch names. You know, when the police pinch me for "keeping a house" I use those names to keep things a little bit quiet.'[51]

Rita met 'Mary' in Hay Street in Kalgoorlie when she called in at her brothel to retrieve a cardigan and poncho for a friend who had recently worked there. This meeting marked the beginning of an unexpected partnership that would see Rita virtually establish and maintain the business for Mary:

> You had to walk on crates to get up into the door...there was no steps even, you know. When I got inside, she started crying and she said, 'Oh, I wish Irene was here! I've had such a bad trot. I've had one lass who came up to work straight away with me when the house arrived, and she got gonorrhoea, and her boyfriend was threatening me...' And she was telling me all her problems, and how she had high blood pressure. I really felt sorry for the woman.
>
> So I agreed, or I got conned into staying there and working with her. So I was her only girl for a while, until we got the house going. Then I got in touch with a few friends, and pulled a few girls over, and got the house going for her. She was quite happy about that.[52]

It soon became clear to Rita that Perth-based Mary was not all that interested in the day-to-day management of her Hay Street brothel, and Rita sometimes found herself managing the business for weeks at a time in Mary's absence, without being paid as a manager. This eventually led to a confrontation between the two women:

> She'd come up every three weeks or something, and stay maybe ten or fifteen days, and go back again. And so it was only that time that I was making any money for myself. That's when we had the argument about the wages. I told her she'd have to give me something for looking after the place for her. I didn't mind doing it at first, as a favour, but she made it a regular thing, and I don't think it was very fair.[53]

Yet despite disagreements such as these, it seems fair to say that Mary was generally fondly regarded by people in both her working and personal lives. When she passed away in 1993 (aged 78), more than 100 mourners, mostly young women, gathered for her funeral at Fremantle Cemetery.[54]

Notwithstanding her reported lack of interest in day-to-day management, Mary had demonstrated a steely determination in establishing the Hay Street premises and business. To clear the way for a brothel to be built on her lot at 129 Hay Street, she first had to negotiate barriers posed by the local council. *The West Australian* reported on 15 April 1970 that the council had refused a development application for a new premises to be constructed, since it feared it would be used for 'immoral purposes'. Mary appealed the council's decision, arguing that the house would only be used for residential purposes. On 18 December 1970, *The West Australian* reported that the council had reversed its previous decision in Mary's favour, and cleared the way for construction of the new dwelling at 129 Hay Street—a move strongly criticised by the Right Reverend D. Bryant, Anglican Bishop of Kalgoorlie. To finance building the new premises, Mary took out an unregistered mortgage with local finance firm M. J. McGrath Pty Ltd in October 1970 by registering a caveat on the property title that included the loan agreement.[55] Caveats were used by brothel owners to secure loans or business deals, because the illegal status of their businesses precluded more common arrangements such as obtaining a loan through a bank.

Another former Roe Street madam who had transferred her business interests to Kalgoorlie following the 1958 abatement of Containment in Perth was Mona Maxwell (see Figure 13). Mona purchased the property at 164 Hay Street from madam Jean in 1959.[56] Val remembered Mona saying that she had worked 'the back lanes' of Roe Street as a 'young girl' and eventually bought 222 Roe Street from madam Josie de Bray during the 1950s. In the meantime, Mona had married a man named Joe Flynn, who had reportedly been convicted of killing a policeman in Perth; he later committed suicide.

Figure 13 *Madam Mona Maxwell, who owned brothels in Hay Street during the years 1959–84.* Courtesy Carmel Migro (*not* Hay Street madam 'Carmel'), private collection of photographs

Elma worked as a cook in Mona's Hay Street brothel for several years during the 1960s, and recalled that Mona tended not to trust people. This caused considerable frustration for Elma, who often found herself locked out of the kitchen pantry when she needed to prepare meals for the workers:

> I told her one day...'If you want me to cook here, you give me a key for that pantry cupboard'. I said, 'I was going to make something totally different for tea for you all tonight'. So I said, 'You either leave that pantry cupboard open or give me a key...'Cause I'll tell you what. I've got as much stuff in my cupboards as what you've got in that. So, why would I punch it?'
>
> She had two grandchildren and...you know, those kids never wanted for a thing. That's one thing I give her.[57]

Former sex workers employed by Mona recalled that they were expected to be available for work at all hours:

> *Val:* You were on duty twenty-four hours a day. If a couple of blokes came off the train at 7 o'clock in the morning, there had to be girls there for them. That's old Mona.[58]

Rita: I didn't mind working for Mona actually, but she just had a lot of funny ideas. You'd be in bed, sort of after working late at night, and you'd be looking forward to having a sleep. And then she'd walk in the room with some bloke. He'd come down early in the morning and she'd come and wake you up for it. And I didn't really like that, you know. Little things like that used to get up my nose with Mona. Otherwise, I used to get on all right with her, you know...I used to fight with her all the time. Yeah, most of the time.[59]

Mona Maxwell's trademark penchant for early-morning 'stirring' certainly comes to mind during one scene in the film *Love in Limbo*, a 1991 Australian comedy set in the 1950s, starring Russell Crowe. The film tells the 'coming of age' story of three young men on a mission to lose their virginity in the legendary Hay Street brothels. They arrive in Kalgoorlie at 7 o'clock in the morning to find a coquettish, middle-aged woman on the verandah of one of the brothels; grinning coyly she observes, 'You're either very early, or very late'. Without missing a beat, she pulls two of them into the house and begins rapping loudly on the sleeping women's doors, insisting that they come out and greet the bewildered young arrivals.[60]

At the same time, Mona often took her workers for Sunday afternoon drives into the surrounding townships. She usually treated them to lunch and then a visit to one of the local goldfields museums. Anyone seeking a bit more adventure could hardly have been disappointed with Mona's driving, as she barrelled fearlessly along the dusty open roads in her colossal black 'Yank tank':

> She took us for drives in her big Lincoln. Oh, she was a terrible driver! She took us out to Coolgardie, we'd go there and have something to eat and a cup of coffee. It was so funny, she was the worst driver you've ever seen. And the Lincoln had a left-hand drive on it. Oh! I'll tell you—most cars got out of the way when they saw that big black Lincoln. They'd give her all the road she needed![61]

One of Mona's long-time colleagues, Allan Young, recalled that her love of the goldfields and the surrounding countryside inspired her to take an active interest in local tourism. Allan had previously founded Goldrush Tours in Kalgoorlie-Boulder, and he shared Mona's interest. He described Mona as a 'real lady' and an 'old-fashioned madam' who tended to be strict with her workers. At the same time, Mona often arranged for Allan to take one or two of her new workers on a picnic or bus tour of Kalgoorlie-Boulder, to give them a pleasant afternoon outside the brothel. On those occasions, Allan discreetly collected the women at Mona's first and returned them to the brothel after dropping off all other passengers at the end of the tour.[62]

Mona's interest in tourism eventually led her to offer free guided tours of her brothel at 164 Hay Street. Allan remembered that he often dropped by with tour groups, visiting politicians and high-profile visitors for an afternoon of Mona's hospitality. A keen gardener, Mona was especially fond of irises and sometimes offered her guests iris bulbs from her garden.[63]

On one occasion, a visiting German sports presenter asked Allan for a tour of the Hay Street brothels. Allan obliged, although having noticed that the 'sports personality' tended to be somewhat abrasive in conversation, he asked the visitor to be 'discreet' and 'behave himself' in Mona's company. He was later appalled when the German loudly asked Mona, 'So, do you still do it?' To Allan's great relief and the German's obvious delight, Mona brightly replied, 'Yes, I do, sonny. I teach all the beginners'.[64]

Mona was hardly joking, despite being well into her twilight years. Former workers Val and Judy remembered well Mona's inimitable prowess, especially with the younger clientele. Mona's soft spot for the young men may well have influenced her decision to marry a charismatic young Spaniard named Pedro in 1969:

> *Val:* She was 78, I think, and if there was only one customer, she'd take him on sometimes. Reckons she could eat an apple and read a book while she was in there.[65]

> *Judy:* She was so funny! She liked the young men. She'd even take all-nighters and she'd get them pissed. Then the next morning they'd turn around and say, 'Oh, how about a Morning Glory, Mona?' And she'd say, 'You had three last night for your hundred dollars!' She reckoned she didn't have sex with many of them, but she used to make them think they did. Very clever lady.
>
> And then she got married. She was nearly 80, and she got married to this young Spanish bloke, you know...the Don Juan type. Yeah, she was madly in love. And we couldn't believe it! Then he left her, and she came back up to her little room, with all the money under her bed.[66]

Like Mona's first husband, Pedro seems to have met with an untimely demise; property documents reveal that Mona was again a widow by the year 1978.

Many goldfields residents also remember Mona for her ongoing support of local charities. Allan Young said that, during the 1970s, she hosted an invitation-only fund-raising charity gala every year at her brothel, during the Kalgoorlie Race Round. The occasion usually attracted around 200 guests, who each paid a $20 donation, and soon became one of the most socially exclusive events of the year for a select group of affluent men in Kalgoorlie-Boulder. Goldfields union official Ray Delbridge recalled:

She had the best carpet in the world there—one of them Axminster carpets. As you'd expect, it was red. She had a bar out the back. A bloke made it, to pay off a debt he had built up over the years. And every year, when the Race Round was on, she used to entertain a few prominent people, invitation only. She'd put the food and the booze on, and would charge so much to get in. After the food and drink was paid for, the rest would go to charity. But if you wanted to go with a girl, you had to pay for it.

One year, they got some coppers to come up from Perth, and they raided the joint. The local magistrate was actually there. It was a Tuesday night, and when they took them to court the next day, there was no one there to hear the first lot of cases, and they actually had to fly a magistrate up from Perth to sit on the bench that day. Nobody knew this mob was coming up from Perth, to raid Mona's big piss-up.[67]

However, key gala organiser Allan Young rejected outright that there had ever been any arrests at Mona's Race Round gala. Although local police officers were never invited, he said that several politicians and magistrates always made the A-list. Allan recalled that Mona continued to host her popular annual gala at 164 Hay Street until she retired in 1984.[68]

Another Hay Street madam known for her traditional approach to brothel management was Stella Strong. Born in Italy in 1935, Stella emigrated to Sydney and then travelled to Perth during the mid-1960s. Like Hay Street madams Mary and Mona before her, Stella had relocated to Kalgoorlie to escape the legal hazards of managing brothels in Perth:

I got sick and tired of all this shifting and doing up new places. Then one day, I heard about a place for sale in Kalgoorlie. To cut a long story short, I came up, bought this one in 1968, and have been here ever since.[69]

Property records indicate that Stella did not actually purchase 143 Hay Street from Nancy until January 1971[70], yet this does not necessarily contradict Stella's version of events. Goldfields residents are known to have been remarkably tardy in registering their land transfers[71], and so Stella may well have bought the brothel in 1968, but did not bother to register the property transfer until 1971.

In sharp contrast to Nancy's relaxed style of management, Stella became known for her dogmatic, hard-nosed approach to running the business. She required all workers to comply with the following list of 'house rules' that were posted in the brothel's common area:

STELLA'S RULES
1.   Girls are on a 50/50 basis.
2.   There is a three minute limit in time for talking to clients at the gate.

3. Clients should not step over line, unless they are going into a girl's room.
4. Girls are not allowed to leave the gate and walk around outside of the line whilst working.
5. Noise must be kept to a minimum whilst girls are on the verandah.
6. There must be no drinking of alcohol whilst working at the gate.
7. No girl should interfere with another whilst they are working.
8. The last girl to finish work must turn off the verandah lights.
9. Girls are allowed to go shopping during the day.
10. Girls are not allowed to enter a pub in town whatsoever.
11. Girls are not allowed to use the public swimming pool or go to the racecourse.
12. Girls must have a weekly medical checkup by a doctor and a 'doctor's book' must be signed.
13. Girls are not allowed to have a man in their rooms unless they are a paying client and are written in the book.
14. No 'boyfriends' and no 'free-bies' are allowed.
15. Anytime a girl has a man in her room, she must have it written in her book.
16. Girls are not allowed to go shopping with their clients. Any relationship between girls and clients must happen in the girls rooms. Their time must be paid for.
17. Everything in the house that is used must be cleaned and thereafter put back in its place.
18. If anything is broken, it must be replaced.
19. During the day girls are asked to be considerate in the house for the girls who are sleeping.
20. When money is taken from a client, it is to be placed in the safe and to be written in the book.
21. Girls who are on a 50-50 basis must be honest with her money. Anyone caught being dishonest with her finances, will have to face the consequences.
22. There are to be no drugs on the premises unless they are prescribed by a doctor.

An addendum also advised that management reserved the right to dismiss any worker for breaching any of the above rules.[72]

To circumnavigate the extreme limitations imposed by local Containment, and sometimes by brothel management, Hay Street women discreetly took taxi trips into town during the mid-1970s to meet with friends who worked in other brothels. Police and madams were obviously unaware of these brief 'underground' journeys. Brothel workers also enlisted taxi drivers to deliver messages to friends in other brothels, as former taxi driver Johnno recalled:

The girls were of course quite regular clients of the taxi industry and they still are. But not to the extent that they were in the 70s.

The madams were very strict back in those days. I can remember picking up one girl, and she was very annoyed with her madam, because her madam would not let her speak to her friend, that came from Sydney with her. She was working in a house over the road, and both those madams were up in arms, I think they were on unfriendly terms, or something. The girls were not allowed to even talk to the girls in the other houses.

I remember with this particular girl, she was annoyed that she was not allowed to even meet her friend, so she rang up and she got me to do this message for her...she said would I drop this over to her friend—after I went around the block. So I drove around the block, took the note in and gave it to this other girl, and they arranged to meet uptown the following afternoon. The girl got me to go down and pick her up and drive her up to town, drop her by the post office, then go back downtown, pick the other girl up, and bring her up to town. And they were quite thrilled that they could be together. They sat in the back of the cab talking for quite awhile.[73]

Although sex workers in Perth were not bound by such austere social restrictions, they constantly risked arrest during the crackdowns ordered by the Tonkin (Labor) and Court (Liberal) governments in the 1970s. Meanwhile, the Containment Policy in Kalgoorlie remained unaffected by police operations in Perth, and business continued as usual in Hay Street.[74]

Jack Hocking, owner and manager of *The Kalgoorlie Miner* during the 1970s, strongly supported the local Containment Policy, in preference to the more complicated 'big city' approaches to prostitution. He regarded highly the vigilant, 'no-nonsense' approach of the local police in enforcing Kalgoorlie's Containment Policy:

I personally think that it's been a great thing for the town. I think it's something in a town where there were a lot of young single men and miners, particularly the foreign element who never had any women friends or wives.

They're not allowed to have any men working in the places. They're all run by madams. There are no men allowed on the job, and there's no chance of anybody getting in there and setting up, you know, the problems they have in Sydney and Melbourne with these people battling for control and what-have-you. There's nothing like that can go on and they're very carefully policed. The police make sure that there's no trouble down there with the riff raff or anything like that. The girls are closely supervised.[75]

Indeed, law enforcement in Kalgoorlie tended to fiercely guard the local Containment Policy from any perceived outside interference—as one hapless social researcher from Sydney discovered while attempting to conduct a survey of Hay Street brothel workers in August 1971. He later wrote:

> I arrived in Kalgoorlie by train on the night of August 24, 1971. At approximately 11 A.M. on the following day I left my motel and went into the red-light district. . .I set off down to the premises which were then known as 'Maria's House' situated at 141 Hay Street (Maria's is no longer at this location and has now moved to a little pink cottage on the other side of Hay Street). I spoke to the madam there, explaining to her that I was doing a survey, and I asked her if she would object to me interviewing some of the girls on her premises at a cost of $40 an hour. She replied by saying that it would be quite alright and she then introduced me to a most unattractive, white-haired and brazen-looking girl from Sydney named Lou. After introducing me, the madam took $30 from me, this being payment for an interview lasting exactly 45 minutes.
>
> I then went into the front room with Lou and proceeded to interview her, but I found her extremely unpleasant and quite resentful of the whole idea of being asked questions. After spending only a short period with Lou I had come to the full realisation that I was wasting my time. However, after only a few minutes, two CIB detectives unexpectedly arrived at the house, having been called to the premises by the madam. Maria's purpose in telling me that it would be alright to conduct interviews on the premises was evidently to have me cornered by CIB police while I was in the room with Lou.
>
> The first thing that I noticed was that all witnesses were hurriedly moved away from the front portion of the house by Maria, which made me wonder what was going to happen next. The two detectives then burst into the front room and abruptly terminated my 'interview', whereupon Lou rushed outside. Had the two men not been driving a police car, I would have assumed them to be a pair of gangsters. Both men were armed with revolvers, they were shoddily dressed and they were rude and overbearing in their manner. Unfortunately, I had one of the questionnaires with me and this was quickly seized by the police as evidence of my activities. The discourse that followed was of a most unpleasant nature:
>
> POLICE: Detective-Sergeant. . .and Detective. . .of the Kalgoorlie CIB (flashing their CIB cards).
>
> MYSELF: Oh, hullo.
>
> POLICE: Now what's all this nonsense about you doing a survey of prostitution, hey?
>
> MYSELF: Oh, I'm sorry, I didn't want to jump on anybody's toes.

POLICE: Listen, somebody might jump on your toes, mate, if you don't watch out. What's all this nonsense, hey? What's all this nonsense? Who do you represent?

MYSELF: I represent. . .

POLICE: You represent yourself. You represent yourself?

MYSELF: Yes but. . .

POLICE: What's your name?

MYSELF: (I gave my name.)

POLICE: How many convictions have you got?

MYSELF: None.

POLICE: Come on, how many convictions have you got?

MYSELF: None.

POLICE: Now give us your real name.

MYSELF: I've already given you my name.

POLICE: What's your wife's name?

MYSELF: I'm not married.

POLICE: Does your wife know you're over here, crackin' on? When did you arrive in Kalgoorlie?

MYSELF: Last night.

POLICE: Well, you'll be gone by tonight. Where are you from?

MYSELF: Sydney.

POLICE: Well, you'll be gone by tonight.

MYSELF: There's no train out of here till tomorrow morning.

POLICE: Isn't there a train out of here tonight? No, that's to Perth. Well, you'll be gone by tomorrow morning, then. And there'll be a CIB car at the railway station to make sure you're on the train.

MYSELF: The CIB in Sydney doesn't seem to be worrying about this survey very much.

POLICE: The CIB in Sydney! You can do what you like in Sydney; that's another country, as far as we're concerned. This is Kalgoorlie!

MYSELF: Look, I think there's been a misunderstanding. . .

POLICE: The situation here is highly explosive; we don't want you asking questions. Who do you work for?

MYSELF: (I gave the name of my employer.)

POLICE: They wouldn't be too happy about you doing this, would they? Crackin' on over here. Where are you staying in Kalgoorlie?

MYSELF: (I named my motel.) I rang up Kalgoorlie police station a few weeks ago to find out if this would be alright, and nobody knew anything about it.

POLICE: Well, you should have spoken to the CIB: you would have saved yourself a trip.

At this point the detective-sergeant picked up one of the questionnaires off the bed, having searched the whole of my belongings, and he exploded into a violent rage.

POLICE: What good's all this silly nonsense, hey? What good is it? What good's it going to do? A survey of brothels!

MYSELF: I don't think that it'll do any harm.

POLICE: Well fuckin' piss oorrff! What good would this do? What good would it do? What's this bloody nonsense? You're a perve. What good's this? Asking girls what they're doing behind locked doors, hey. What good will it do!!! You bloody perve! If you went before a magistrate, he'd take one look at this bloody rubbish and say you're a bloody perve. Anyhow, how did you know there were brothels here in Kalgoorlie?

MYSELF: I've been here before.

POLICE: Well, how did you know there were brothels?

MYSELF: I've been here before.

POLICE: You've been here before! Crackin' on! What would your parents think of you, hey, crackin' on to birds in Kalgoorlie?

MYSELF: I'm not cracking on to anybody. . .

POLICE: Well, you won't be doing it around here. You can do what you like in Sydney but you can't talk to the girls around here—and we've told them not to.[76]

The researcher's letter of complaint to the superintendent of police in Kalgoorlie was met with a stern reinforcement of the attending officers' warnings that he 'had no right at all to be conducting a survey of prostitution in Kalgoorlie, especially since he did not represent any organisation'.[77]

Another most unwelcome 'outsider' discovered the Kalgoorlie brothels during the mid-1970s: the Australian Taxation Office (ATO). While sex workers in Perth had paid taxes since at least the early 1970s (as employees of 'escort agencies' and 'massage parlours')[78], madams and prostitutes in Kalgoorlie had apparently previously avoided declaring their earnings and paying taxes.[79]

Rita said that during the mid-1970s the ATO ordered all Hay Street businesses and workers to pay their estimated tax bill dating back seven years. Rita was ordered to pay $52,000, which fortunately she had saved over the years while working in Hay Street; however, it did effectively force her to shelve her plans to purchase a property in Western Australia's Wheatbelt region.[80]

Former Hay Street madam Irene recalled that she was one of the first Hay Street madams to be audited by the ATO in June 1975—three months after taking over the lease of 129 Hay Street from Mary Scrimgeour:

> Soon as I got there, the first three months or something, the taxation department got me. Now, I can tell you, I know exactly when it was. It was the Queen's Birthday 1975—the tax got me. I got caught straight away by the tax, then I said to myself, 'If I've got to pay tax like every other citizen, I got the right like every other citizen'.[81]

While Irene did not actually purchase 129 Hay Street for another three years, she lodged a caveat on 20 February 1975 to register her first option to purchase the property, should Mary Scrimgeour decide to sell it. Irene said that she had learned while previously leasing Mona's brothel that it was well worth taking out 'a bit of insurance' on Hay Street:

> [Mona] was just a character. Actually, her and I didn't talk. We did at the start, with my first brothel. I knew to be very wary of her. And I bought 129 [Hay Street] for my insurance. . .in case she ever did to me what she did to all the others. She got them to do the places up, and then she kicks them out and takes over. And sure enough, she tried to do it to me. But she ended up with the short end of the stick.
>
> Well, I beat her by her own tricks. She was from the old rules, she thought she could conquer everything with the fist, and I beat her with the law, fair and square.[82]

Even under the Containment Policy, law enforcement was not always consistent or predictable, and the brothels were occasionally raided and the women charged with criminal offences. In one case, Kalgoorlie police raided a Hay Street brothel in May 1978[83], only to find that their actions did not receive the support of local justice Ray Finlayson (also Kalgoorlie's mayor at the time). In the Kalgoorlie Court, Mr Finlayson dismissed charges against two 22-year-old women who had been arrested for 'assisting in the management of premises for the purpose of prostitution'. He later commended the local Containment Policy in *The West Australian*:

> We know the houses are there. They are well-run and well-controlled. To my knowledge there are no men living off the earnings of prostitution in Kalgoorlie. The police do a very good job. The way the houses are conducted shows a lot of common sense and balance.[84]

Despite these public reassurances about 'order' and 'balance', Hay Street women still faced considerable uncertainty and discrimination throughout the 1960s–1970s. Their occupational hazards included the possibility of arrest and criminal conviction, STD infections and pregnancies, and abuse and injuries from young 'pranksters'. Meanwhile, under the unofficial local Containment Policy, the women remained 'cloistered' in the Hay Street brothels and were subjected to extreme restrictions on their movements about the town. It seems safe to say that the public perception of order and balance under the Containment Policy contrasted sharply with reality for the Hay Street women.

CHAPTER 5

Business as usual: Madams' Stories

From the 1970s to the 1990s, Kalgoorlie's time-honoured Containment Policy and the Hay Street brothels continued to resist 'outsider' scrutiny and interference. Yet by then, the print media in Western Australia had begun to strongly support a legal framework to replace the (still unwritten) Containment Policy, having all but abandoned its preoccupation with the 'social evil'—perhaps in tandem with changing community attitudes. Certainly, editorials that appeared in Perth-based popular newspapers had become highly critical of police crackdowns on the sex industry in the capital city, where allegations of police corruption continued to surface. In the meantime, there had been relatively little change in the lives of women working in Kalgoorlie's Hay Street brothels.

Former madam Irene (see Figure 9), who managed and owned various Hay Street brothels during the 1970s and 1980s, recalled that her approach to brothel management embraced the 'old rules' of Containment. Born in Germany, Irene arrived in Melbourne in 1962 and initially found work as a bakery assistant and a domestic servant. A few years later, she moved to Sydney with her boyfriend and took a job as a waitress in Sydney's Kings Cross, where she first encountered sex workers who worked as streetwalkers in 'The Cross'.[1]

When Irene first visited Kalgoorlie in 1969, she took in the customary drive-by tour of the Hay Street brothels, and found that the lively scene immediately appealed to her business sense. Then in 1975 she arranged to lease the brothel at 141 Hay Street from madam Mona Maxwell, whom Irene described as an unpredictable business associate at the best of times. Irene puts her own success on Hay Street down to her providing a friendly and professional working environment for the women:

> Well, the first time I saw the brothels, I thought: 'If I ever have the opportunity of being a madam, I'd treat the girls how I'd like to be treated myself'. And then I knew I'd be successful. One thing was that the madams were just not approachable. They laid down the law. Reminded me of my father...'You'll do as I tell you'.[2]

The restrictions of Containment often led Irene and her workers to joke of life on Hay Street as a form of imprisonment. Nevertheless, Irene preferred to remain focused on running an orderly and profitable business:

> It was hard work. I knew madams that, you know, had good times. And they had parties all the time...but I wasn't that kind. I went there for a purpose, to make my money. And I wanted girls that were interested in making money, not in parties and good times. They make their money and go home. And I intended on making my money and going home. Nothing more, nothing less. Really, it was like living in gaol, only good pay—that's all.[3]

During the mid-1970s, standard Hay Street fees included $30 for half an hour, and $50–60 for an hour's booking, with the customary fifty-fifty split between workers and 'the house'. Irene recalled that, in her first years managing Hay Street brothels, she often found that 'well-timed' popular tunes helped her to keep track of the workers' shorter bookings with clients:

> It started at $6 for a short time and $10 for a strip. That was the length of one song on a big LP...[Laughter]...I remember that was the cue, when the record started. When the song was finished, it was time to tell them to wind up. [Laughter][4]

Irene remembered that the women usually arrived for work with their own radios or phonographs and popular records. Meanwhile, each room came furnished with a double bed, a locking wardrobe, a dressing table with mirror, a bedside table and a washstand stocked with basic hygienic provisions:

> The washstand consisted of a little cupboard where they had all their short time towels in there...little hand towels...and on top they had a dish where they washed themselves and the clients. They were aluminium bowls, with

coating and flowers on them—if you dropped them, they could chip but not shatter. And then they had two water jugs, one for hot water, one for cold water. They got the jug of hot water when they put the money away.[5]

Irene generally assumed the tasks of cooking and cleaning for the workers, to avoid having to pay domestic servants. Although she said she did not really mind the long working hours, early-bird Irene never quite adjusted her habits to that of a night-owl:

I slept on the verandah behind the door. I had a mattress on the floor, because I couldn't stay awake...especially since I had done the washing, the cooking, the cleaning, everything most times. It was always hard for me, because at 3 o'clock I couldn't stay awake any longer. I just couldn't hack it all night. I never made it till dawn.[6]

Since madams were not allowed to advertise for sex workers, prospective workers usually learned about the Hay Street brothels through word of mouth in Perth and in interstate brothels, and women tended to contact Hay Street madams by telephone before making the trip to Kalgoorlie. Irene tried to select workers she sensed would be friendly but 'sensible', and often loaned women the $111 airfare to get from Perth to Kalgoorlie. She avoided hiring women who she thought were 'too rough around the edges':

There was plenty other madams that were taking them sort of girls, so I wanted the girls to be a bit nicer, so they would last the distance. I knew the coppers were very strict with me, so my girls had to be reasonably sensible to stand the grind.[7]

While most of the women tended to work in Hay Street for durations of four to six weeks before leaving Kalgoorlie

some stayed a few years. I used to make them go away, after three months, to have a break for a week. So they didn't get burnt out. And when they had their periods, they had the days off.[8]

As required under the Containment Policy, sex workers were also suspended from working if they tested positive for any STD. Irene said she took her role as madam and carer very seriously:

I remember when girls got hepatitis, girls got VD, I had to keep them. I nursed them back to health. They stayed in the house, and I fed them. One girl had hepatitis, and she was off for six months. She stayed with me. Well, what can you do? You can't chuck them out. It's all right, I got my pay. [Laughter] All good things come to those that do the right thing.[9]

Generally speaking, Irene never ventured outside the traditional rules of Containment, though she did not stop her workers from discreetly 'getting out' of the brothel for the afternoon to one of the out-of-town goldfields hotels:

> Yes, [the women] sneaked out, but for me that wasn't worth the risk. I remember my birthday—I asked the coppers once, 'It's my birthday. Can we go and have some meals somewhere?' And he said to me, 'If you didn't ask me, you could have gone'. I didn't want to take the risk of getting into trouble because they were always on me. But I don't care, I didn't pay them either. *[Laughter]* [10]

Irene recalled hearing that some Hay Street madams paid police to enforce a number of 'extra-Containment' rules to control their workers, and that those rules were always enforced under the guise of the local Containment Policy.* At the same time, she sympathised with the police, who she felt had an unenviable task in policing illegal brothels. To Irene, the local CIB seemed 'firm but fair' during her years as a Hay Street madam:

> I can't complain about the coppers. We knew where we stood with each other. But I also had a very hard time with the coppers, I have proof of that. But if they said, 'This is the line you're going to walk on', I walked on it. And they knew if they'd come to me and I'd say 'It was black', then they knew it was black. [11]

In 1975 one shocking and particularly sinister tragedy in Perth fixed the spotlight firmly on the relationship between law enforcement and the sex industry in Western Australia: the as-yet unsolved murder of Perth madam Shirley Finn. The discovery of Shirley Finn's body on 22 June 1975 in her car at the Royal Perth Golf Club in South Perth, bearing two gunshot wounds to the head, sent shock waves through the local sex industry and the general community, amid widespread rumours (that persist even today) that the police were involved in her murder. [12]

The month following Shirley Finn's murder, *The West Australian* announced that the State Cabinet had approved a strategy to 'tighten the law on prostitution' by increasing penalties five-fold for prostitution-related offences and broadening the legal definition of 'brothel' to include vehicles such as cars and boats. These proposed changes were reportedly the state government's response to a failed prosecution the previous year. [13] In any

---

* As noted in the last chapter, a number of people interviewed for *The Scarlet Mile* related hearsay evidence of corruption in Kalgoorlie and, although it is difficult to confirm how much of this is based on speculation and how much is based on actual knowledge, this evidence has been recorded where reported.

event, given the relatively punitive nature of the proposed changes, it seems reasonable to suggest that the timing of this announcement could unfortunately have served to drive 'underground' the very people who might otherwise have come forward with information to help solve the Finn murder case. *The West Australian's* editorial on 25 July 1975 called on the Court government to abandon its heavy-handed approach and introduce workable prostitution law reform. A world away in Kalgoorlie, it was business as usual in the Hay Street brothels, which remained unaffected by the turmoil in Perth.

Later in 1975 a Royal Commission investigated the relationship between law enforcement and prostitution in Western Australia. Evidence presented indicated that the Vice Squad in Perth had been operating an unofficial policy of 'selective policing' in the capital city, although the commission did not confirm allegations of corruption within the Vice Squad itself. Instead, Chief Justice Norris concluded that an unofficial policy of 'containment' offered the next best option to police in the absence of workable prostitution laws.

Following the announcement of the Royal Commission's findings, police authorities unofficially reintroduced the Containment Policy in Perth. In doing so, police extended criminal immunity to twelve brothels and four escort agencies operating in Perth, as well as the four remaining Hay Street brothels in Kalgoorlie, provided that they complied with the standard Containment rules, including police registration and compulsory health examinations for workers, and the exclusion of men from managing or financing businesses. Notably, the 'second-wave' Containment Policy in Perth did not include the personal restrictions that were still being enforced in Kalgoorlie, such as the workers' forced residence in the brothels.[14]

The first official report to challenge the human rights abuses enshrined in the Containment Policy was commissioned by the Human Rights Commission of Australia in 1984. Dr Judy Edwards researched and produced this study, entitled *Prostitution and Human Rights: A WA Case Study*. Edwards concluded that these human rights abuses had been created, perpetuated and accommodated by the sex industry's illegal status in Western Australia.

Edwards also argued that the Containment Policy itself permitted a variety of abuses, not only because it had never been written down but also since state laws and the unofficial Containment Policy had historically been selectively applied by police. Furthermore, there had never been any provisions for appeal by workers or management denied the unofficial 'right' to operate within the protection of Containment. Edwards also strongly criticised the restrictions on sex workers' personal freedom under local

Containment in Kalgoorlie. With respect to the general working conditions for sex workers in Western Australia, a number of human rights abuses were listed, including the following:

- Police registration and photographing of sex workers are degrading and constitute a degrading invasion of their privacy.
- Compulsory health checks for workers, and not clients, discriminates against a mostly female work force.
- Taxation without the basic right to operate creates unfair double standards for those people (mainly women) who work in the sex industry.[15]

Then on the evening of 1 July 1984, the human rights abuses attending the Containment Policy paled into insignificance. The previous night, a young Indonesian woman had arrived from Perth to work for Irene at 129 Hay Street, when her menacing former boyfriend appeared. As Irene recalled:

> That girl was only there for one day. She was from Perth. See…she brought her troubles with her. I said to her the night before, because he was hassling her, I said, 'You go tomorrow, and sort your things out, and when you sort it out, you can come back'. But it was too late.[16]

The man had ordered the young woman to leave with him, but she responded, 'No, you go!' Later the man was seen throwing eggs at the brothel, before trying to kick in one of the doors. As one witness told *The Kalgoorlie Miner*:

> He was acting crazy. He went across the street to his vehicle, did a U-turn and parked outside the brothel. He got out of the vehicle carrying a sawn-off shotgun.[17]

Having failed to persuade his former girlfriend to leave the brothel with him, 29-year-old New Zealander Gregory John Emery (of Southern Cross) shot the 23-year-old woman twice in the head as she crouched in a cupboard in her room. He then turned the gun on himself, but not before overturning a kerosene heater on the woman's bed, which soon erupted into a roaring inferno.

Irene was at home a few blocks away when her brothel manager, 'Thelma', rang with news that the man had returned with a gun. As Irene rushed into the brothel, she spotted the overturned kerosene heater on the woman's bed but was afraid to dash into the room to retrieve it, fearing that the gunman was still there. She was unable to see that he already lay dead on the floor, on the other side of the bed. Irene remembered clearly the sense of terror and helplessness she felt amid the chaos, afraid even to go into the back garden to get a fire extinguisher in case the gunman was hiding there:

> If I had known he was lying there dead, I would have just picked up the heater and moved it out. Then, the girls always mucked around with the fire extinguishers, and chased men away, and it was quite a lot of money to get them filled up at the fire station all the time. So I took them [the fire extinguishers] out the back. But then I thought the bloke with the gun was out the back. I thought, 'Well, I'm not going to get shot for a heater'. So I went next door to 'Marlene's', and I said, 'Give me a fire extinguisher'. And she said, 'We haven't got one'.[18]

According to Rose (who was still living across the back lane from the Hay Street brothels), nearby residents would also have found it impossible to forget that evening:

> The night Irene's brothel burnt down was the most frightening incident that I can recall ever happening in Hay Street. Terrible screams and gunshots could be heard as it must have been this poor girl's final realisation she was about to die, as her crazy boyfriend started to shoot. The house caught on fire and was totally destroyed with them still inside.
>
> Irene and her other girls had thankfully managed to escape and were safe and well as neighbours comforted them. We were all shocked and frightened, scared that this crazed gunman would shoot at anybody that moved. It was total panic for everybody in the vicinity.
>
> Guys wearing only their underpants came over the back fence of Irene's brothel and sprinted for their lives up the back alley to safety.[19]

ABC Radio journalist John Bowler had just wrapped up his Sunday evening broadcast in Kalgoorlie and was preparing to leave the studio, when he received a telephone call from a fellow journalist with news of a police 'standoff' with a gunman on Hay Street. Moments later, Mr Bowler was at the scene, cooling his heels:

> I was one of the first there, it was about 11 o'clock. There was sort of a standoff, and one shot had been fired, I think. Somebody told us, 'Someone's got a gun, and you don't want to go in'.
>
> A mate of mine, a police officer, was called to the scene. It was Georgie Mills, and an Aboriginal police aide, Preston Thomas. And they walked in, sort of casual, thinking it was a drunk hassling over the price, you know, 'Here we go again' sort of thing. George walked in and turned the corner, and there was this guy frothing at the mouth with a shotgun pointed straight at his belly. Now George never wore a sidearm, because he said if the police wear weapons

it sort of escalates the whole crime scene, and he says it's probably one of the reasons he's still alive now. Because if he had had a gun, and the guy sees a gun on his hip, he might have pulled the trigger. And there's no way George could have got to the gun anyway to save himself, because the guy had his finger on the trigger and he could have pulled it in a tenth of a second.

So George just backed away, and he said Preston turned white. And George—this little fat policeman—beat Ben Johnson's record for the hundred metre dash, because they just ran! They dashed out and got back to the station and came back with reinforcements. And then the fire started, and we were all standing back at that stage because we didn't know whether the guy was still alive or what, and the police weren't going to rush in...[20]

Police stopped the fire brigade from entering the burning brothel, for fear that the gunman might still be alive inside. At the height of the blaze, 30-foot flames melted the brothel's tin roof as the entire corrugated structure began to buckle underneath. The smouldering ruins of 129 Hay Street had cooled sufficiently by 1.00 am to permit armed police to search the premises. They found the charred body of the young murdered woman still crouched in her bedroom cupboard, while Emery's remains lay on the floor across a 12-gauge shotgun with one cartridge still in its breech. Both had died of gunshot wounds to the head.[21]

That night Irene took her six remaining workers home to stay with her. The following day, she told *The Kalgoorlie Miner* that the murder-suicide was a tragic 'domestic incident' that 'could have happened anywhere'. As a mark of respect for the young murdered woman, all the Hay Street brothels remained closed on the evening following the tragedy.[22]

Following the murder-suicide and the razing of the brothel, Irene did not rebuild on the site; she instead sold the corner property to a local furniture manufacturer. Having commenced negotiations to purchase Mona's brothel at 164 Hay Street in the months preceding the tragedy, she arranged to lease the premises at 143 Hay Street from Stella in the short term. Then in August 1984 Irene finally purchased 164 Hay Street from Mona Maxwell, as her old arch-rival prepared to retire.[23]

The West Australian reported that Mona had decided to sell up for 'private reasons' after twenty-five years on Hay Street, adding that Kalgoorlie's oldest and most famous madam was approaching 100 years of age. As Mona welcomed troops of reporters and travel agents through her 'house of hospitality' for the last time, she did not betray any bitterness:

Opening the Spanish iron gates of the house was the short grandmotherly-looking woman in a yellow track suit. She had auburn-tinted hair, thick glasses and an energetic, cheerful manner. It was none other than Mona Maxwell herself.

She took [the group] around the house, going first to the two spacious living rooms furnished in tan and brown with low slung lounge chairs, bars and soft lighting. Then it was off to the bedrooms which were surprisingly old-fashioned and homely, decorated with pastels and department store bedroom suites.[24]

Meanwhile, at the opposite end of the red-light district, madam 'Trudy' (see Figure 14) had been operating Nancy's brothel at 181 Hay Street since 1983. Former nurse 'Abbey' remembered that she began working for the ever-struggling, yet affable, madam Trudy in 1984, after they met while working together at a Containment brothel in Fremantle. Having been accustomed to the more discreet 'lounge room' system in Perth brothels, Abbey began soliciting on Hay Street with some trepidation:

Of course I was daunted at the reputation of Kalgoorlie, because the blokes up here were considered to be pretty rough, compared to Perth. I also didn't like the idea of standing out in front, and hooking people in. That was a bit daunting.

But a lot of times men came in from the bush, and quite often they didn't even have sex. I mean, I can remember blokes saying to me, 'I just want to lay

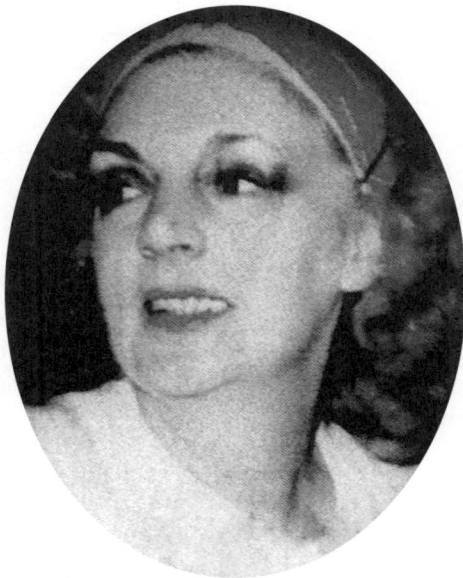

Figure 14 *Madam 'Trudy', who owned the brothel at 181 Hay Street during the 1980s.*
Courtesy Irene, private collection of photographs

next to a woman', because they'd been out bush for months on end, and they just wanted to be with a woman. Some of them paid hundreds of dollars, and they didn't even have sex. We used to say that Kalgoorlie was the only place that could happen.

The men are very macho, and they carry on like pork chops, but mostly that's all bullshit. When you're in the room, it's a whole different story.[25]

Over time, Abbey observed that the clients in Kalgoorlie preferred women they could relate to easily, and many a regular client viewed his favourite Hay Street woman as his 'surrogate girlfriend'. Abbey fondly recalled that she formed unusually friendly relationships with some of her regular clients, who even sought her help in selecting gifts for their female relatives:

For example, one client might give me $20 and say, 'It's me Mum's birthday next week. When you're downtown, can you pick out a nice birthday present'. There were a couple of clients where the mother actually knew my name.[26]

On the other hand, Hay Street women needed to be well prepared for 'problem' clients. Abbey explained one simple but effective code used by the women:

Now there were some bad characters around this town, and we all knew them. We used to have a system…the girl on the end, if she knew a bloke was one that none of us would see, she would say, 'Has that call come through from John yet?' And that was a warning to tell us 'Close your door'.[27]

All things considered, Abbey said her earnings in Kalgoorlie compared favourably to her earnings in Perth. She recalled that in 1984, Kalgoorlie's prices were set at about $10 higher than standard prices in Perth, with 181 Hay Street charging $30 for a 'short time' service, $60 for half an hour, and $90–100 for an hour's booking. Kalgoorlie workers could also charge overnight clients up to $500, while there was no equivalent earning opportunity for brothel workers in Perth. In the end, the higher earning potential for sex workers in Kalgoorlie generally appears to have meant longer working hours, as Abbey explained:

In the winter you had to be out there from 6 until about 2 or 3 perhaps. On Friday and Saturday nights, well, you'd work all night then. And of course Sundays we closed at midnight. We didn't have nightclubs open then, and every-thing closed at 9. And so you picked up that bit of business after 9 o'clock. After a couple of hours it was just dead anyway.

We also did a lot of overnighters, we did heaps then. And so on a Friday or Saturday night, you would work all night, and then you'd take a long overnighter or a short overnighter. A long overnighter was from about midnight until 7 in the morning, and you'd charge $500 for that. Or you could take a short overnighter, say from 2, for $250–400. That was good because you did good business anyway, but you got these bonuses on the end of the shift.[28]

In keeping with industry custom, women who worked at 181 Hay Street for madam Trudy gave 'the house' 50 per cent of their earnings, and were provided with accommodation and meals:

Well, we didn't pay rent, it was just a fifty-fifty split, although we paid $20 a week for electricity. There was always an evening meal, which we didn't have to pay for. A girl can't work twelve hours without eating a good meal, and they could be really stuffed if they didn't eat and look after themselves.[29]

In 1987 the Health Department of Western Australia recommended compulsory condom use in the sex industry (as part of the broader, collective strategy of Australian public health authorities) to stem the spread of HIV/AIDS in the community. Abbey proudly recalled that, even prior to this recommendation, she was among the first Hay Street women to insist on using condoms with all her clients, which she managed despite the initial resistance she encountered from clients and madams:

Yes, I actually brought the condom rules in. Kalgoorlie is hardened un-condom territory, because they're all macho men here. You know, 'never used a condom in their lives', and all this rubbish. It was a big no-no, right? So anyway, I enforced the condoms myself for about a month, without telling anybody. It was only by chance that [a client] came out and mentioned it to [another worker] that whenever he saw me he used a condom. I was trying to prove the point that it could be done in such a way that they didn't even know they had had one on. It's very easy to do, especially when they're pissed, like most of them are. The trick was, I didn't make a big issue of it.

By then there was increasing publicity, and so everyone could see that what I was saying made sense. It was the AIDS publicity that did it—because most men's knowledge [about sexual health] is pretty obscure. The important thing was, you needed to prove that you didn't lose money. And even if you did lose your job over it—well, so what? Your health's more important.[30]

Meanwhile, Hay Street women continued to have weekly medical examinations under the provisions of the Containment Policy. Abbey remembered that workers sought the services of private doctors instead of attending the community health service in Kalgoorlie:

We had a doctor that everybody preferred to go to, rather than the clinic. See, because if you got, just say thrush, which is annoying but it's not terribly drastic, [the clinic] will put you off for a week. He would only put you off for twenty-four or forty-eight hours, something like that. I mean, there was also gonorrhoea around then, and other things. If you caught something, once you've taken twenty-four hours of tablets, you're not infectious to anybody. You've got to take the whole course for your own sake, but you won't infect anybody.

So basically, the girls would go to him and if they had caught anything, they would get the tablets and might take two nights off work, then go back to work, whereas the clinic would put you off for ten days. In those cases the girl would have to go back home, because we couldn't live in the town and occupy working rooms if we weren't working. It didn't happen that often, but it did happen.

And it was mandatory that you were checked, because the coppers used to come in every week, to check the medical books. We all had a card, and the card had to be signed by the doctor. And the D's came in to check that, usually Fridays. They knew that any new girls would be there.[31]

After working at 181 Hay Street for two years, Abbey leased the brothel from Trudy during 1986–87 for $1,500 per month. Although she estimated that the business occasionally turned over $4,000–5,000 on a busy week—when she had four to six workers 'on the door'—these periodic peaks were offset by the constant challenge of attracting new staff:

I was in fairly new territory and I didn't have many connections, and at some times I only had one or two ladies working for me. I was leasing the place for $1,500 a month, which doesn't seem like much, but I had only one or two ladies working, as well as covering the costs and outgoings of the place, and also it was traditional that you put a meal on the table at night as well.[32]

Abbey explained that one major weekly expense lay in the need to purchase several cartons of tinned beer to serve to the brothel's male visitors, not all of whom were paying customers. It had been a time-honoured Hay Street tradition that all men who visited the brothels were welcome to relax and have a few beers 'compliments of the house', even if they were only in the company of a visiting client. Abbey said that meeting this expectation cost a considerable sum on an ongoing basis, yet she knew that failing to honour the tradition would have cost her more in business in the longer term:

It was a give-away, they didn't have to buy it. That's why the Liquor and Gaming [Squad] didn't worry us, because we only gave it away. I mean you'd spend a few hundred per week on beer, but it was worth it from a business point of view.[33]

While men were encouraged to 'let go' and 'live it up' on Hay Street, Abbey felt that life in Kalgoorlie's brothels presented a stifling restriction for the women. In an effort to lighten up the atmosphere a little, she threw monthly parties for her workers and a few invited clients, usually on Sunday evenings after closing:

> When I first came up here, you couldn't go anywhere, you couldn't go out to tea. You weren't allowed to go to pubs or anything.
>
> When I was managing 181, I used to have a party night, usually about once a month, you know…because most all the girls were sweet on one or two of their clients. And you used to close at twelve on a Sunday, anyway. So from 12 o'clock on a Sunday we'd have a party. And I let them invite who they liked to invite, and have a bit of a rage.[34]

Abbey left Kalgoorlie and resumed her nursing career when Trudy finally sold the corner property at 181 Hay Street in October 1989.

News that Trudy's bank might force a sale of 181 Hay Street spread like wildfire through the sex industry in Western Australia. First to offer to take the brothel off Trudy's hands was Mary-Anne Kenworthy (see Figure 15), a naive yet fairly ambitious Perth escort agency owner. Having arrived in Perth from New Zealand six years earlier, Mary-Anne was well familiar with running businesses both inside and outside the Containment Policy in Perth. She was also a former associate of Perth escort agency owner Sue Devereaux, who had reportedly recruited workers for madam Stella Strong during the mid-1980s.[35]

Even during the period for settlement on 181 Hay Street, Mary-Anne was not provided with the usual disclosures and liberties one would expect in the transfer of a 'mainstream' business:

> I contacted [Trudy], and we came to a price arrangement that I was happy with—$25,000 deposit and I paid her $1,000 a week for the first year…The purchase price was $185,000 if I recall rightly. I wasn't allowed to look through the premises before the purchase date.
>
> Then the police weren't happy for me to buy it…they reasoned that you couldn't buy two Containment licences. So I actually had to buy it through a secondary party and a trustee, who I bought out about eighteen months later.[36]

Following the settlement, Mary-Anne and her business partner had only two weeks to renovate the dilapidated premises and recruit workers before Kalgoorlie's annual Race Round commenced. The upgrading also enabled them to set prices that exceeded Hay Street's standard fee structure by $20 across the board (see Figures 16–20). Mary-Anne maintained that

Figure 15 *Madam Mary-Anne Kenworthy, who has owned the brothel at 181 Hay Street since 1989.*
Courtesy Mary-Anne Kenworthy, private collection of photographs

the renovations and higher fees were necessary to attract workers from Perth. The new 'Club 181' charged clients $90 for a half-hour booking, and $140 for an hour's booking. All earnings were divided between workers and 'the house' in the customary fifty-fifty split.[37]

Like many a Hay Street madam before her, Mary-Anne encountered chronic difficulties in attracting staff. Many of the women who worked at her Perth escort agency initially refused to go to Kalgoorlie, explaining that they were intimidated by the prospect of soliciting openly in the doorways of the brothel's hallway that ran along Hay Street. Mary-Anne remained convinced that her Perth business could provide a reliable recruitment pool for her Kalgoorlie brothel, if only she could manage the open soliciting problem that made the women feel uncomfortable. This led her to introduce a more discreet mode of operating, to make the women feel more comfortable:

When we bought the place, we had to put heating in, we had to knock out walls, we extended the lounge—and we had two weeks to do all this before the Race Round. It was a pig sty. I don't think the houses kept up with the standards. In Kalgoorlie, they want nice facilities. . .they want the works. After operating three days with only one girl, we realised it wouldn't work, and so we closed it down for ten days.

By that time I was able to convince the girls to give Kalgoorlie a go, by improving the standards on Hay Street for them. I think the girls also felt better about themselves because we were higher priced than any of the others—the average house was charging $120 an hour. But to get the girls up there, we had to get it off that [Hay Street] hallway. Then I had the police come down and tell me I couldn't do it—that it was a tourist attraction. Well, I disagreed and said I could do it.

The first three years in Kalgoorlie, we actually didn't have the girls out the front. We closed the front off, and [clients] just rang the doorbell and came in, down to the lounge, and chose their girls from the lounge. I couldn't've gotten a lot of girls to go to Kalgoorlie with halls, because we had quieter, shy girls who much prefer to work the lounge system. They wanted the discretion.[38]

Nowhere else but in Kalgoorlie does it seem plausible that the local police would step in to reverse a madam's efforts to tone down open soliciting by her workers. It would appear that Hay Street's status as a much-feted local institution and tourist attraction could have played a role in such a directive. This of course contrasts sharply with the mission of police in the early twentieth century, to minimise the visibility of 'harlots'.

Mary-Anne is believed to have been the first Hay Street madam to openly allow her workers to live and socialise wherever they pleased when not working, despite police orders under Containment. She also discussed hearsay evidence that local police had historically enforced personal restrictions on the workers for the benefit of the madams in Kalgoorlie:*

I argued for the girls' right to live out if they wanted to, although we were always seen to be obeying rules. But I used to let the girls go out quite freely. I used to let them live out if they wanted to, but it was never lied about. If we were ever asked by the police, we would just tell them outright.

The Containment rules in Kalgoorlie were illegal. They were against the rights of human beings, human decency. Those were madams' rules, they were never police rules. I've heard that those rules were all set up by the madams, and they used to pay the police to enforce those rules. But [the rules] worked for the town as well, so they became accepted.[39]

---

* It is not clear how much of this evidence is based on speculation and how much is based on actual knowledge.

Figure 16 *Front view of 181 Hay Street, 1999.* Courtesy Mary–Anne Kenworthy, private collection of photographs

Figure 17 *Workers' Hay Street doorways and waiting area.*
Courtesy Mary-Anne Kenworthy,
private collection of photographs

Figure 18 *Kitchen with original stove.*
Courtesy Mary-Anne Kenworthy,
private collection of photographs

Figure 19 *Outdoor entertaining area at rear of brothel.*
Courtesy Mary-Anne Kenworthy, private collection of photographs

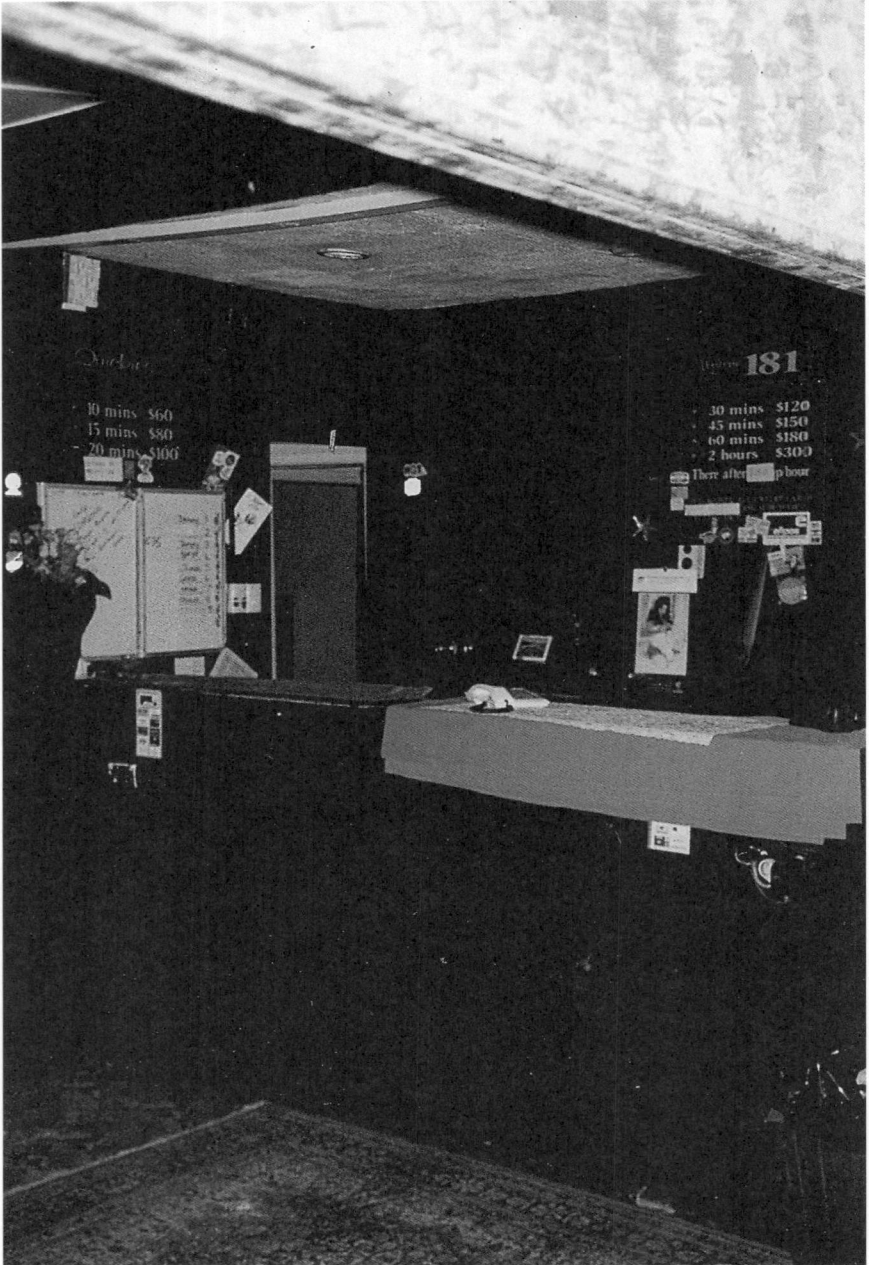

Figure 20 *Reception area and office, with the brothel's service/fee structure prominently posted, 181 Hay Street, 1999.* Courtesy Mary-Anne Kenworthy, private collection of photographs

Mary-Anne noted that most of her workers still chose to live on the premises, to avoid Kalgoorlie's notoriously inflated property rental market. They paid her $100 per week for their room and board, and slept in private and secure 'dongas'* located at the rear of the property, all equipped with a single bed, wardrobe, bedside table, desk, television and air-conditioning/heating. These were the women's private rooms, to which clients and other workers did not have access.[40]

During the late 1980s Abbey was 'headhunted' by Mary-Anne to return and manage Club 181. While Abbey enjoyed managing the business for a brief time, she bristled at Mary-Anne's open defiance of Containment:

> When Mary-Anne took over this place, and she started bringing in this looser sort of attitude, I found it really hard to work like that. I thought the [traditional Containment] system worked quite well, to be honest. Mary-Anne came in and started standing up to the police, and ruffled them a bit. And so I found it very hard to accept Mary-Anne's policy, which was 'Bugger all that, you're allowed to do what you like'.
>
> Basically, we'd all run the houses the way the D's wanted them to be run, which as far as I was concerned was no problem, because that kept them off your back. But Mary-Anne sort of changed all that, and that was really hard for people like me to take, you know, who had been running houses a certain way. So we didn't see eye to eye all the time.
>
> Well...I mean, I agree with her. You know, you shouldn't be a second-class citizen, and you should be allowed to do what you like. But the system worked. And so for years we saw a system work, and then suddenly somebody was coming in wanting to change it. That's a little bit daunting, that is.[41]

During her early years in Kalgoorlie, Mary-Anne did carry on one Hay Street tradition that had well and truly begun to fizzle out by the 1980s: she hired a cook to prepare daily meals for her workers. She explained that this helped her to ensure that her workers were healthy and productive, so that earnings would be maximised. She also often provided breakfast to clients and other early-morning visitors to the brothel:

> They didn't have [cooks] in other houses, but we had a cook for the first two years. She used to prepare a dinner meal, and we've always had cleaners; the girls have never cleaned in any of my places. I used to go up every weekend or second weekend, and we used to have a lot of clients stay over. We'd be busy

---

* 'Dongas' are extended caravans that provide a row of single-room accommodation units; used widely at mining sites.

until 7 or 8 in the morning in those days, and I mean at 6 o'clock we'd cook breakfast for clients and girls and whoever else was around.

Actually, the first couple of years in Kalgoorlie were great. You held court at 6 o'clock in the morning, and a lot of people would just come down and talk to you, to say hello. Clients would even look after my daughter for me, and gave her a bottle if I was busy. It was a very family atmosphere.[42]

While Mary-Anne worked furiously to build her new business in Kalgoorlie, she estimated that her Perth escort agency lost 35 per cent of its market share. Mary-Anne believes that this was mainly due to her frequent staff recruitment drives to bolster the business in Kalgoorlie, as well as her extended periods away from managing the Perth agency. Then one day, soon after Mary-Anne began operating in Kalgoorlie, former business associate Sue Devereaux organised for Mary-Anne's Perth escort agency to be burnt down (for which Devereaux was later convicted and gaoled), as Mary-Anne matter-of-factly explained:

We had had one of those lulls in the [Perth] market place, and business dropped off dramatically. You get two or three months where your business halves overnight, and there seems to be no logical reason for it And Sue had heard that we were doing better, and burnt it down purely from a business point of view.

So Lucy rang me up about 6 in the morning and said, 'I've got some bad news for you. The Agency's been burnt down'. Luckily, the owner next door had been trying to sell his [non-sex industry] premises. So I said to Lucy, 'Get in touch with him, and see if we can rent. If we can rent it, then we'll buy the bloody thing off him'.[43]

By 4 o'clock that afternoon, Mary-Anne was on the scene, managing damage control. On arrival, she rang her Telecom technician, who inspected the ruins and discovered that the cables in the Telecom box at the rear of the freshly gutted premises had not been damaged by the fire. Thus they could easily be connected to the telephone lines at her newly acquired offices next door. At the end of the day, a combination of amazing good luck and resourcefulness had put Mary-Anne back in business in time to catch the evening trade.[44]

Generally speaking, Mary-Anne expected the same level of determination that 'the show must go on' from all of her staff. But Abbey found that while she was managing Club 181, she could not implement what she considered Mary-Anne's 'hard-nosed', profit-driven approach to brothel management. Abbey conceded that her instincts had often led her to turn away 'rowdy' clients for the sake of the workers, a practice she believed would not be endorsed by Mary-Anne:

If there was a bloke that came in and he was an arsehole, and he was just going to be trouble, I'd just say, 'Right. Nobody's here'. Whereas Mary-Anne would have somebody see him.[45]

Mary-Anne maintains that this is a 'load of shit' and insists that she'd never pressure any worker to provide services to a client whom the worker would rather refuse. However, she had always considered the bottom-line profit the primary performance indicator for her managers and workers. She also said that she liked to see workers departing her employ with substantial savings. Having noticed that a number of her workers in Kalgoorlie seemed to be spending their income almost as quickly as they earned it, Mary-Anne introduced a restrictive system of payment to ensure that the women left Hay Street with reasonable savings:

> We used to pay them weekly, but then we started paying them fortnightly or when they left. We ran a card situation for them, and at the end of the night, we put what they earned onto a card. Any money they owed us would come off the card. I actually liked the girls to get a cheque when they left town. We let them 'sub' up to $50 a day. Anything over that, we question it. If a girl had to pay her rental payment in Perth or something, she could sub it.
>
> But I was very strict the first couple of years, of what they could pull their money for. One: it discourages the drug addicts. And two: it was impor-tant that when they left town, I could write them out the fattest cheque possible. I mean, there was one girl I had to write a cheque out for $43,000. After all her taxes were paid, after everything was paid, she had $43,000 left.[46]

Mary-Anne said that mature-age women consistently proved more capable of maintaining regular clientele in Hay Street, which seems to sup-port madam Rita's earlier observations. Mary-Anne recalled that one of her most popular workers was a woman in her late 40s, the softly spoken 'Vanda', whose professional acumen and charming nature always seemed to secure for her a substantial share of Club 181's trade:

> Vanda was one of the best workers I've ever seen, in the way she treated her clients. She'd bring them up to the counter and she'd be touching them. And when she brought them out of the room she'd be kissing them on the cheek. I've never seen anyone who worked as well as her.[47]

Back on the north side of Hay Street, madam Irene sold her premises at 164 Hay Street to New Zealand–born madam Teriapii King-Brooks in 1989. Irene used her $600,000 settlement money to purchase the central Perth railway station newsagency. While being a newsagent appealed greatly to Irene's early-bird work habits, she ended up managing the demanding central city business for only one year before selling up and retiring to the relative tranquillity of the Blue Mountains in New South Wales.[48]

There was to be no such 'great reward' awaiting madam Teriapii when she departed Hay Street the following year, under rather more troubled circumstances. Her difficulties with the law began in August 1990, during Kalgoorlie's annual Race Round. The Kalgoorlie CIB and the Customs Office raided the brothel in a joint exercise code-named 'Operation Rex', after police sniffer dogs Rex 3 and Rex 5. During the raid, the 'snoopsome twosome' netted their masters 80 grams of cannabis and 5.5 grams of methylamphetamines, which resulted in the arrests of all seven brothel workers and madam Teriapii herself. Teriapii was charged with possession and intent to sell or distribute the drugs—her first offence—for which she was later convicted and gaoled for six months. Following the August raid, police immediately ordered that the brothel remain closed for one month.[49]

Then on 28 September 1990, six days after the brothel reopened, police again closed it down—reportedly on special orders from Chief Superintendent of Police Les Ayton of the Internal Affairs Unit in Perth.[50] This second closure seems to have been related to earlier police comments in August, when Kalgoorlie CIB officer Mal Scott told *The Kalgoorlie Miner* that 164 Hay Street would remain closed pending an investigation into 'questionable money' involved in the brothel's purchase. It was later revealed that police suspected that Teriapii's purchase of 164 Hay Street may have been partially financed by men, and male financial involvement in brothels was strictly forbidden under the Containment Policy.[51]

The financial involvement of local men in the brothel's purchase was confirmed in a letter dated 13 September 1990 from Brian Singleton, QC, to local solicitor David Johnston, excerpts of which were published in *The Kalgoorlie Miner* on 23 March 1991. In this report, Mr Singleton's client—a prominent Kalgoorlie businessman code-named 'Mr X' in the report—said that he had headed the syndicate of investors who financed the purchase of 164 Hay Street in 1989. He claimed that no money had been repaid on the uninsured loan (for an undisclosed amount), and that he had unsuccessfully sought to have ownership of the property transferred into his wife's name—a request he believed had been obstructed by police.

Meanwhile, Teriapii also owed a reported $200,000 to the Westpac Bank on the property's mortgage.[52] Finding herself facing overwhelming pressures to repay both loans, Teriapii defied police orders to keep the brothel closed and worked alone from 164 Hay Street during 12–14 October 1990. Local police again arrested her, and this time charged her with keeping a brothel and living off the earnings of prostitution. These charges were later dismissed by Magistrate Peter Malone, who ruled that Teriapii had not broken the law by working alone from her place of residence.[53]

In *The Kalgoorlie Miner's* report on the court case, Detective Sergeant Richard Anderson of the Kalgoorlie CIB warned that the decision had 'paved the way' for prostitutes to work alone from private homes in the suburbs of Kalgoorlie-Boulder: 'It would be to the detriment of Kalgoorlie, and we would lose a prime tourist destination, if prostitution went into the suburbs'.[54] However, there is no evidence that prostitutes sought to operate in the suburbs of Kalgoorlie-Boulder as a result of this case.

Meanwhile, Teriapii had also mounted a Supreme Court challenge to the Containment Policy in a joint action with Ingrid Pluktchy, a Perth private agent who had been arrested several times by the Vice Squad while working from her home in a wealthy Perth suburb. In July 1991, the full Supreme Court of Western Australia, led by Chief Justice David Malcolm, concluded that the legal status of the Containment Policy was doubtful at best. However, the court dismissed the women's bid to have the Containment Policy scrapped, since there was no official documentation of the policy, which made it impossible to determine whether the policy was lawful and whether the women had been unfairly treated under its provisions.[55]

The Containment Policy had also come under legal scrutiny the previous year, when Police Minister Graham Edwards tabled the final report of the Community Panel on Prostitution in October 1990. The panel, headed by Beryl Grant of the Uniting Church, investigated the sex industry in Perth and Kalgoorlie, and had reported on a total of twenty-one submissions received from police and health authorities, local councils, women's interest groups, churches and private citizens. It its final report, the panel concluded that the Containment Policy was illegal and discriminatory, and that law reform was needed to clarify the rights and responsibilities of sex industry participants and various regulatory authorities in Western Australia.[56]

The City of Kalgoorlie-Boulder's submission to the panel appears to have proposed the state's virtual adoption of the Containment Policy, as several of the following recommendations seem to suggest:

1. Brothels

(a) That brothels be licensed.

(b) Ownership of land and improvements in respect of brothels should be vested in a female person only (not a corporation).

(c) Owner of a brothel to be the Licensee, who also must reside on the premises. Applications for leave of absence to be made to a magistrate.

(d) Male persons not to be involved in management of brothels or to reside on the premises.

(e) Prostitution to be licensed.

(f) Sale of liquor on these premises to be prohibited.[57]

The city council's submission obviously pleased staunch traditionalist madam Stella Strong, whose praise is recorded in notes along the margins of the document (provided by the council), including the following comments:

> Thank you from the bottom of my heart to Mr Ray Finlayson and his counelleurs [sic] of the City Kalgoorlie Boulder. The only department with common sense, compassion and guts and understanding with clear sight of the present & more important the future of The Goldfields.[58]

Vehemently opposed to any changes to local Containment, Stella also came out swinging against the Community Panel on Prostitution's recommendations (which had obviously been supported by the council) in *The Kalgoorlie Miner*. She claimed that any licensing system for brothels would be a disaster, and said she was particularly concerned that men might be allowed to own brothels in Western Australia. She warned that 'Canberra bureaucrats' could not be trusted to understand the needs of people living in a country mining town like Kalgoorlie, and insisted that Hay Street women would always need to be confined to the brothels for their own protection. She also said that any reduced police role in the administration of the sex industry in Kalgoorlie would be an invitation for drug dealers and violent criminals to take over the town.[59]

Madam Stella and other staunch supporters of local Containment need not have worried. The Lawrence (Labor) government took no action on the panel's recommendations.

Back in Hay Street, business at Club 181 had dropped dramatically following the forced closure of 164 Hay Street in late 1990. As it happened, closure of the only brothel located on the north side of Hay Street had significantly altered the meandering patterns of men in the red–light district.

> When 164 [Hay Street] closed down...we only had the four houses, and guys would come up the street from that [eastern] end, they'd walk past those two houses, over to [164] then they'd see our lights and come across the road. Well, our business dropped dramatically, so we actually had to go back on the hallway system. And it's still on the hallway today, because it does work for Kalgoorlie.[60]

Club 181 was being managed by Mary-Anne's sister, Sally Kenworthy. Mary-Anne said that Sally was a good manager, although she could be 'a bit of a soft touch' with the women. However, former Club 181 worker 'Taylor' argued that Sally's understanding nature had created a much-needed supportive environment for the workers:

> Sally was excellent. She understood that you had certain times when you just couldn't work. And Sally used to take us down to the nightclubs herself. We'd take it in shifts, and you could go with Sally from 11 till 1, or maybe 12 till 1 another three girls would go down.[61]

Sally Kenworthy appears to have been the first Hay Street madam to accompany her workers for a few drinks at Kalgoorlie's pubs and night-clubs—outings strictly forbidden under the local Containment Policy. Like Mary-Anne, Sally believed that Hay Street women were entitled to enjoy an evening out, like anyone else in Kalgoorlie. Then Sally departed Hay Street in 1993, leaving another unconventional madam to take the helm at Club 181.

Leigh Varis-Beswick (see Figure 21) certainly set a notable precedent in Kalgoorlie, being Hay Street's first transgender madam. Leigh was born Harry Varis in Kalgoorlie in 1950, served two years of a plumber's appren-ticeship during the mid-1960s, briefly considered a career as a policeman, and then finally made the decision to start working as a drag queen for Perth madam Shirley Finn in 1969. Leigh proudly recalled that her clients rarely realised that she was 'still a boy' in those days:

> Nobody knew, you know. We were good at what we did. We didn't look like men in dresses, we looked like young girls. But we were boys. Clients didn't know.
>
> We didn't usually have sex. We used to offer oral and hand relief and massage. Every now and again somebody would come in wanting to go to bed with a boy.[62]

Leigh later toured Australia with the cabaret companies 'Les Girls' and 'Les Coquettes'. She then worked as a streetwalker in Sydney's Kings Cross, until one evening when she and a workmate were threatened by standover men demanding protection money. Leigh immediately packed her bags and headed back to Western Australia.[63]

Over the next fifteen years, Leigh worked in the state's North West as a barmaid, office cleaner and hotel manager. Having built up the neces-sary savings, she travelled to Singapore in 1986 to have transgender surgery. Leigh then set out to build a successful career as both a 'working girl' and a manager in several Perth brothels over the next seven years.[64]

Figure 21 *Madam Leigh Varis-Beswick*. Courtesy Mary-Anne
Kenworthy, private collection of photographs

When Leigh decided to return to Kalgoorlie in 1993 as a 'Hay Street woman', she applied to work at Club 181 through Mary-Anne's escort agency in Perth. But she was refused a placement by the interviewing staff, who felt that Hay Street was perhaps not yet ready for a transgender 'working girl'. Undeterred, Leigh soon began working for madam Stella Strong at 143 Hay Street, where she encountered several men she had grown up with in Kalgoorlie:

> It was weird! Guys that I knew were coming down the street, but they didn't know who I was. And a lot of guys that I played football against, and played cricket against as a young man. I was taking them in the room, and they were on top of me, and I'd look up...and I'd know who they were, but they didn't know who I was. And obviously for different reasons I couldn't tell them who I was. You know, what they don't know won't hurt them.[65]

Sally Kenworthy's boyfriend happened to be Leigh's nephew, and within the month Mary-Anne had contacted Leigh and invited her to temporarily manage Club 181, on the advice of Sally:

> Leigh ended up taking over from Sally, and it's been the best thing since sliced bread. She's great at management. She's got an advantage...you know, a lot of females aren't logical. But Leigh, having a bit of both, is logical. I feel that Leigh is completely female, I can't think of her as anything else, but she's got that logical advantage with her. I won't interfere if they make over so much money a week. The dollars tell me whether she's doing a good job.[66]

Arguing against this heavily profit-driven approach to brothel management, former Club 181 worker Taylor found that Leigh often pushed her to work 'past her limit'. Taylor also resented that Leigh often seemed unsympathetic with respect to the women's most basic needs:

> Because she's not a woman, she doesn't understand your mood swings and your time of the month. She wants you to get out and work, and she doesn't like to take 'No' for an answer. Down there [at 181], you just about have to ask to go to the toilet. At 3 o'clock in the morning, you come in and sit round the table...maybe the other girls are busy...and she thinks you're slacking off, and she's there to make you work. Which is just so much bullshit. If my body's had it, I can't continue to work.[67]

Leigh responded that she herself remained on duty twenty-four hours a day, seven days a week, and she expected the same commitment from her workers.

> Girls come up to Kalgoorlie for the specific task of making money. Now if I've got lots of girls here, girls get two nights off a week if they want it. Say I've got eight or nine girls, then they get their night off. But like tonight, I've got six girls on. Well, I can't afford to let anybody have the night off. I need at least six girls out the front. I've got another lady coming back tomorrow night, so I'll be giving one of these girls the night off tomorrow night.
>
> But a lot of girls come up here and say, 'I'm here for ten days, or three weeks, and I want to work every night. I'm here to make money'. And they'll tell you, 'I don't want a night off'—which is up to them. I have one lady who works seven days a week. She does not have a day off. She hasn't had a break now for about seven weeks.[68]

While Leigh remained focused on turning a good profit at Club 181, she insisted that she always felt protective of the workers:

> Well, you have just about one [troublemaker] every week. But they're not really a problem. My job is to get them to the front door. But I haven't had a blue in

here for ages…where I physically attack somebody. I haven't had anybody like that for ages. But I make short shrift of them. If they misbehave, I come the heavy at them, and my job is to get them off the premises, with as little fuss as possible, without involving the police.

I've hit guys, don't get me wrong. I'll protect mine. If they hurt the girls, I'll go in and hurt them. They're my girls. One girl said, 'You treat us just like daughters'. And I said, 'Well, yeah. In a way that's what you are to me. If anybody hurts you, I'm going to be like a mother hen, and protect my brood, you know?'

You'll get the odd drunk come in, and he'll abuse you and swear at you. But you're sober, they're drunk. You can stand up and they can't.[69]

In an effort to reduce the brothel's expenses, Leigh put an end to the time-honoured custom of providing complimentary beer to guests who had not made a booking with one of the workers. Leigh maintained that her 'no nonsense' management approach actually helped to build a more solid client base at Club 181, while also reinforcing the brothel's sound working relationship with the local police.[70]

Leigh's decision to 'turn off the tap' might well have been influenced by the economic recession of the early 1990s and its negative impact on Kalgoorlie's economy. For the first time in a hundred years, Kalgoorlie had suffered the same economic downturn as the rest of the country and the state, and thousands of goldfields miners had been laid off. This had significantly affected business in the Hay Street brothels.

Hay Street's severe recession might also have played a role in madam Stella Strong's drastic decision to terminate all her workers at 143 Hay Street in early 1992, reportedly for breaching (unspecified) Containment rules. The following month, *The Kalgoorlie Miner* reported that five women between the ages of 22 and 28 years would soon be arriving from the eastern states to reopen the brothel.[71] It seems safe to suggest that Stella would have been less likely to have taken such action had business been reasonably good at the time.

In April 1992 both Stella and Sally commented in *The Kalgoorlie Miner* that business on Hay Street remained remarkably quiet. Stella complained that the introduction of the gold tax in Western Australia had hurt Kalgoorlie's goldmining industry.[72]

Thus the economic realities of the 'outside world' had closed in on Kalgoorlie and even on the Hay Street brothels. In the years that followed, social and legal realities would begin to chip away at the local Containment Policy itself.

CHAPTER 6

Foreshadowing the end of an era

Hay Street's popularity as a local and tourist attraction continued to gather momentum during the early 1990s, apparently with the blessing of local authorities; this contrasted sharply with the historical efforts of the local police and council to reduce the visibility of the sex trade in Kalgoorlie. Then in February 1994 the Hay Street brothels landed firmly in the spotlight when Kalgoorlie's new Centennial Theatre launched its inaugural season with *The Starting Stalls*, a play set in a Hay Street brothel (see Figure 22).[1]

Popular fascination with Kalgoorlie's 'scarlet women' made *The Starting Stalls* an instant hit and the toast of Western Australia's theatre circuit. The play sold out its three-night season at the 640-seat Centennial Theatre before the curtain rose on the first performance, and later played to sell-out audiences in Perth, as well. *The Starting Stalls* presented a light-hearted glimpse into the lives of women trying to beat hard times with a 'tour of duty' on Hay Street. The dialogue highlighted the financial hardships, family commitments and resilient humour that united the diverse group of women, as well as the tensions that arose from living and working together within the cramped confines of a Hay Street brothel.[2]

Feted by audiences and theatre reviewers in both Kalgoorlie and Perth, *The Starting Stalls* also had its critics. These included Penny Lyall, executive

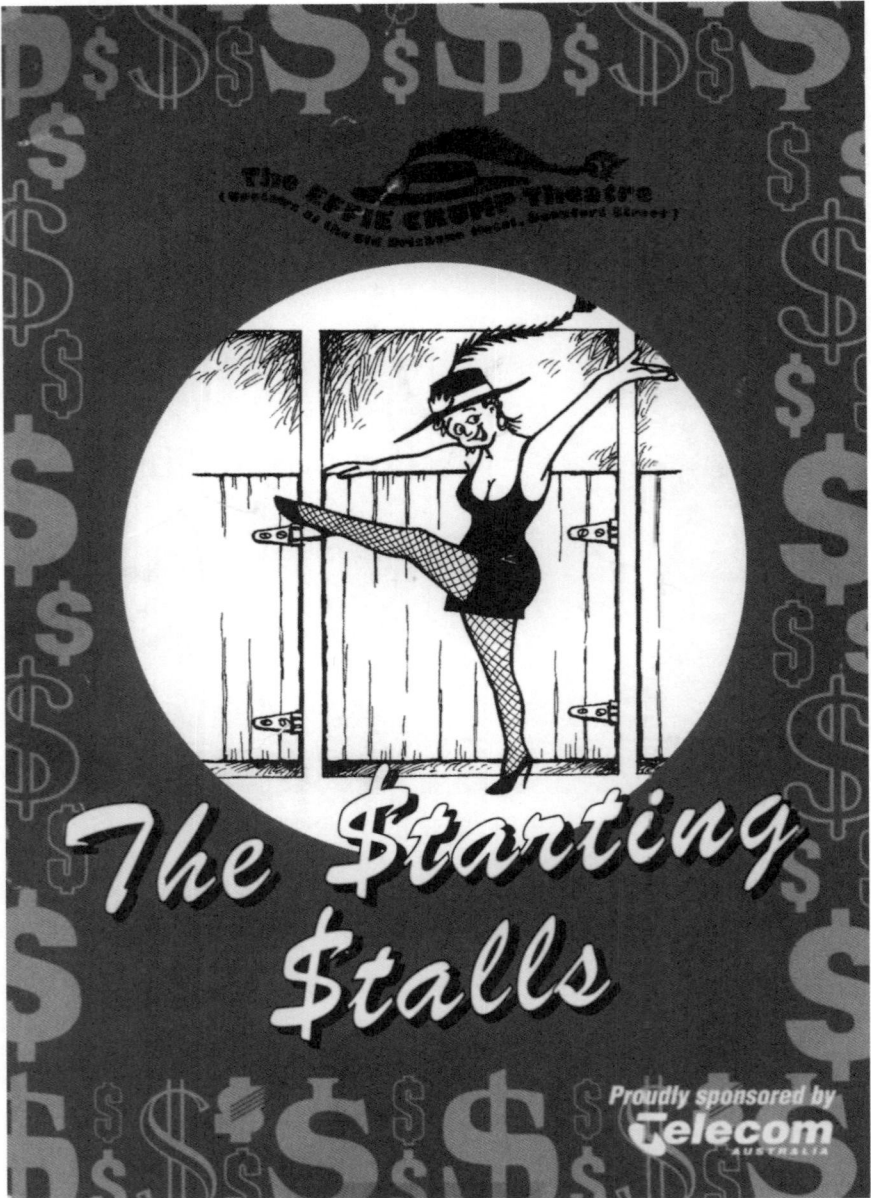

Figure 22 *Program cover for* The Starting Stalls, *1994.*
Courtesy Adrian Kenyon, Phoenix Communications

director of the Perth-based sex worker Support, Information, Education and Referral Association (SIERA). She argued that *The Starting Stalls* had ultimately dehumanised sex work and had failed to take a stand on the illegal status of the sex industry in Western Australia. Lyall's scathing review, published in SIERA's newsletter *Working for a Living*, noted that many sex workers had complained to SIERA that they were left feeling angry and confused by the plot's implausible resolution; this involved a 'two-for-one special', two bookings with a worker for the price of one, ostensibly to improve business. Lyall concluded that the play was under-researched and ill-informed and had trivialised the women and their work.[3]

On the evening that I attended a performance of *The Starting Stalls* in Perth, it was obvious that the mainly middle-class, middle-aged audience found the 'two-for-one' concept enormously funny. On the other hand, sex workers I spoke to immediately after the performance said that they had enjoyed the play until the 'bargain-bin' finale, which they had found degrading. They nevertheless hoped that the generally sympathetic character portrayals would help to 'humanise' the community's perception of sex workers.[4]

Perth playwright Cate Smith gathered background information for *The Starting Stalls* during a number of brief visits to Kalgoorlie in 1992–93. She spent most of her time chatting to workers and observing them at Stella Strong's brothel, the Red House (143 Hay Street), which had long been nicknamed the 'Starting Stalls', owing to its trademark frontage that looks for all the world like a row of horseracing pens (see Figure 23).

Over a cup of coffee, Smith had convinced Stella to allow her to conduct informal research for a few evenings; she was then forbidden by the workers to keep even a notepad handy. Smith duly agreed to take only mental notes while sitting unobtrusively in one of the 'stalls', quietly observing interactions between the workers and clients, while passing the time with her passion for quilting.[5]

As a tourist in Kalgoorlie during the 1970s, Smith had caught her first glimpse of a Hay Street woman, sitting under coloured lights in a doorway, knitting while she waited for clients to arrive. She retained this image and resolved that one day she would write a story about Hay Street women.[6] Twenty years later Smith sat, almost Madame Defarge–like, quietly quilting in the shadows while surveying each worker, client and passer-by.

In later interviews, the playwright revealed that she had often been confounded by Stella's mysterious ways and mood swings. For example, although she had always stayed at Stella's private residence during her visits, she had never been trusted with a key to the house. Apart from finding herself locked inside the quaint Kalgoorlie bungalow on a number of occasions,

Figure 23 *The Red House, the brothel on which* The Starting Stalls *was based.*
Courtesy Nucolorvue Productions

she was sometimes locked out; Smith once had to enlist local police to locate Stella, so she could collect her luggage from the house in time to catch her flight back to Perth. Their obviously tenuous 'friendship' ended abruptly on the eve of the premiere of *The Starting Stalls* in Kalgoorlie, and Smith continued to be baffled by Stella's sudden 'cold shoulder' for some time afterwards.[7]

We should not forget the human heart beating at the local police head-quarters, in the midst of so much ado about *The Starting Stalls*. In keeping with the spirit of this light-hearted event, local CIB chief Garry Annetts gave the green light for the 'real stars' of Hay Street to attend local performances of *The Starting Stalls*.[8] This is believed to have been the first occasion in the Containment Policy's ninety-year history that local police permitted Hay Street women to leave the brothels during the evening hours.

Sergeant Annetts confirmed in *The Kalgoorlie Miner* that the local Containment Policy continued to segregate sex workers from 'normal social activity' in the town. He also commented that restrictions on the workers' movements in Kalgoorlie had historically been 'important to the madams, since they would lose money if their employees were able to earn income outside the brothels'.[9] The latter comment appears to support claims by some former Hay Street workers and madams that a number of local Containment rules had actually originated with madams.

Nevertheless, police continued to enforce the local Containment Policy to the (unwritten) letter, as Mary-Anne Kenworthy learned when she stepped in briefly to manage Club 181 in April 1994:

I told Leigh to go away for the week, and I'd come up and run the place. I wasn't up there for 24 hours when somebody rang up for an escort. I said, 'Not a problem. I'll send you an escort'. I mean, running escorts is a natural part of my business. I don't know that I even considered that we weren't allowed to do escorts in Kalgoorlie. And even if I had considered it, I still would have done the same bloody thing.

I got a phone call an hour later, 'We've got one of your girls down at the police station, and you've just been nicked'. And the first thing I thought was, 'Oh, no. What's Leigh going to do to me?' [Laughter] So anyway, I get down to the police station and they said to me, 'You have to close down for a week, and we're going to charge that girl'. And I said, 'Look, you're wasting your time charging that girl, because you didn't give her any money, did you? So she can't be living off the earnings. It's just going to run up a lot of legal costs, and you should be charging me'. They said, 'You will not tell us what to do—you are closing down for one week!' And I said, 'Get fucked'.

And I got myself back [to the brothel] and pulled all the girls together and told them what happened. I said, 'Vice have told me I can't operate, but you are all registered to work in Kalgoorlie. While I think on this, we'll close reception down tonight, and whatever you earn, it's your money'.

After a few phone calls to the solicitors the next day, I decided, 'Shit. I'm going to have to go with this ban, but I'm not going to close my doors'. So I thought, 'Well, we're going to renovate'. Because the only way I could keep my doors open and my lights on was to be painting, and I needed the doors open for the paint fumes to go out. It was the only thing I could think of. At the same time, everybody that walked past, I'd drag them in and make them have a cup of tea or coffee for an hour. And the police were cruising up and down, they didn't know what the hell was going on! [Laughter] I expected them to come in, but they never came in and never rang me to ask what was going on.

I did have the TV station turn up about three days later and they said, 'Oh, we see you've been closed down'. I said, 'What a load of bullshit—we're renovating'. But then again, I was able to turn it to an advantage by doing the upgrade. I put the prices up again. Within two weeks, I actually had my money back from the closure.[10]

In the Kalgoorlie Magistrates' Court on 25 October 1994, defence counsel Jon Redman argued that there was no evidence that 'Melissa' had actually earned any income on the evening of 30 April, as she had not received payment from either of the detectives. Magistrate Deborah Bennett-Borlase agreed that there was no case to answer and dismissed the charge of living off the earnings of prostitution. The following day in *The Kalgoorlie Miner*, Kalgoorlie CIB chief Garry Annetts suggested that police and brothel operators would perhaps need to be 'more flexible in their interpretation of Containment', but denied any inconsistencies between the policy's operation in Perth and in Kalgoorlie.[11]

Meanwhile, police authorities publicly appealed to the state government for workable prostitution law reform. While police in Kalgoorlie faced increasing resistance from workers and madams who challenged the extreme restrictions under local Containment, the Vice Squad in Perth struggled to regulate dozens of massage parlours and escort agencies that had been established throughout the metropolitan area. Along with the attending strain on limited resources, the situation of police administering an illegal activity left them vulnerable to allegations of corruption. It is hardly surprising that police authorities strongly supported the introduction of a workable, transparent and robust legal framework to replace the unofficial Containment Policy.[12]

Early in 1994 the Court (Liberal) government announced that its Coalition Justice Committee (composed of Liberal and National Party Members of Parliament) had commenced an investigation into the local and interstate sex industries, with a view to recommending a law reform model for Western Australia.[13] In June Police Minister Bob Wiese told *The West Australian* that he and the committee were reviewing the law reform models and experiences of Victoria and the Australian Capital Territory. The committee had also called for submissions from police and health authorities, local councils, sex industry representatives and community organisations in Western Australia. The Minister acknowledged that the Containment Policy was 'now open to abuse and corruption', and that it had failed to address changes in the sex industry over time. In the same report, Detective Sergeant Kym Kramer, head of the Perth-based Vice Squad, agreed that Containment had reached 'the end of its life as an effective means of control', and said that prostitution law reform was urgently needed to provide appropriate regulation of the sex industry.[14]

Meanwhile, all this talk of abandoning the old ways had again galvanised the last of Hay Street's 'steam-powered' madams into launching her own resistance campaign. In a written submission to the City of Kalgoorlie-Boulder in July 1994, Stella Strong made clear her fierce opposition to any changes to the local Containment Policy, and further urged the council to persuade the Coalition Justice Committee that the state government should endorse the Containment Policy rather than pursue prostitution law reform.[15]

Stella's submission to the council included a list of long-standing rules for workers (see pages 75–76), as well as the following self-styled 'edict', which she had recently posted for the workers' information:

This [sic] rules are given to me by C.I.B. and Mayor of Kalgoorlie and some are my own. I do respect them and keep them till taken from me officially. Up to now everyone including council, police, townspeople and girls have been in agreement and happy with these rules which have worked very well to everyone's mutual benefit. We are on good terms with townspeople so do not care what any other houses do in Hay Street. While it suits you to stay in Kalgoorlie, you are respected and accepted like any public servant—if you don't agree, you are welcome to leave—any time, without explanation. But do not underestimate me! I do respect everyone professionally but will not give my word for 'amateurs'. Kalgoorlie is no training centre—so take my word for it and try—it works to take good and bad or 'up and down' in the long run![16]

This document also provides a record of basic operational information. Stella's July 1994 council submission included her brothel's service and fee structure, as well as her requirement that all her workers be 'on the door' by 6.00 pm in winter and 7.00 pm in summer. The brothel closed at 2.00 am most nights, but remained open until 5.00 am after the busier Friday and Saturday evening shifts. It is not clear whether Stella claimed a percentage of the workers' income from all-night bookings, since the notice only 'advises' a minimum fee for such bookings, which apparently did not commence until after official business hours:

OFFICIAL PRICE LIST (MENU 143 HAY STREET)

TIMES IN ROOM W. CLIENTS

Treatment	Time	Amount
S/S (straight sex)	20 mins	$ 60.00
S + M (sex and massage)	20 mins	$ 70.00
Part O + S (oral and sex)	20 mins	$ 70.00
S/S	45 mins	$ 80.00
S + M	45 mins	$ 90.00
S + O	45 mins	$ 90.00
S/S	60 mins	$ 150.00
S/M	60 mins	$ 160.00
S/O	60 mins	$ 160.00

All Night—Starting 2 a.m.—Till 8 a.m.
By your own discretion—But advisable not less than $500.[17]

Above all, Stella remained staunchly opposed to any changes to local Containment in Kalgoorlie. When news broke in *The Kalgoorlie Miner* in October 1994 that the case against Club 181 escort worker Melissa had been dismissed, Stella closed her doors in protest and immediately offered two workers at Club 181 the keys to her brothel under a six-month lease. The startled women, April and Ann, had secretly been trying to obtain the lease from Stella for months, and had repeatedly been refused. Stella's sudden change of heart could well have been timed to flick a fly in the soup of her Hay Street nemesis, Club 181 owner Mary-Anne Kenworthy, still basking in her victory at the Kalgoorlie Magistrates' Court. In any event, Stella's move swiftly relieved Mary-Anne of two workers and elevated them to management positions in a competing brothel.[18]

April had lived in Kalgoorlie since the age of 10, having moved with her family from rural New South Wales in 1980. As a teenager, she had joined friends for the occasional drive past the Hay Street brothels to shout abuse at the 'fucking whores' sitting in the doorways. In early 1993 single motherhood and chronic poverty led April to begin working at Club 181; she said that, as a long-term local resident, she found the prospect of soliciting in Hay Street particularly intimidating:

> I knew the cleaner from 181 through my baby-sitter, and so I went around there one day with her. I said, 'Well, what do you do?' So she rang up Sally and arranged for an interview. I went in and talked to Sally, and she said, 'Well, you can start tonight if you want'. So I did. I sat out on the stool that night, with my head hung down, and my hands around my face. I was so paranoid that someone would see me…I was really scared. And then I didn't see anybody I knew for six months.[19]

By mid-1994 April and co-worker Ann had retired their personal debts and acquired some savings. When rumours surfaced that Stella would not renew her lease with Perth-based escort agency Elegant Liaisons, April and Ann began to discuss leasing Stella's brothel. Both women lived in private accommodation away from Club 181, and this greatly facilitated their four-day brainstorming session to hammer out a business plan and proposal:

> Well, first we brought a medical certificate in to Leigh, saying we had gastro. This gave us four days off, and it was in that four days that we plotted it. We put it on paper and worked it out, between going to the race meetings, of course. [Laughter] And the first time we went over to see Stella she knocked us back. She said, 'No way in the world! I don't even know you! You two are Kenworthy's girls, and she's trying to get the lease through you'.
>
> We talked to three girls from Stella's house, and they helped us get the lease. They said, 'Stella, don't give it to the mob that had it before [Elegant Liaisons], it was horrible. Don't let them have it'. Because we had showed these girls at the Red House the proposal for the business, what we were going to do, then they came over to Stella's with me. And still she knocked us back again and again.[20]

April and Ann had given up all hope of leasing 143 Hay Street, and were caught off guard on the afternoon of 25 October:

At 3.00 pm, Stella rang at [Club] 181 and said, 'Be in Perth by 7.00 am tomorrow morning. I'm going to sign the lease to you'. And we just went, 'What! What the fuck?' You know, because I had forgotten about it, Ann had forgotten about it. But Stella must have been thinking about it.

When Ann got the news, she came and told me [in a Kalgoorlie cafe]. I told the girl I was sitting with that we had gotten the lease, and we were offsky. Then Leigh and Mary-Ann came into the diner, and I was talking to them as well. But they had found out the night before, and they had taken us on the side and said, 'We've found out, we know what you're up to'. They said, 'Don't interfere with our business, and once you walk out that's it. There will be no looking back. And don't try to steal our girls'. And we thought, Hey, you know, you should be proud of us. And I didn't think we had anything on Mary-Anne Kenworthy, because she's the biggest business owner in Perth.[21]

They set out immediately for the seven-hour drive to Perth, and rose early the next morning for their meeting with Stella at 7.00 am at her accountant's office. At the meeting, Stella presented a six-month lease agreement for 143 Hay Street that set the rent at $5,000 per week, effective from 31 October. The heads of agreement also included the condition that 'all aspects of the operation must comply with the Containment Policy', yet these terms were not specified. Then Stella advised the women that she had temporarily misplaced the account-keeping books for the business:

When she laid out all these heads of agreement, we said, 'Stella, we can't afford to pay $5,000 a week. That's a bit rich'. And she goes, 'Oh, you've got nine rooms there. That's one thousand per girl per room per week. No worries'. But that hasn't happened at all. And she didn't have the books present, either. She told us that she'd lost them. And as for the $5,000—that was not negotiable. She told us to take it or leave it. And we thought, 'Well, we've come this far'.

Stella handed us a toilet bag full of keys, and said, 'There you go'. [At the brothel] everything was dark, no one was working, and a sign had been put up by CIB in front of the house saying, 'CLOSED UNTIL FURTHER NOTICE'. It was dated from the day before.

So anyway, first we had to find the keys. Eventually we found the back gate key—but what we had to do was go out to the nightclub, because we knew the girls would be there. So we got one of the girls' keys to the back gate, but the back door was *bolted* from inside. One of the girls was still in there. We were bashing and screaming, 'Let us in!' [Laughter][22]

April and Ann were dismayed to discover the interior of the brothel in a gloomy state of disrepair that included holes in the walls, worn carpets, shabby linen and broken fixtures. It would thus appear that the premises had seen little of the $5,000 per week profit that Stella claimed she collected from the business. Bearing in mind the difficulties that they would encounter in recruiting staff, April and Ann immediately made a short-list of basic repairs and improvements to create a more livable environment.[23]

The following week April placed advertisements for workers in *The West Australian*, and began canvassing Perth private agents listed in the paper's 'Personal' column. The latter strategy delivered the most promising results and within the week, two private agents had arrived from Perth. April had also persuaded another former Club 181 co-worker (by then working at a Containment brothel in Perth) to come back to Kalgoorlie to help her get the new business started. Meanwhile, the three workers who remained during the management transition had agreed to stay and work.

With this group of six workers, the business soon earned up to $7,000–8,000 per week for 'the house', based on the customary fifty-fifty split in earnings with workers. For the first two months, April and Ann continued with the existing fee structure at 143 Hay Street. But they soon increased this, in order to recover their expenses from repairs and renovations. In November–December 1994 the fee structure was:

- 20 minutes $ 80
- 30 minutes $ 110
- 45 minutes $ 130
- 60 minutes $ 160.[24]

April said that the weekly income of $7,000–8,000 had paid for little more than the $5,000 rent and an average of $1,000 per week for the brothel's other outgoings; these included utilities, building maintenance, cleaning services and the provision of condoms and other 'safe sex' supplies to workers. Any remaining profits were divided between April and Ann and the occasional hired receptionist.[25]

Three months into the lease agreement, Ann decided to leave the business and April assumed sole responsibility for managing the brothel. A long-term resident of Kalgoorlie, April said that she was fortunate to have had the support of her mother, who often helped with receptionist duties or looked after April's 6-year-old son. April maintains that her mother played a critical role in enabling her to successfully manage the business for the duration of the lease.[26]

Meanwhile, Kalgoorlie's third remaining brothel, at 133 Hay Street, was operating under the management of a very private madam. In 1992 the recently widowed 'Carmel' (see Figure 24) had purchased the brothel known as 'Questa Casa' from madam Marlene for $420,000. Carmel recalled that she then spent a further $40,000 on renovations to create a safer and more comfortable living and working environment.

The extensive improvements included insulation throughout the building, new wiring and lighting, new carpeting, a new kitchen and bathroom, new furniture and a slow-combustion wood-burning heater for the lounge room. Carmel had also transformed the backyard into a pleasant garden and patio area. The finishing touches to Questa Casa included soft pastel colours throughout the interior and a rather lively touch to the exterior of the premises.[27]

By day or by night, Questa Casa presented a striking vision—resplendent with enormous hand-painted tulip buds that appeared to grow out of the planted greenery at ground level, beautifully taming the corrugated iron canvas (see Figure 25). This rather ethereal image contrasted sharply with the rest of Hay Street, including the madam-next-door's stark, siren-red frontage and the surrounding industrial storage yards that dominated most of the streetscape.[28]

Chatting happily about her recent trip to Perth to visit her daughter and granddaughter, the quietly spoken Carmel seemed a poised and

Figure 24 *Madam 'Carmel', standing in one of the doorways of her brothel at 133 Hay Street.* Courtesy *The West Australian*

Figure 25 *Questa Casa, 133 Hay Street, 1995.*
Author's private collection of photographs

educated woman. Unlike any of her Hay Street contemporaries, Carmel resided permanently at her brothel, yet she did not monitor the workers' shifts, working hours or incomes. Instead of collecting the standard 50 per cent of their earnings, she charged each woman a flat rate of $700 rent per week, and usually retired to her private room between 9 and 10 o'clock at night. Although she did not hire a cook to prepare meals for the women, Carmel provided the meal herself one to three times per week, and each worker took her turn once a week to prepare dinner for the others, at the provider's expense. All workers at Questa Casa were expected to take the evening meal together, and dinner was served promptly at 6 o'clock.[29]

Questa Casa worker Taylor, a young mother from New Zealand, revealed that she could generally depend on earning between $1,500 and $2,500 most weeks, and this averaged $500 more than her take-home earnings from Club 181.[30] Certainly, Carmel's flat-rate arrangement would appear to have made Questa Casa considerably more profitable for the workers. Taylor had worked at all three Hay Street brothels since 1992, and said she preferred Carmel's approach to management:

> She's very motherly, she's not your boss. She never bosses you around. I had heard she was a real bitch. But no way—she is not. I wouldn't work anywhere else on Hay Street now. She's really motherly...she's nice. I just can't understand why people aren't queuing up to get in here. On a Tuesday night at 143,

if I had made $300, I thought I was doing well. If I did that now, it would be $100 for the house and $200 for me. If I had been able to work for Carmel first, I would have been out [of the sex industry] by now. After this weekend I'm going to buy a new fridge, washing machine and a dryer, and I've only got a few bits and pieces to take care of before I'm ahead again.

I don't mind it [living at Questa Casa]. I wouldn't live out anyway, even if I had the choice, because for example to get a decent place in town, you're looking at $200–300 a week. And that's just for a reasonable unit. And then in Kalgoorlie there is the problem of burglary and rape—it's just too much to worry about. Here, I lock my door, there's an alarm on the house, and the back gate's locked so if I want to go out and sit in the garden for a while, I can. I wouldn't live out. I would if I worked at 181 or 143—I'd want to live out, because it's not a nice environment. But 133's lovely, and it's got the nice garden. It's just more peaceful generally.[31]

Above all, Taylor valued the freedom to determine her own working hours. At the same time, she also found it difficult to adjust to Carmel's strict 6.00 pm curfew at Questa Casa, having enjoyed the occasional evening out while previously employed at Club 181. Yet she believed that the more profitable financial terms and the refreshing domestic environment at Questa Casa were well worth the sacrifice of the odd night out. She worked longer hours when business was steady, sometimes until 6.00 am or 7.00 am, and occasionally during the afternoon. When business was quiet, she retired early. Regardless of the pace, Taylor always took time out to relax with her favourite television shows, such as *Star Trek*:

I work every night, six to eight hours depending on how I felt, and what the money's like that night. And I'm still doing better than I was down the road. Oh yes, definitely. I open my door at lunchtime, because you get a few guys coming along in the afternoon. Then it gets to midnight and I think, 'Oh, I can't be bothered' and I just go to sleep. It's really good that way.

If I'm really tired, I just go to bed. On Tuesday nights I shut my door and go and watch *Melrose Place*, and on Friday nights I watch *Star Trek* and then I go back to work. You do what you want, basically. If I don't want to work, [Carmel] doesn't care as long as she gets the rent. So it's really good, and it's so nice having the gardens out the back.[32]

Another Questa Casa worker, 'Mary'—a youthful, radiant and softly spoken woman in her early 40s—also strongly supported Carmel's style of management, which she said allowed workers genuine autonomy to pace themselves and screen their clients. Having 'seasonally' worked in Hay Street brothels for fifteen years, the focused and articulate Mary said that Carmel's alternative to brothel management had more of a 'human touch':

I work for particular goals, and once I've reached a goal, I go and do something else. I contracted with Carmel how much is reasonable for me to pay, and then what I make is my own business. If you're given the freedom, you tend to take your time, and be careful with the amount of people you're seeing. You have to be in control. You need to be calm and aware of what's happening, so that you can handle any situation, and making sure that a service is provided, and that they leave happy. This is the aim. It's a professional attitude. If you can maintain a client, in a manner that you can handle, you can have a reasonable amount of fun yourself. This is especially true of regular clientele.

I have several regular clients, where many very young girls just don't get the regular clients. My goal is not to make a million dollars. I think it is to preserve myself while pursuing my goals, according to my experience, my age and my lifestyle, and just work within certain bounds. So it gives me the chance to choose, to use this time in my career to safeguard myself and pace myself while I make money.

[The customary fifty-fifty split] is just the greed of the madams. They get every single dollar they can. That's why workers are forced to see men they don't want to see. It's very hard, it's disgusting. The lack of choice is very degrading. Then you pay tax on top of the 50 per cent commission. So out of $100, a worker might get $30–40. That is very degrading. But I think as far as money goes, workers at other houses make the same amount of money as us, or more, because you're forced to work the hours, and forced to see the men.[33]

Questa Casa worker 'Phillipa' arrived in Kalgoorlie in early 1990, shortly after receiving her redundancy notice from the Northern Territory's public service. She worked briefly in all four Hay Street brothels, including the former business of madam Teriapii King-Brooks, who Phillipa said expected workers to be 'on the door' seven nights a week from 6.00 pm to 6.00 am. She also said that the women were not allowed to refuse any clients. Phillipa recalled that she immediately found Carmel's management more reasonable:

It also helps because if you're not in the mood for work, if you're too tired, it's better if you're not outside [on the door]. Because a client won't come back again if he doesn't have a good time.

We also have the choice of who we see. In other houses, if a guy comes in and picks you, that's it, it's you who has to see him. And some guys, it's not that they're even drunk or anything, but they've got the wrong attitude to start with. You know, sometimes you can tell they will probably get a bit rough. You can normally tell right at the door, exactly what they're going to be like.[34]

Working conditions seem to have varied considerably on Hay Street, depending on the management approach of the brothel. Yet with respect to these conditions overall, it would soon become obvious that the dismissal of charges against escort worker Melissa in October 1994 had been a most significant event. Police authorities conceded that Containment had ceased to provide an effective means of regulation, and continued to campaign for workable legislation to replace it. With their public 'vote' of no confidence, the ninety-year-old Containment Policy now faced a new level of uncertainty.

CHAPTER 7

The stormy demise of traditional Containment

After ninety years of relative seclusion under the long arm of Containment, the Hay Street brothels became an overnight media sensation in 1995, when the traditional Containment Policy unravelled in a spectacular demise. Senior police authorities had decided that the time had come to abandon a number of Containment's archaic practices in Kalgoorlie, a decision taken for a number of reasons but prompted by the unsuccessful prosecution of escort worker Melissa in October 1994. While police authorities would surely have expected an initial backlash to this historic operational decision, few could have predicted the sustained 'war by media' that followed.

The stage had been set in January 1995, when Detective Sergeant Brian Cunningham arrived in town as Kalgoorlie's newly appointed officer-in-charge. A seasoned veteran of twenty-two years' service with the Western Australian Police, including several years as officer-in-charge in country towns in the state's South West, Sergeant Cunningham recalled that he had been instructed by his appointing superiors to implement changes to the *still unwritten*—yet previously immutable—local Containment Policy:

> There were a couple of meetings with the Crime Executive, in relation to the Containment Policy, and when I took over here, my predecessor gave me a complete briefing on the policy, and what was operating in Kalgoorlie.

It [the change in policy] relates to unsuccessful prosecutions in the past. The fact is that there were escort agencies running here, and my predecessor could see that there was a necessity to bring Kalgoorlie into the 1990s, and have it operate the same as in Perth. Escorts, as such, the age of the girls working in the industry…and the fact is, as far as the girls being able to socialise, and live outside the premises, needed to be changed and relaxed.[1]

Kalgoorlie's new officer-in-charge seems to have hit the dust running; within two weeks of his arrival, he had advised management of all three Hay Street brothels that:

- Hay Street brothels were now permitted to provide escort services to hotels and private homes in Kalgoorlie-Boulder.
- Hay Street workers were now free to reside and socialise off brothel premises.
- The minimum working age for sex workers in Kalgoorlie had been lowered from 21 to 18 years.[2]

While madam Mary-Anne Kenworthy toasted the changes as a hard-won gain after years of resisting local Containment, the other two Hay Street madams did not welcome the news. Madam Stella Strong had made her views abundantly clear to the council the previous year, when rumours of changes to Containment first surfaced. Stella continued to oppose any modifications to the ninety-year-old policy; however, she kept a relatively low profile in early 1995, due to temporary illness. Meanwhile, madam Carmel and acting manager Phillipa at Questa Casa went to extraordinary lengths to reverse the changes.

Phillipa remembered well the day she learned of the Containment changes:

Carmel was away when the changes were brought in, and I often watch the house while she is away. The CIB phoned me and asked me to come down, because they wanted my opinion on something they were considering doing. I gave my opinion, and when I finished they turned around and said, 'Well, we've decided to go ahead with the changes, effective from today, for a six-month trial period'. And I said, 'Why did you get me up, drag me down here, when this is something you've already decided without consulting us. Thank you for wasting my time'.

The police blamed the courts [for the changes], which is ridiculous. Because that escort charge that was laid here, they worded the charge wrong, and that's why it was dismissed by the court. It was the police's fault. They said the courts would not uphold the Containment Policy. That was their excuse. It is just their way of passing the buck.[3]

Furious at the lack of consultation, Phillipa stormed out of the Kalgoorlie CIB office and into the offices of *The Kalgoorlie Miner*, where she stunned chief of staff Nigel Tapp with the news that radical changes to local Containment had been secretly introduced by the police. Mr Tapp, however, found that police in both Kalgoorlie and Perth refused to acknowledge the Containment changes until a few days later, when official confirmation came from the Vice Squad's headquarters at the CIB in Perth.[4]

On the morning of 25 January 1995 *The Kalgoorlie Miner* ran its page-one exclusive under the simple banner headline, 'Police relax brothel containment policy'. In this report, Detective Sergeant Kym Kramer (chief of the Perth-based Vice Squad) confirmed that police had relaxed Containment in Kalgoorlie to bring it in line with the policy as it operated in Perth. Sergeant Kramer also commented that it was no longer appropriate for police to enforce the virtual incarceration of sex workers in the Hay Street brothels:

> You can't expect someone not to live as a normal person. We are bringing it up to the same standard we have in Perth. It is recognising the needs of the workers more than anything else and that's what we're considering.[5]

Having been tipped off by Phillipa days before the story broke, Carmel cut short her holiday in Queensland and returned in time to fire the first salvos at the Containment changes in the same report. She declared her absolute opposition to any system that allowed sex workers in Kalgoorlie to live, socialise or provide services outside the Hay Street brothels, and called for an immediate reversal of the police decision. She warned that any relaxation of traditional Containment would also make it difficult for madams to keep brothel workers under control and ensure that they attended weekly medical examinations.[6]

That morning, the mayor of Kalgoorlie-Boulder awoke to the news like most local residents, having received no prior notification of the changes from either the local police or *The Kalgoorlie Miner*. Even so, Mayor Ron Yuryevich took only passing notice of the newspaper's page-one exclusive and its explosive potential.

> Well, I quite honestly just read it about 6.30 that morning. Read it, put it down, and went about my business. It wasn't until about 8.30 the phone calls started coming thick and fast—from irate ratepayers, of course. I've always held the view that where [the brothels] exist now, it has worked well. There's no two ways about that. So why change something that has worked perfectly well? Well, I won't say perfect...nothing's perfect. But reasonably well, and is accepted by the community at large.[7]

Mayor Yuryevich estimated that he received 500 telephone calls at his council office and at home during the days that followed *The Kalgoorlie Miner*'s front-page story. He also wryly observed that the volume of calls and correspondence generated by the Containment changes far exceeded residents' protests against a previous proposal to locate a nuclear waste dump at the Kalgoorlie town site:

> Well, the radioactive dump that somebody wants to be established here—that was a very big issue. But I must admit that this issue has overtaken that, and I'm absolutely flabbergasted by it. . .it was pretty vicious at the time. I mean, I know I'm an elected spokesperson, all this sort of stuff—but I do draw the line at being abused. We got blamed for all this, on the basis that council were letting things go. And I had to explain that we had nothing to do with it, so I had to go on the defensive a lot.
>
> The majority of [complainants] I would class as people who have come in, they've invested in a house, bringing their kids up. . .[Complaints] were mainly from the 30–35 year-old group with young kids. They pointed out to me that they owed huge mortgages. . .and the following problem if a sex worker sets up shop next to their $200,000 house. They were worried about land values and loss of amenity.[8]

Mayor Yuryevich, in *The Kalgoorlie Miner*, condemned the Containment changes, vowing to vigorously pursue a reversal of them with police authorities at the highest level. He also blasted the Court (Liberal) government for allowing the Containment Policy to break down in the first place, and for failing to introduce workable legislation to regulate prostitution.[9]

At the next council meeting, held on 30 January 1995, Mayor Yuryevich voiced his concern that if Hay Street women were allowed to live in private accommodation, it could result in the council having to police dozens of illegal brothels in the suburbs of Kalgoorlie-Boulder. On the other hand, the mayor and councillors did not take issue with Hay Street women socialising in the town's hotels and restaurants, nor did they object to the brothels' providing escort services to clients in hotels or motels—though they were opposed to such services being provided in private homes. The lowering of the working age in Hay Street to 18 years did not attract significant attention from the council at this meeting.

The council resolved to write to Police Minister Bob Wiese to demand that he urgently review the Containment changes, with a view to ensuring that all sex workers in Kalgoorlie be required to live in the Hay Street brothel premises, and that Hay Street brothels be banned from providing escort services to private homes.[10] While the relevant resolution was passed without difficulty, the minutes also noted Councillor Buchhorn's apparently dissenting comment that 'the ladies should be able to live to the same standard as other citizens'.[11]

Not all Hay Street women would agree with Councillor Buchhorn. The next morning's *Kalgoorlie Miner* ran the page-one headline 'Change upsets brothel worker'. In the accompanying report, Phillipa stepped up the public campaign to reverse the Containment changes, insisting that local residents would not tolerate having prostitutes as neighbours. She also predicted that escort workers would leave a trail of broken relationships throughout the suburbs of Kalgoorlie-Boulder. In this report, and in a later interview for *The Scarlet Mile*, Phillipa seemed to espouse the staunch traditionalist 'Hay Street—Love It or Leave It' school of thought:

> The people I have spoken to…don't want someone living next door to them having frequent calls from prostitutes. After all, no woman wants to return from a weekend in Perth visiting family, to the smell of another woman's perfume on her bed or have a neighbour inform her that a working girl from Hay Street has been there during her absence.
>
> It has always been an unwritten law that if you wish to work in Kalgoorlie you abide by the town's desire—work only on Hay Street. If you are unable to accept these minor considerations then you choose to work elsewhere. Being allowed to live out is an invitation to work privately.[12]

Hot on the heels of Phillipa's cover story in *The Kalgoorlie Miner*, Carmel (see Figure 24) argued the following day in *The West Australian* that sex workers in Kalgoorlie should be permitted to live and work only in the Hay Street brothels. Carmel echoed Phillipa's concerns that the Containment changes would destroy the traditional peace that had long existed between Hay Street women and the rest of the town:

> Everybody knows everybody else in Kalgoorlie and if girls are permitted to go to private homes it is going to be noticed by the neighbours when a man's wife is away and a girl comes to visit. At the moment, everything is confined to Hay Street and if anybody wants a bit of fun they go down Hay Street and it doesn't affect the rest of the town.[13]

On the other hand, this report also included the comments of managers at the other two Hay Street brothels, who said they strongly supported the Containment changes, despite their relatively minor impact on business. 'Jesse' at Club 181 reported that business had increased only slightly since the brothel had begun advertising escort services; she also confirmed that most of Club 181's workers continued to live on the premises rather than in private accommodation, because the brothel's living arrangements were more convenient and economical for them.[14]

Meanwhile, the Containment changes continued to draw a strong response from local residents. *The Kalgoorlie Miner's* chief of staff, Nigel Tapp, recalled that, like the complaints received by the mayor, letters to the editor regarding the Containment changes had expressed fierce opposition in unusually strong language:

> I'd say we've received about twelve to fifteen letters. I think that's a strong response for any issue. There was definitely a strong public feeling, and certainly there's no doubt that most of the public were against the changes for various reasons. Some morally, some [concerned] about the future of Hay Street as a tourist destination, some concerned about hotels being used for soliciting. A big point was the lowering of the [working] age from 21 to 18, that health checks would not be kept up privately, and that prostitution would encroach on suburbs as a result, because no one is going to know if prostitutes are operating alone from home or not.[15]

The Kalgoorlie Miner also surveyed the opinions of passers-by in Hannan Street, three of whom were featured in the paper's 'Hearsay' column. The daily format of 'Hearsay' included a photograph of the respondent 'du jour', with his or her name and a brief statement of opinion appearing below (known as 'vox pop' in newspaper parlance). Ms Lorri Clark expressed her fears that the Containment changes would 'lead to prostitution in the suburbs, and that is not appropriate to the family situation'.[16] Mr Ted Forken also believed that local police should return to the former Containment Policy 'for the girls' own safety'.[17] While these two residents (who appeared to be in the 35–45 year age group) strongly opposed the Containment changes, an apparently much younger resident, Mr Craig Cloughley, clearly supported the changes and argued that 'it is a matter of their [sex workers'] personal freedom of choice'.[18]

While Madam Stella Strong continued to sidestep the unfolding 'war by media', she threw her weight behind traditional Containment in a letter to the editor of *The Kalgoorlie Miner*. In a clear show of support for Carmel, Stella warned that Hay Street workers should never be allowed to live outside the brothel premises:

> I believe the containment policy that had operated in the past was the best for Kalgoorlie for many reasons. Recent changes will mean the girls are not policed by madams and regular health checks will not be carried out. There is now the threat of private houses being used for prostitution. There is also the threat soliciting will happen at hotels. Policing would be much easier if prostitution was contained in Hay Street. With escorts we will see bouncers being used as protectors and collectors.
>
> Stella Strong, 143 Hay Street, Kalgoorlie[19]

Madam Mary-Anne Kenworthy had remained conspicuous by her absence from the early public debate on the historic Containment changes. This was no doubt a sound strategy, given her perceived status as Hay Street's 'victor' in the relaxation of the local Containment Policy. Yet Stella's letter to the editor seems to have motivated Mary-Anne to throw her hat into the ring to defend the changes. Three days later in *The Kalgoorlie Miner*, Mary-Anne shot back at opponents of the Containment changes, arguing that the changes did not go far enough. She proposed that brothel premises should be regulated by the local council according to the same standards as other businesses, and said that the Hay Street brothels and the surrounding area should be upgraded, particularly as the district had become a major tourist attraction.[20]

Mary-Anne also used this opportunity to break new ground in discussing the occupational health and safety of sex workers. First, she flatly rejected Carmel's and Stella's claim that Hay Street madams would be unable to ensure that workers who lived off the premises attended weekly health examinations.[21] It is important to note that in Perth, sex workers have not lived on brothel premises since 1958, yet Containment brothel and agency owners have never experienced difficulties collecting weekly medical certificates from their workers, in compliance with the Containment Policy.[22] Second, Mary-Anne revealed that all her workers in Kalgoorlie and Perth also attended occupational health training seminars:

> Whether they are eighteen or twenty-one the girls are still green. There are a lot of bad habits and myths about sexual problems perpetuated through talk. It is important that houses provide the correct sexual [health] education. Often, if the girls don't ask for advice it is not given to them. It is in our interest to keep our girls fit and healthy.[23]

In 1987 the Health Department of Western Australia had begun providing health education workshops for sex workers, in addition to its recommendation for compulsory condom use in the sex industry. These two initiatives were strongly supported by sex workers. The Health Department's pilot outreach project in 1987 aimed to educate and support sex workers, encouraging them to examine all clients carefully for visual signs of infection, and to use condoms with all their clients.[24]

The pilot project's overwhelming popularity with sex workers convinced the Health Department to foster the development of a community-based organisation known as SIERA. Based in Perth, SIERA received matched funding from the Western Australian and Commonwealth health departments to continue outreach to Western Australia's sex workers, who operated mainly in the Perth metropolitan area and Kalgoorlie. Complementing its educational role, SIERA provided an environment where sex workers felt welcome to drop in for a chat with staff and other workers; the organisation also produced a quarterly magazine for its members entitled *Working for a Living*.[25]

SIERA executive director Penny Lyall praised Mary-Anne Kenworthy's progressive health management strategy in *The Kalgoorlie Miner*'s report and announced that SIERA would soon take its health education workshops on the road to the Hay Street brothels for the first time: 'There has been an assumption across the industry that the girls are educated. In this day and age it is impossible. Safe sex is quite a complicated issue'.[26]

In March 1995 Penny Lyall and SIERA's outreach and education officer Tarna Bulman travelled to Kalgoorlie, where they received a mixed reception from Hay Street management and workers. While Leigh at Club 181 and April at the Red House were happy to arrange for their staff to attend in-house seminars, Carmel refused and explained that the women at Questa Casa were subcontractors and not her employees. In a later interview, Ms Bulman described the practical format of SIERA's health education seminars:

> We go through the range of STDs and types of transmission, from body-to-body to blood-borne viruses like Hep B and HIV. And I have as much to learn from them as they do from me. So you want them to be interactive, and to talk a lot. I take them through the pictures and talk about the different diseases, and how you get them, and what to look for.
>
> Then the second half is practical stuff. I use a blow-up doll, he's called 'Big John'; he has an eight-and-a-half-inch penis. I whip him out, and then I get all the girls to show me how they check their clients. They take it through, and I give them pointers about things they might have missed and things that might be useful and different techniques. Then from there I show them all the range of safe sex products they can use on the job, and tell them how to use them.[27]

Meanwhile, the progressive provocations in *The Kalgoorlie Miner* on 18 February had prompted madam Carmel to step up her public offensive against the Containment changes. Within the week, she had lined up a dazzling broadside. A report in *The Australian* featured an arresting photograph of two women casually exposing their buttocks at Questa Casa in Hay Street. This sensational image occupied nearly two-thirds of the page and dwarfed the feature story entitled 'Proper madams'. The first few paragraphs of the story related the unfortunate account of an obviously intellectually impaired young woman whom Carmel had recently taken 'under her wing':

The woman was, as they say in those parts, 'not the full quid'. She had the mental and emotional maturity of a girl, and there was concern for her welfare. She had been involved in a 'gang bang' with a group of men in town—and it was not the first time.

There was no use pressing charges—the woman had invited and enjoyed the incident, according to the word around town. Her parents and the local CIB detectives, discussing the dilemma in the West Australian goldfields town of Kalgoorlie four years ago, had to find a different response.[28]

Carmel maintained that she had taken charge as the woman's brothel madam and surrogate mother. This bizarre case study, along with the confronting photograph that dominated the page, provided the only representations of sex workers in *The Australian*'s feature story. One (unnamed) female shop owner in Kalgoorlie, who commented in the report, seemed to regard the Hay Street brothels as social quarantine units:

Under containment everyone knew their place. The girls are down on Hay Street and they don't get in anyone's way. They serve a purpose and they make the women in town feel safer, and Hay Street is a real tourist attraction. But if they start doing business in the hotels or in the suburbs, I don't think people will like it.[29]

This feature also claimed that one of the Hay Street madams had successfully lobbied police authorities for the local Containment changes; presumably the unnamed madam was Mary-Anne Kenworthy:

The changes were forced by the madam of one of the brothels, who owns escort agencies in Perth and who successfully convinced senior police that the discrepancy in operating rules between the two places was illogical and unfair.[30]

The report also announced that Deputy Police Commissioner Les Ayton would visit Kalgoorlie the following week to discuss the Containment changes with local community representatives. On the morning of 2 March 1995, Mr Ayton chaired a predictably tense meeting with Kalgoorlie-Boulder mayor, Ron Yuryevich, the town clerk, Peter Strugnell, state Members of Parliament Ian Taylor and Julian Grill, a representative for federal Member of Parliament Graeme Campbell, and president of the Kalgoorlie branch of the Australian Family Association, Robert Hicks. Madams Carmel of Questa Casa and April of the Red House were also present at this meeting[31], although madam Leigh Varis-Beswick declined to attend, following a late night managing Club 181.[32]

In the course of defending the Containment changes, Kalgoorlie-born Les Ayton found himself battling a relentless chorus of uncompromising demands that police immediately reverse the Containment changes. Only

April sat silently during the stormy exchange, perhaps as the only local representative who supported the Containment changes. Carmel argued firmly against the changes throughout the meeting; then when Mr Ayton declared that the Containment changes would remain effective for the duration of the six-month trial, she stood up abruptly and announced, 'Well, gentlemen, I can see I am wasting my time here', and walked out.[33] The following day, *The Kalgoorlie Miner* ran an article entitled 'Ayton refuses to budge on containment changes', in which the Deputy Police Commissioner said that the meeting had been a success and that he had 'laid to rest suggestions that corruption was a motivation for the changes to the policy':

> These people now understand why we've taken the actions we have. If we did not agree, at least we mutually understand the situation. Modifications were needed so there could be at least some degree of acceptable control between the parties [brothels and police]. [34]

Meanwhile, Mayor Yuryevich did not view the Deputy Police Commissioner's tough-luck response as a success. In a report in *The Sunday Times* entitled 'Kal's girls get the green light', he again condemned the unpopular Containment changes and renewed his pledge to fight for their reversal. In particular, he made a point of emphasising local residents' concerns that small brothels would begin operating in residential areas, which could adversely affect social amenity and property values:

> If they go into the suburbs, they'll find that they might have to employ protection and that conjures up all sorts of ideas and problems. I don't believe we really need heavies sitting on the street corners in suburbia—minders, pimps, anything you'd like to call them. I believe if you are going to buy a $200,000 house, mortgage yourself up to the eyeballs then find there's a brothel next door, you're not going to be happy.[35]

However, Club 181 madam Leigh Varis-Beswick hit back in the same report that sex workers preferred the security of working in a brothel; those women who chose to go home after working in the Hay Street brothels would not want to invite clients into their homes. She also said that it was time for the town to accept and respect Hay Street women as human beings: 'You can't keep the girls cooped up in a house full of women all the time. It's time we let people know, we're here, but we're human'.[36]

The Sunday Times's report also included the comments of Fiona Patten, president of the Canberra-based Eros Foundation. Ms Patten lashed out at Containment traditions such as the Hay Street women's virtual imprisonment in the brothels, which she said raised 'horrendous civil rights issues which would be unheard of in any other occupation'.[37]

Nevertheless, in the following day's *Kalgoorlie Miner*, the mayor continued to praise that old-time Containment while Phillipa passed the ammunition. The mayor announced that he had received a petition containing 2,054 signatures from local residents who opposed the Containment changes, and he intended to present the petition to Commissioner of Police Bob Falconer to negotiate a reversal of the changes.[38]

The principal petitioner was none other than Phillipa, who had drafted the petition in the weeks immediately following the January 1995 changes. She had then distributed copies for local residents to sign at supermarkets, chemists and other shops throughout Kalgoorlie-Boulder, as Mr Yuryevich later recalled:

> The petitioner organised 2,054 signatures in a very short time, basically advising that Hay Street has existed in Kalgoorlie for over a hundred years, and forms a major part of Kalgoorlie's tourist attractions. It says 'If you are against escorts operating in Kalgoorlie in private homes, hotels and motels. If you are against prostitutes living anywhere except in Hay Street, sign here'.[39]

Phillipa's petition requested that the mayor personally deliver the document to Police Commissioner Bob Falconer; however, the mayor was unable to arrange an appointment with Mr Falconer, and so he met instead with Police Minister Bob Wiese. At their meeting, the mayor was dismayed to find that the Police Minister stood solidly behind the operational decision to relax Containment in Kalgoorlie. The Minister added that, in any event, he was in no position to interfere with police operational matters. In *The Kalgoorlie Miner*, a furious Mayor Yuryevich accused the Court government of dereliction of duty and political expedience in the lead-up to an election, and called on Police Minister Wiese to resign:

> He (Mr Wiese) has basically said that the law courts are not backing up the police. He said no Government is going to look at a controversial issue like this in the lead-up to an election campaign. And if Mr Wiese is not prepared to stick by his portfolio and deal with these problems, he should look for another job.[40]

The following month, Carmel continued to campaign publicly in *The West Australian* for a reversal of the Containment changes:

> When I came here three years ago, the rules were clear-cut. Now it seems anyone can start up a business and the police seem powerless to act.
>
> I thought restricting the girls, or the curfew if you like, was a good idea. The girls, if caught in a night-club or pub, were warned once and the second time asked to leave town for a month. This is a small town. What happens when one of our clients is taking his wife out for dinner and he looks across

the table to see one of our girls waving happily at him? There could be absolute hell to pay.

With the escorts, I think it is exploiting the town. When the sex industry was confined to Hay Street, the town accepted it. The town has been very gracious to the industry. We didn't leave Hay Street, and the clients came to the doors. So it was their choice, not ours. As it is now, it's our choice, we go out to them. It seems to say to the town, 'Well, whether you like it or not, we're here'.[41]

Carmel also revealed that she would continue to resist lowering the working age for women at Questa Casa, insisting that working in the sex industry was not for the faint-hearted or under-20s. She said she believed that young women needed first to gain some employment experience in the 'formal' work force before considering sex work:

The lowering of the age is against my idea of what's right. I had two girls ring me from Sydney the other day looking for work. They were nineteen. I told them to ring me in a year's time. I don't care what people say, 18 and 19 year-olds are too young in this business. It's too hard a game for girls that age, and although they can earn excellent money, it really cuts out any other avenues for them to take career-wise later on in life.[42]

Despite the initial storm of public protest against the historic Containment changes, their six-month trial ended without further incident. On 20 July 1995 Assistant Police Commissioner (Crime) Mel Hay announced in *The Kalgoorlie Miner* that the Containment changes had been made permanent, since no substantiated complaints had been received by local police as a result of the trial:

We had minor alterations made to the existing policy in Kalgoorlie-Boulder. We still have containment. In essence, the draconian principle of staying on the premises had to be lifted...[and] people are adults at eighteen, working in escort agencies and massage parlours at eighteen, we gave them the option.[43]

In a later interview, Robert Hicks of the Australian Family Association criticised the lack of community consultation on the issue, and said there certainly had been complaints made to police about the new policy:

The six-month trial was a stunt to allow the outrage to cool down. Now they drop the bombshell to say the relaxed policy is indefinite. The police have an audacity suggesting there was no public backlash.[44]

Mayor Yuryevich also rejected the six-month trial as a sham, and protested that the police decision to make the changes permanent amounted to 'installation by stealth'. Carmel joined forces to publicly condemn, in *The Kalgoorlie Miner*, the now-permanent Containment changes, and vowed to continue to run Questa Casa according to local Containment tradition:

> Right from the word go I have never approved of escorts in Kalgoorlie. I could see a place for them if the girls only went to hotels and motels but the girls go to night-clubs, pick up blokes and take them home. They are operating at home. This is still a small place, despite being a wonderful place, and girls get known here. In the past, they have still had the run of the town, going to pubs and out to lunch, but I have always believed that at night the town should be given back to its people. The six months [trial] was there to throw everyone off. I agree with the Mayor right down the line. There was no intonation [sic] that this was going to happen at all.[45]

At the next council meeting, held on 24 July 1995, Assistant Police Commissioner Mel Hay and Kalgoorlie Regional Chief Superintendent Gary Booth assumed their respective hot seats to officially defend the unofficial (and unpopular) local Containment changes. The Assistant Police Commissioner assured the council that brothels and sex workers were still firmly under police control in Kalgoorlie, and listed a number of Containment rules that local police would continue to enforce:

> Mr Hay also read the rules under which the brothel premises could operate:
>
> 1. No drugs on the premises or on [sic] any person under the influence of drugs to be found on the premises.
>
> 2. No alcohol, or any person under the influence of alcohol to be found on the premises.
>
> 3. Workers not to receive social security while they are working on the premises.
>
> 4. Workers may reside outside the house, but on the following conditions:
>
>   (a) no person to live off the earnings whilst living outside the house,
>
>   (b) no males to reside in the house that the girls live in,
>
>   (c) the address to be recorded with the local CIB.
>
> In this way, control is achieved.[46]

In this official detailing of the Containment Policy in Kalgoorlie, police authorities renewed their commitment to Containment's historical objective of maintaining a realistic degree of control over prostitution. This outline also revealed that, in keeping with the traditional Containment

Policy, the women were not permitted to live with or financially support their male partners while working in the Hay Street brothels.

However, Rule 2 raises more questions than it solves, for it is highly doubtful that at any time police had ever seriously hoped to make Hay Street an alcohol-free zone. Apart from the Hay Street brothels' custom of serving complimentary beer to their clients and other guests[47], the brothels could hardly be expected to turn away men who were affected by alcohol, as the above claim appears to suggest. At the same time, it has never been uncommon for Hay Street women to consume a measure or two of alcohol over the course of their shifts.[48] In any case, alcohol consumption in the Hay Street brothels was the least of the council's concerns that evening.

Mayor Yuryevich led the assault on the police representatives: he openly questioned the integrity of the six-month trial and bitterly protested the lack of community consultation on the issue. During the ensuing melee, no indignity was spared as councillors took a 'grand stand' against the Containment changes. Councillor Tom Kendall declared that the 'industry had been captured by its regulator' and complained of an 'uncomfortable feeling that the Police Department were acting as pimps to increase the size of the brothel industry'. Equally interesting was Councillor Kendall's speculation that if police lowered the working age to 18 years, there would be 'no stopping them from registering 12 year-olds to work as prostitutes'. Assistant Police Commissioner Hay and Superintendent Booth held their ground throughout the occasionally hysterical exchange and emphasised the only point on which the police and the council could agree: that workable prostitution law reform offered the only long-term solution for regulating the sex industry.[49]

The council resolved to write to Police Minister Bob Wiese to request that legislation urgently be drafted to enable local councils to regulate brothels. The council also instructed that the City of Kalgoorlie-Boulder conduct an extensive media campaign to further shore up public support for reversing the Containment changes, including full-page advertisements in the council's monthly newsletter, *Your City* (see Figure 26), and the quarterly *Goldfields Magazine*.[50] Months later, the 'underwhelming' public response to both these appeals convinced the council that no further action should be taken on the matter.[51]

It appears that local residents' fears regarding the Containment changes had dramatically decreased since the January 1995 announcement, in the absence of evidence that prostitutes had begun to operate from homes in the suburbs or to solicit in the hotels where they socialised. In fact, with the exception of Phillipa of Questa Casa, the 'notorious' Hay Street women themselves had remained all but invisible throughout the raging controversy.

CITY OF KALGOORLIE-BOULDER
PROPOSITION TO CHANGE THE CONTAINMENT POLICY OF PROSTITUTION IN KALGOORLIE-BOULDER

The Western Australian Police Service, has relaxed the
Containment Policy of Prostitution which has worked effectively
within Kalgoorlie-Boulder for many years.

The relaxation has seen a number of changes which it is believed will be detrimental to the sex industry workers and residents of the City of Kalgoorlie-Boulder. The Containment Policy has been changed to allow the following:

1. The age of sex workers has been reduced from 21 to 18 years.
2. Sex workers will be able to live off-site; i.e. no longer on the premises of the brothel.
3. The brothels are allowed to operate escort services away from the premises.

Council is concerned that the above changes will have a significant effect on the Community and the well-being of Kalgoorlie-Boulder generally. This is your opportunity to tell the Police Department what you want to operate within the City of Kalgoorlie-Boulder.

To have your say please complete the coupon below and return it to the City of Kalgoorlie-Boulder via any suggestion box located at the following:

Davidson Street
Boulder Town Hall
Eastern Goldfields Community Centre

Kalgoorlie Town Hall
William Grundt Memorial Library
or by Freepost no later than 1st September 1995.

Alternatively you may wish to make a more detailed submission in writing which is to be received by Council prior to the above date.

Please note: If you wish to take advantage of the Freepost facility please record at the top of the address Freepost No. 28 and no postage stamp will be required.

THIS IS YOUR OPPORTUNITY TO HAVE YOUR SAY

NAME _____

ADDRESS _____

1. I support the previous Containment Policy under which Prostitution was
   managed within the City of Kalgoorlie-Boulder   YES ☐   NO ☐

2. I support the relaxation of the Containment Policy and the changes recently
   implemented by the Western Australian Police Service.   YES ☐   NO ☐

3. Other comments _____
   _____
   _____
   _____

Figure 26 *City of Kalgoorlie-Boulder questionnaire for residents, featured in the* Your City *newsletter, August 1995.* Courtesy City of Kalgoorlie-Boulder

Despite the local policy changes, Carmel continued to manage Questa Casa according to the 'old school' of Containment: all workers still resided on the premises and observed a nightly curfew of 6.00 pm. Carmel also continued to insist that workers be at least 21 years of age, but she later relaxed her ban on escort services and left this to the discretion of the individual women. On the other hand, Club 181 and the Red House continued to take advantage of the Containment changes: advertising escort services, lowering the working age to 18 years, and allowing the workers to live off the brothel premises.

While the historic Containment changes of 1995 appear to have had little demonstrable impact on life in Kalgoorlie-Boulder, life in Hay Street had changed significantly for the women, who historically had been virtually imprisoned in the brothels; they appear to have enjoyed their new-found liberty in the town without incident. Hay Street's status as Kalgoorlie's much-feted red-light district had remained entirely intact; it might even be argued that the stormy controversy had in fact enhanced Hay Street's notoriety. Meanwhile, the Court government's failure to introduce prostitution law reform also ensured that the brothels' illegal status, and thus much of Hay Street's infamous appeal, would not change in the immediate future.

CHAPTER 8

The politics of new Containment

During the mid to late 1990s, the Hay Street brothels remained the focus of the sex industry in Kalgoorlie, and continued to attract a strong and steady custom, as well as a reliable stream of voyeurs who preferred to survey the women from the sanctuary of their cars or tour buses. The location and structure of the sex industry in Kalgoorlie had not altered significantly as a result of the 1995 Containment changes. Yet the lifting of extreme personal restrictions on workers had obviously changed life for Hay Street women.

As I embarked on research for *The Scarlet Mile* in 1995, a priority was to determine the effect of the Containment changes on sex workers. Management at Club 181 allowed me to formally survey its workers, while management at Questa Casa and the Red House refused to allow copies of the questionnaire to be distributed. While it is unfortunate that this made it impossible to collect a complete set of data, the survey responses received from workers at Club 181 nevertheless provide a valuable snap-shot of life on Hay Street immediately following the historic Containment changes.

All seven workers at Club 181 completed the survey in mid-1995. Of these, five were 25–30 year-olds, one worker was under 21, and the other was in the 35–40 age group. Six had been born in either Perth or New

Zealand, and one woman had migrated from Ireland. Six of the workers had English or Celtic ancestry, and there was one Aboriginal woman.[1]

While most of the workers were single, separated or divorced, one woman reported that she was happily married (with children) to a man in the state's South West. Of the three women who had young children (under 6 years old), two had arranged for the children's father to care for them during their mother's brief 'tour of duty' in Kalgoorlie. Meanwhile, another young single mother, the only worker who lived in private accommodation, had hired a nanny to look after her 2-year-old daughter during her working hours. Each woman had told relatives that she was working temporarily in Kalgoorlie in a different occupation—hairdresser, domestic cleaner (a 'cover' used by two of the women), office receptionist, chef, real estate agent or public servant. These had actually been the women's previous occupations. In most cases, the women had never discussed their sex work with their family or friends, except for their partner.

When asked about their reasons for working in the sex industry, all said they had investigated sex work as a result of severe economic crisis, and five of the seven were paying off mortgages. Most of the women surveyed had been in the sex industry less than two years, working first in brothels, escort agencies and massage parlours in Perth, where one worker had previously operated as a private agent. All said that they had come to Kalgoorlie for the gold, like everyone else, intending to earn as much money as possible in the shortest period of time and then go home. Most worked between five and seven nights per week, sometimes earning $350–800 on a good night, but occasionally nothing on a very bad night. Their clients were generally Australian-born men in the 25–40 age group. Other prominent client groups included men from New Zealand, the United Kingdom, the United States and South East Asia.

As one might expect, the long hours and the lack of time off necessitated a break away from Kalgoorlie at least once every three months, for all workers. Most of the women reported that they worked from ten to twenty-one days and then travelled back to their home in Perth or the country to spend time with family and friends before returning to Kalgoorlie.

The women responded differently on the issue of job satisfaction. While three workers reported that they were satisfied with the work and conditions at Club 181, one worker felt indifferent and another dissatisfied. The remaining workers chose not to respond. There was a similarly divided response on the issue of living on the premises. Four workers said they were satisfied with living on the premises, while one was indifferent and another dissatisfied. The remaining worker lived in private accommodation. While there were no workers planning to change their living arrangements, all believed that sex workers should have the choice to live in private accommodation.

There was general support for the Containment change that allowed 18-year-olds to work in Hay Street. All workers expressed concern regarding the protection of young workers, and the extension of basic civil liberties to sex workers. On the other hand, three workers felt strongly that private agents should not be allowed to operate in Kalgoorlie, citing the lack of worker safety outside brothel premises. Two workers thought private work should be allowed, with one conceding that its popularity could be unfavourable for Hay Street. The remaining two workers did not respond.

The issue of worker safety outside brothel premises received a similar response when workers discussed their feelings about escort work, now gaining in popularity in Kalgoorlie-Boulder. All except one worker surveyed provided escort services. Most workers still lived in-house, and generally responded that escort bookings afforded them a break from the brothel, which they often inhabited twenty-four hours a day. Another worker looked forward to escort jobs, as she was nearly always tipped. Nevertheless, all seven workers expressed strong concern regarding the lack of security for workers on escort bookings.

Four of the seven women had short-term plans to solve various economic crises and leave the industry permanently within two years. Only one worker expressed a strong desire to remain long term, with a view to running her own brothel in the future. For most, however, the aim was to enrol for further study and practise in different professional areas (for example, as a naturopath, a child psychologist or a nurse for the elderly). One woman proudly wrote of her plans to build a secure future for herself and her 4-year-old child:

> I'm in the industry for a short time only, too [sic] make some quick money, so I can study, be a mother, and have a stable 9–5 pm job, which is security for my child's upbringing. I do this work now so my child will never have to.

While most workers reported that they now took advantage of Kalgoorlie's hotels, nightclubs, cafes, cinemas and festivals, they conceded that they rarely had more than one night off and usually just stayed in their rooms watching television or reading. One worker, who had not yet ventured out for a sampling of Kalgoorlie's nightlife, felt somewhat apprehensive about leaving the brothel at night: 'It would be good if you could do so without any problems'. Meanwhile, another worker summed up her reasons for working seven nights a week on Hay Street: 'I'm here for the money and nothing else'.

Local barmaid Natassia, who worked in a Hannan Street nightclub around the corner from the Hay Street brothels, said she believed that the women should be allowed to socialise 'like everyone else' in the town, if they chose to do so: 'I don't have a problem. They work like everyone else, and they're entitled to have a drink and go out and have a good time'.[2]

On a daily basis, tourists asked Natassia to direct them to the Hay Street brothels. She also said that whenever miners were taking a new workmate out for a night on the town, a visit to the Hay Street brothels usually completed the initiation:

> Usually they've got someone new in town, and they're going to take them down to 181 on Hay Street and show them what it's all about. When you've got new guys in town, they normally say, 'Well, we've been here and we're going there, and then after that we're going to go to Hay Street'. 181 is normally the main topic—that seems to be the popular one.[3]

Former Club 181 worker Taylor solidly supported the Containment changes and had enjoyed the odd night out with other workers, despite an icy reception from one publican's wife:

> I think it's good. They should have done it years ago. [Containment is] a breach of civil liberties, if you ask me. Just because I do what I do for a living doesn't mean that I can't go to the pub.
>
> I had a lot of hassle with one hotel in Boulder. We used to go for drinks there, and the publican's wife just hated us. And this one night we ran into each other in the hallway and I asked, 'Do you have a problem with me drinking in your hotel?' Because we were spending about a hundred dollars every time we went there, the three of us. The barman loved it, and I guess the guys liked watching the girls enjoying themselves, because there's a shortage of women in Kalgoorlie.
>
> And I just said to her, 'We're not here to pinch your man or upset your hotel'. And she said, 'Everybody knows you're sluts and I don't want my children exposed to it'. Rah, rah, rah. And we had this big screaming match. I had to say, 'Do you know how much money a week I spend in here?' I pointed out to her that when we work and then go out, we don't want to work.
>
> So we left and went somewhere else, and her hubby must have talked to her. Now she's nice as pie to us. But she used to look down on us, and now she realises we're just normal human beings. She's been really nice to me ever since. She's the one who put all the food out for my birthday party. . .now how many pubs would do that?[4]

One young Hay Street regular named Robbie strongly believed that Hay Street women deserved the same freedom and welcome as any other resident or visitor in the town. Well educated and forthright, Robbie spoke with respect about the women and offered his own insights into his gravitation towards them:

> It is an erotic experience. It's meeting this new person and feeling you're relating to this new person...because everybody loves that. New shapes, new concepts. Men love that erotic special thing. You walk up to the door, and you see a woman...she's doesn't even have to so much be beautiful, but she's accepting. She wants you to be there. Whether for business or otherwise, somehow you're just drawn, you know? You are going to be able to, within five or twenty minutes, be naked with this new woman, doing something erotic, which is almost in the realm of the fantasy, basically. Just being in their environment. You want to be accepted.[5]

Looking back, Robbie said that his most enjoyable experiences at the Hay Street brothels involved charming women who shared his interests. Although he now feels entirely relaxed when he visits the women, he described his first visit to Hay Street as anything but encouraging:

> In my head, I was rushed. I walked around the block. I walked through the alley-way, and around the block. *[Laughter]* In complete nerves. The first time, it just didn't work...I was shaking and nervous. So I thought, 'Well, I may as well do it properly'. I walked around the block again, and...it worked. *[Laughter]*
>
> Later I met Paula. We talked about Apple Mac computers. *[Laughter]* For some reason, we just got on so well. And I didn't sleep with her. It just didn't feel right. I had made a...non-erotic attachment with her. It was just a friendly attachment. I could *not sleep* with her. She was my sort of sanity there. She was so friendly, and it was such a beautiful feeling, to have someone invite you into their environment, into their personal place.
>
> In a sense, there is a degree of mothering. You know, 'Come on in, put your clothes there, here's the shower, here's your towel, make sure to do this, and I'll see you in a minute'. So polite. That's what I've experienced. Gentle, no rush. Then within ten or twenty minutes I think, 'Hey, you're someone I can relate to'. That's what I like, to get to a personal level. Even for Kalgoorlie, it's so laid back. And I'm sort of proud of these girls, in a special, different way. They've earned respect here.[6]

Another young Hay Street regular, Andy, said that he highly valued the services provided by the Hay Street women, especially as a man who usually worked in remote locations:

> I've worked in remote locations over the years at the mine sites. You stay for three or four weeks at one of these sites, and the only females you see work in kitchens or cleaning or whatever. You're paid very well for your job, your

average bloke works long hours. And you need sex and companionship. Short of that, you just have sex. Hay Street beats the bullshit in the nightclubs and the pubs. In Kalgoorlie, you know where it is, and you haven't got all the hassles with the bullshit.[7]

Andy had a strong preference for visiting Club 181 because it was the only brothel with an outdoor spa, and was the house with the most stringent rules regarding hygiene. He also strongly supported compulsory condom use:

> I suppose if I had to pick a brothel, it would have to be 181. Because you go up and you pay, saying 'I want to go with Leanne', or whatever, for an hour. You have a shower, then she comes and meets you, and you jump in the spa for five or ten minutes, then you go to the room and that's it.
>
> Other places you can have a shower, but you have to request it. At 181 you have to have a shower, 'Here's your towel, fuck off and have a shower. She'll meet you'. Normally, she's in the spa waiting. 'Hello, Andy.' And I don't know. They all know what to do.
>
> Well, if they don't practise safe sex, say they accept $100 more for unsafe sex, they deserve to catch something. That's stupid. If the clients try that sort of thing they deserve to have the workers say, 'Fuck off'. You don't need that sort of shit. They're just slack fuckers, you know? Society has changed. Nowadays that's an insult. You look after the business properly, and then get on with it.[8]

In plain bush-speak, Andy made clear his respect for Hay Street women and seemed annoyed at some of their working conditions and financial terms of employment:

> I think the girls don't get paid what they're worth. From what I've heard they get paid half of what you pay; the house takes the rest. To me, they [sex workers] do the hard work; they can't pick and choose who they go with. Some houses, OK, but I hear they don't have much choice. They're forced. They need some sort of regulation, something to help them control who they see. Because you don't need some drunken asshole come in and say, 'Here's a hundred bucks. Let's go'.[9]

The issue of regulation had resurfaced in November 1995, when the Australian Labor Party (WA) released a discussion paper on prostitution law reform in Kalgoorlie—a locational decision no doubt influenced by intense media interest in the Hay Street brothels following local Containment changes earlier in the year.[10]

The discussion paper recommended that an independent board be appointed to license brothels, management and sex workers. The recommendations proposed new criminal offences for activities such as street soliciting, employing under-age workers and offering or encouraging commercial sex without a condom.[11] The paper also recommended extending occupational health and safety regulations to cover sex workers, including compulsory medical examinations and health education for sex workers.

Labor's discussion paper seems to have been based mainly on the recommendations of the Community Panel on Prostitution (1990) and an academic submission that proposed free, compulsory health education seminars for sex workers.[12] The idea of 'statutory' condom use appears to have been taken from the Australian Capital Territory's *Brothels Act 1992*, which had reportedly served to reinforce the ability of sex workers to negotiate condom use with all their clients.

The launch of Labor's discussion paper on page 1 of *The Kalgoorlie Miner* featured a photograph of shadow police minister Nick Catania outside Club 181 in Hay Street. In this report, Mr Catania said that the state government had not been courageous enough to deal with the issue of prostitution law reform. In the same report, Police Minister Bob Wiese hit back at these claims and said that the matter was under review:

> I have publicly stated that the containment policy in the State is inadequate. A review of the legislation and suitable controls is taking place and will be presented to Cabinet in due course. The Opposition's attempt at producing a discussion paper on legislation to control the sex industry in WA is nothing new, but simply stoking the coals on a controversial issue they should have extinguished with proper laws years ago.[13]

The discussion paper attracted strong support from madam Leigh Varis-Beswick of Club 181 and Delia Riley, a senior nurse for the Goldfields Public Health Unit. On the other hand, Robert Hicks of the Australian Family Association remained opposed to any attempt to decriminalise or legalise the sex industry in Western Australia:

> The AFA opposes legalised prostitution because it inevitably entangles the State in approving and licensing activity that is detrimental to marriage, to the family's efforts to impart good values to their children, to the status of women and the safety of the community.[14]

The media's interest in prostitution law reform lasted all of one week, but included an impressively steady stream of newspaper articles, talkback radio discussions and television news. Several television reports began with sensational images of scantily clad street workers walking through Sydney's Kings Cross, and then crossed to Hay Street women sitting or standing in their doorways. These reports also often began with the same file footage—a montage of Hay Street women's legs, crossed and well-heeled, swinging gently. The procession of images usually concluded with a file clip of an obviously tired and possibly inebriated young man making his unsteady way past the Hay Street brothels.[15]

While law reform was far from becoming a political reality in November 1995, one Hay Street woman obviously decided to take the law into her own hands later that month, in an incident that apparently related to a pay dispute. At 6.30 am on 29 November, former Club 181 worker Roberta repeatedly slammed a four-wheel drive vehicle into the front of the brothel and succeeded in collapsing its entire frontage (see Figure 27). Kalgoorlie CIB Detective Senior Constable Tom Cogan further confirmed in *The Kalgoorlie Miner* that police had been forced to smash the driver's window in order to stop Roberta and the moving vehicle.[16]

Roberta's early morning drive followed her termination and eviction from 181 Hay Street the previous evening. Upon her termination, she had allegedly threatened staff and stolen money from the brothel office, and then broken into the premises a few hours later. Having also proceeded to cause an estimated $40,000 damage to the premises with the four-wheel drive she had 'borrowed' from a local relative, Roberta appeared later that

Figure 27 *Frontage of the brothel at 181 Hay Street following a former worker's ram raid with a four-wheel drive vehicle.* Author's private collection of photographs

day in the Kalgoorlie Magistrates' Court, charged with burglary and wilful damage. She was released on $10,000 bail and remanded to appear again on 13 December.[17]

It is indeed fortunate that all staff were asleep in their dongas at the rear of the property when Roberta began levelling the frontage with one almighty crash after another. In the aftermath, the front hallway and the three rooms facing on to Hay Street had sustained extensive structural damage: massive supporting beams lay felled across dusty debris, twisted electrical cables dangled precariously from collapsed ceilings, and a thick layer of dust and assorted debris covered the furniture and floors. Despite its 'disaster area' appearance, Club 181 was open for business that evening, with some workers taking clients into their dongas out back, to cope with the sudden room shortage.[18]

Within the month, another Hay Street woman made history, this time by taking legal action against her former employer. In September 1996, former Questa Casa worker Phillipa sued madam Carmel in the Industrial Relations Court in the (Western Australian) sex industry's first unfair dismissal case.[19] The true identities of Carmel, Phillipa and witness Vanda were suppressed in the court proceedings. Apart from recording the details of this legal precedent, judicial registrar Mark Ritter's sixty-eight-page judgment also contains a valuable snapshot of life at Questa Casa during the mid-1990s.[20]

Phillipa's legal representative, Sally Gaunt, argued that Phillipa had been summarily dismissed on 7 November 1995 in contravention of several sections of the *Industrial Relations Act 1988* (Cwlth). In her testimony, Phillipa told the court she was fired after advising Carmel that she would not be taking up an offer to lease Questa Casa, which the two women had been negotiating for months. Phillipa said Carmel had responded furiously that her plans had been wrecked, and that 'she could not bear to have me on the premises any longer, and I was to pack and leave immediately'.[21]

Representing herself, Carmel disputed this account of events, and claimed that Phillipa had been intolerably drunk and abusive when she was told to vacate the premises.[22] Carmel also countered that she was not Phillipa's employer, but in fact a landlady who rented rooms to women for the purpose of their being self-employed. She argued that, even if a relationship of employment had existed between herself and Phillipa, no contract of employment could be considered legally binding, because the sex industry itself is illegal in Western Australia. Carmel also submitted that, should the court determine that Phillipa's dismissal had been unlawful, reinstatement would not be practicable, and compensation would be the only appropriate recourse.[23]

Phillipa agreed that the women paid Carmel a fixed amount each week for their rooms, no matter what their earnings, and Carmel did not pay the workers. Yet she argued that Carmel maintained a sufficient degree of control over the women's lives to constitute an employer–employee relationship:

> [Carmel] had always let it be known that she was The Boss, and we had to live under her regulations, do exactly what she told us to do, but for taxation purposes she preferred to call herself a landlady.[24]

Carmel agreed that she enforced house rules that were additional to the local Containment Policy. She conceded that these rules included a 6.00 pm curfew for the women, as well as the requirement that all workers take the evening meal as a group with Carmel. Each woman was rostered to take her turn providing the meal for the rest of the brood. Former Questa Casa worker Vanda further testified that Carmel enforced other extreme restrictions on the personal lives of the women:

- No visitors (male or female) were allowed in the workers' rooms at any time (apart from clients).
- Workers were not allowed to have male partners living in the town.
- Questa Casa workers were not allowed to socialise with women who worked in other brothels.[25]

It was agreed by all parties that the service and fee structure at Questa Casa had been set by Carmel, following consultation with the workers, although the women were not strictly bound to this fee structure when negotiating with clients. Phillipa testified that Carmel had insisted on mediating all workers' disputes with clients and that she 'quite often' refunded the client his money, after taking it back from the worker. Carmel had also made it clear to the women that only she was allowed to call the police in the event of a disturbance.[26]

As further evidence that Carmel had been her employer, Phillipa noted that Carmel collected weekly PAYE (pay-as-you-earn) taxes from the workers for the ATO.[27] Carmel, however, argued that she collected taxes from the self-employed women at Questa Casa as a voluntary tax agent for the ATO, and that this voluntary role did not make her the women's employer. Carmel also told the court that she had signed Phillipa's 'Separation Certificate' for the Department of Social Security out of goodwill, but had made a point of crossing out all sections of the form that referred to her as 'The Employer' and Phillipa as 'The Employee'.[28]

Justice Ritter requested guidance on state prostitution laws and the Containment Policy in his letter to Attorney General Peter Foss. However, the Attorney General declined to provide guidance—a response that Justice Ritter found disappointing:

By letter dated 23 May 1996, Mr Foss QC said, 'As the issues raised focus upon the application of the Industrial Relations Act 1988 (C'th), I do not intend to apply for leave to intervene.' In my view, this was a pity. The issues raised focus upon the state of the law in Western Australia about the relationship between a brothel madam and a sex worker, and whether the latter can enforce legal rights arising out of the relationship...and the containment policy in Western Australia. I think the views of the Attorney General would have been helpful in understanding the law on these issues in Western Australia. It is therefore, as I have said, a pity that the Attorney took the restrictive view of the Court's request that he did.[29]

In his final judgment, Justice Ritter considered the range of unusual conditions before him, as well as a number of legal precedents involved in defining the employer–employee relationship. He said that changes to the Containment Policy in Kalgoorlie in 1995 had also played a critical role in his judgment, since Carmel's strict control over the women at Questa Casa could no longer be justified under local Containment provisions.[30]

On 10 September 1996 Justice Ritter announced his decision that there had been a legally binding employer–employee relationship between Carmel and Phillipa, and that Carmel had unfairly dismissed Phillipa. He awarded Phillipa a total of $5,375 in costs, compensation and damages, to be paid by Carmel within twenty-one days:

> There is the consideration of preventing injustice and the enrichment of one party at the expense of the other. To deny the applicant jurisdiction in this case would be such a situation, in my opinion. The respondent is quite aware of the legal status of her relationship with the applicant and the other sex workers. She derives a benefit from the employment relationship by the payment to her of the rental by the sex workers. Yet, she comes before the Court and asks the Court to deny the applicant jurisdiction because the employment relationship is tainted by illegality. To allow this argument to succeed, particularly in light of the containment policy in Kalgoorlie could rightly be described as the respondent unjustly enriching herself at the expense of the applicant and the other sex workers. The respondent would be entitled to the benefit of the employment relationship, the payment of the rental, the protection from prosecution that the containment policy allows, yet be immune from the unlawful termination of employment provisions of the Industrial Relations Act because the employment relationship infringes the letter of the law.[31]

The following day, *The Kalgoorlie Miner* carried the front-page headline 'Local sex worker in landmark victory'. In this report, Phillipa said that she was overwhelmed by her unexpected victory, and hoped that the judgment would lead to better conditions for sex workers in Hay Street. The same report included Justice Ritter's criticism of the Court government's political inaction on prostitution law reform, which he said was needed to remedy 'the status quo, with all its uncertainties, contradictions and scope for police abuse and corruption'.[32]

Meanwhile, Mary-Anne Kenworthy continued to develop her brothel business with a view to capturing a share of Kalgoorlie's tourist market. Unable to get council approval to rebuild her premises, she had attempted to move to better premises in 1992, when she first proposed the idea of turning 181 Hay Street into a prostitution museum:

> Yes, I offered the council—I would give them 181 if I was allowed to move across the road and operate from Mona's [former brothel], and they could...turn 181 into a museum site...they could do whatever they liked with it. I would own the land, they would have operational rights to the building. And at the end of the day, I thought there might be a 5 per cent return or so. Then I approached the Tourist Commission, who were very interested. But the police wouldn't allow us to move our licence across the road, and so we couldn't look at it. And you know, the tourists haven't got enough to do up there. I estimate that [with a prostitution museum] we'd get 60–70 percent of the tourist market.[33]

Then, in May 1996, the City of Kalgoorlie-Boulder issued planning consent for a backpackers hostel to operate at 164 Hay Street. The development application succeeded despite strong objections from both Carmel and Mary-Anne. While Carmel argued that 'young impressionable' visitors would be given a 'map to moral poverty...in brothel territory', Mary-Anne said she was more concerned that the hostel would bring 'undesirable elements' into the neighbourhood, which would upset the existing 'quiet and good order'[34] and destroy Hay Street's historical amenity.[35] The hostel has continued to operate at 164 Hay Street, apparently without having raised further opposition from its neighbours.

The historical and tourist value of the Hay Street brothels has certainly not been lost on tour operators in Kalgoorlie-Boulder. All bus tours of the town by day or by night feature a drive down Hay Street, with this attraction usually saved for the finale.[36] When I took a day tour of Kalgoorlie-Boulder, I could not help but notice that the bus (packed with tourists) slowed down to a kerb-crawl as 'Hay Street' was announced and the vehicle rolled quietly past the brothels, which seemed starkly understated in the light of day. Nevertheless, all passengers immediately assumed the craning position, some standing up in the aisles and crouching forward to get a better glimpse of the legendary dens of infamy. Notably, there was rather more chuckling and chattering between passengers for the last five minutes of the tour.[37]

Yet behind the scenes, Hay Street women continued to labour in an unregulated industry, hoping to provide a secure future for themselves and their children. One former worker, 'Madison', who worked on Hay Street from 1993 to 1995, proudly recalled how she had won her struggle to break the cycle of poverty for the sake of her daughter:

> My daughter is very smart, very laid back and well-adjusted, and she's going to finish her education and go on to further training and get a good job. She doesn't get into trouble, she's a very good kid. I'm very lucky. She's been brought up to believe it doesn't matter what people do, or the colour of their skin, everybody's human.
>
> My mother worked three jobs, she was bringing up three kids by herself. She worked three jobs so us kids wouldn't go without. And I've worked two jobs much of the time, while my daughter was growing up, mainly so that she won't have to go through what my mother went through, or what I went through. I've got my house, and then there's my mother's house, and those will be my daughter's one day. So she is secure in her future, and if I can pay off another one, she will have three houses. So she won't have to go through what we went through and her children won't have it so hard.
>
> Because they say that if you grow up hard, and come from a broken home, that that's what your kids will be like, and all the rest. That's a load of bullshit, because you can stop the cycle and you can change it, so that your kids don't have to do it. I'm not complaining about what I've done, I'm not ashamed of what I did, but I'm just determined that she won't have to do it.[38]

Hay Street worker Taylor also felt determined to build a secure future for herself and her young daughter. The hostility she encountered in Kalgoorlie-Boulder after the Containment changes had further raised her awareness of the powerful social stigma associated with prostitution. Taylor appealed for people to understand that universal economic imperatives drive ordinary women to work in the sex industry, and for many women this is their only means of escaping long-term poverty:

> I'd like people to realise that we're just normal women. Just working people who've got economic goals to meet. Maybe we're going to uni or trying to buy a house or furniture—you've got to have a goal. It's not like we're forced to do it, you know. We choose to, and people should not be judgmental. I think that probably will change, but it will take time.[39]

CHAPTER 9

Scarlet women in the new millennium

The sex industry in Western Australia has undergone major changes in recent years. In Perth, the Containment Policy was abandoned altogether during the mid-1990s after ninety years (beginning with the Roe Street red-light district), because most of the sex industry in the metropolitan area was by that time operating outside its parameters. By October 1995 the Vice Squad had registered dozens of businesses under the new policy in Perth and regional areas of Western Australia.[1] As with Containment, this new policy is unwritten and is administered according to the discretion of police authorities, with no system of appeal. And like so many other major changes to law enforcement policy in Western Australia, the changes did not affect Kalgoorlie. The remaining Hay Street brothels—Langtrees 181 (181 Hay Street), Questa Casa and the Red House—still operate under the local Containment Policy in Kalgoorlie.

Yet the Kalgoorlie Containment Policy has also changed, with the mid-1990s ushering in something of a new era for Hay Street in Kalgoorlie. As discussed in previous chapters, when some local Containment conditions were relaxed in 1995, brothel workers on Hay Street were allowed for the first time to move freely about Kalgoorlie-Boulder and live in private accommodation. The same year, Phillipa at Questa Casa became the first sex worker in Western Australia to take her employer to court in an unfair dismissal charge. Then in May 1999, Leigh Varis-Beswick (Hay Street's first transgender worker and madam) was elected to the council of the City of Kalgoorlie-Boulder.

These events were heralded in the local media as important victories for sex workers—in contrast to the shrill whispers of the 'scarlet stain' and the 'social evil' that titillated readers during the late nineteenth and early twentieth centuries. It seems fair to say that while early historical press reports reflected the Victorian attitudes of their readers, the media of the latter twentieth century and (so far) the new millennium have generally embraced more tolerant contemporary attitudes. This change in community attitudes was clearly documented in *The West Australian*'s June 1999 West Poll, in which more than 80 per cent of Western Australians surveyed responded that they supported decriminalising the sex industry.[2]

Mary-Anne Kenworthy had a significant victory in October 1999 after a four-year battle with the local council and the state Heritage Council, when she was granted approval to demolish her deteriorating premises at 181 Hay Street to build a new brothel (see Figures 28, 29). As soon as the new structure had been completed (at a reported cost of $2.8 million), she commissioned Perth artist Elaine Leonard to create a range of historical themes throughout the new Langtrees 181 in Kalgoorlie—including an erotic Romanesque mural in the Roman Orgy Suite, geishas in the Eishen Room (dedicated to early Japanese prostitutes), and camel drivers and belly dancers in the Afghan Boudoir (see Figures 30, 31, 32). The new brothel also houses a prostitution museum and a cafe, and conducts tours of the premises to cater for curious locals and tourists.[3]

The reinvention of 181 Hay Street stirred up further enthusiastic reports in the local press. Among them, *The Kalgoorlie Miner*'s 'Controversy Corner' columnist, Billy Kerr, declared Hay Street a 'revered icon' in Kalgoorlie, and

Figure 28 *Hay Street frontage, 181 Hay Street, following the brothel's demolition and rebuilding, 2000.* Courtesy Mary-Anne Kenworthy, private collection of photographs

Figure 29 *Reception area, which replaced the Hay Street 'doorways',*
181 Hay Street, 2000. Courtesy Mary-Anne Kenworthy,
private collection of photographs

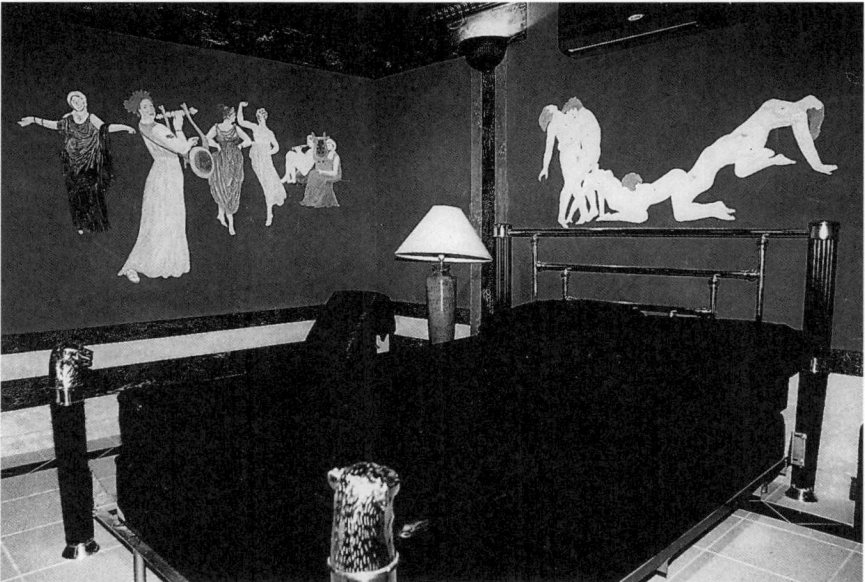

Figure 30 *The Roman Orgy Suite, 181 Hay Street, 2000.*
Courtesy Mary-Anne Kenworthy, private collection of photographs

Figure 31 *The Afghan Boudoir, 181 Hay Street, 2000.*
Courtesy Mary-Anne Kenworthy, private collection of photographs

Figure 32 *The Eishen Room, 181 Hay Street, 2000.*
Courtesy Mary-Anne Kenworthy, private collection of photographs

heartily gave the new premises at the corner of Hay and Lane streets his stamp of approval:

> At the end of the day—and despite the inevitable criticism—this is a unique and exciting development that is further proof that here in the Goldfields we dare to be different and we do it successfully.[4]

Mr Kerr's proud cultural observation highlights one of the themes recurring throughout *The Scarlet Mile*: that Kalgoorlie is a fiercely independent, isolated goldfields town determined to conduct its own affairs as it sees fit.

The Court (Liberal) government became acutely aware of the town's proud resilience when it introduced the *Prostitution Act 1999* (WA), which at first appeared to threaten the sanctity of the Hay Street brothels. The government had actually targeted street prostitution in inner-city Perth with this narrow piece of legislation that gave police unprecedented powers to conduct searches without warrants and detain suspects without evidence. Western Australia's state police authorities, who had lobbied the Court government for years to introduce a broad-based law reform model, were not impressed by the new legislation. They threw down the gauntlet and threatened to follow the letter of the law, which raised the possibility of crackdowns on long-sanctioned brothels in Perth and Kalgoorlie.

State Member of Parliament Mark Nevill told *The Kalgoorlie Miner* that the draconian measures proposed in the Prostitution Act had been designed to appease conservative Court government backbenchers, who reportedly formed the major political bloc that prevented the government from introducing progressive prostitution law reform.[5] Then, in a famously forthright parting shot, Police Commissioner Bob Falconer told *The West Australian* that the Court government did not 'have the balls' to introduce genuine prostitution law reform—a view supported by Deputy Premier Hendy Cowan.[6] The new Police Commissioner, Barry Matthews, soon chimed in with yet another public appeal to the government for workable, broad-based prostitution law reform.[7]

Several organisations publicly opposed the Prostitution Act on the basis that prohibition laws had been universally unhelpful in addressing occupational health and safety issues—in particular, sex workers' ability to enforce compulsory condom use with all their clients. These organisations included the WA AIDS Council, Family Planning WA, the Australian Democrats, the Greens and the Western Australian Municipal Association.[8]

Back in Kalgoorlie, the local branch of the Australian Family Association welcomed any prospect of closing down the Hay Street brothels or even having the women removed from public view. In one report in *The*

Kalgoorlie Miner, local branch president Robert Hicks threw the association's support behind the legal view that the Hay Street brothels should not be exempted from any state prohibition laws:

> We draw parallels with the people of Northbridge [inner-city Perth] who forced this legislation...because they were sick and tired of seeing prostitutes soliciting on their streets. The situation in Kalgoorlie is in a sense no different, so why should it be allowed to continue? [9]

One Hay Street woman, 'Yvette', hit back in *The Kalgoorlie Miner*, saying that any attempt to eradicate brothels in Kalgoorlie would be futile but could well spell the end of Hay Street as a unique local attraction:

> It [the legislation] won't stop the industry, but it will ruin Hay Street. We are not street walkers. For 100 years the ladies have sat out the front of Kalgoorlie's brothels...the beauty of Kalgoorlie is that it is unique. [10]

In an extraordinary move, Police Minister Kevin Prince gave his assurance in *The West Australian* that Kalgoorlie's brothels would not be affected by the new state legislation. He also said that the Court government would be prepared to redraft the Prostitution Act, if necessary, to ensure that the Hay Street brothels were protected. [11] As it happened, this was not considered necessary, and business continued as usual in Hay Street, Kalgoorlie, unfettered by political interference from Perth.

The Prostitution Act also specifically prohibited sex industry business owners from sponsoring sporting teams, artistic endeavours and public events. This provision seems to have been aimed at the fairly high-profile sponsorship activities of Mary-Anne Kenworthy, a long-time backer of rugby teams and local sporting events in Perth and Kalgoorlie. [12] She also financed the recording of a CD by popular Perth comedy duo Novak 'n' Goode in November 1999. [13]

Mary-Anne again fell foul of the law in November 2001, this time in the Western Australian Industrial Relations Commission, when an unfair dismissal case was brought against her under the *Industrial Relations Act 1979* (WA) by Suzanne Parker, a former receptionist at the new Langtrees 181 in Kalgoorlie. Mary-Anne testified that she had dismissed Suzanne for failing to follow instructions and for refusing to wear the uniform colour of black while on duty; she also claimed that Suzanne had not been available for weekend shifts as required by her employment contract. Representing herself, Suzanne countered that she had always (at least partially) worn black while at work, that Mary-Anne had failed to properly explain certain data entry instructions to her, and that she had always been available to work on weekends, except on two occasions.

Commissioner J. F. Gregor found that Mary-Anne's summary dismissal of Suzanne had occurred in the heat of the moment and without warning, and could not be justified. Suzanne was awarded $2,825, which included compensation for income lost until she found alternative employment, as well as $1,000 for injury suffered.[14] In what appears to have been a direct reference to the social stigma still associated with prostitution, Commissioner Gregor said that Suzanne's injury had been exacerbated by the fact that she had been working in a Hay Street brothel:

> It is clearly open to conclude from her evidence and I do, that she did suffer stress and humiliation. This was more than normally experienced in a dismissal because of [the] nature of her employment, the occupation and the industry of her employer and the location of the employment in a country town...[15]

The commissioner's comments clearly recognise that, despite the change in community attitudes, a stigma continues to stain the 'scarlet women' and their associates.

This much had been made abundantly clear earlier in the year, when *The West Australian* 'named and shamed' seventeen men who had been found guilty in the Perth Magistrates' Court (Petty Sessions) of 'seeking a prostitute in a public place'. The front page featured a photograph of a man who appeared to be running from the camera. Arrested during a 'street sex sting' in inner-city Perth, the men included accountants, courier drivers, factory workers, boilermakers and construction workers. While such harsh and intrusive media treatment had been meted out to sex workers and madams from time to time, clients had historically been spared. It is safe to suggest that the 'naming and shaming' of clients in the state's daily newspaper almost certainly served to reinforce the harsh social stigma still associated with prostitution in Western Australia.

This powerful stigma is one of the most important factors affecting sex workers' attitudes towards how the sex industry is run and regulated. Yet this was apparently not well understood by the Gallop (Labor) government when it set out to reform the state's antiquated anti-prostitution laws. In November 2002, forty delegates from the Scarlet Alliance (Australia's peak body of sex worker organisations) attended a forum in Perth and took the opportunity to comment on the forthcoming draft legislation. They told *The West Australian* that they were concerned about rumours that the Western Australian Government's much-anticipated law reform model, the Prostitution Control Bill, would include individual worker licensing and identification cards. One forum delegate from Victoria, Alison Arnot-Bradshaw, said that these measures would only add to the marginalisation and stigmatisation of sex workers:

Any law reform must aim to reduce this marginalisation and stigmatisation. From the research I have conducted with sex workers in Victoria it has been shown it is these two issues that have the greatest negative impact on their working and private lives.[16]

The following day, a 28-year-old Perth sex worker supported this view and appealed to the Police Minister in *The West Australian* to understand that the social stigma associated with prostitution made it impossible for workers to accept identification cards or any form of registration on a central government database:

> We're not being defiant, but there's just no incentive to do it. The simple fact is that this is an adult, intimate sexual service. As much as we would love to be part of a legal system and not risk prosecution, it's not worth losing our anonymity and so much of our lives.[17]

Police Minister Michelle Roberts refused to respond to suggestions that registration of individual workers and compulsory identification cards would drive the industry underground, and said that sex workers were criticising legislation they had yet to see.[18]

However, when the draft legislation was released for public comment on 26 November 2002, it did (as expected) include compulsory licensing and photographic identification cards for sex workers, which confirmed the workers' worst fears. Nevertheless, the Gallop government championed the legislation on the basis that it would extend to sex workers protection under the Western Australian *Industrial Relations Act 1979*, the *Minimum Conditions of Employment Act 1993*, the *Long Service Leave Act 1958* and the *Workers Compensation and Rehabilitation Act 1981*. The proposed legislation also aimed to ensure that brothel madams could not sidestep industrial laws by classifying their workers as subcontractors.[19] Yet by ignoring the powerful social stigma attached to prostitution, the government created a major barrier to worker participation, which in turn would result in a substantial pool of illegal workers who would not be protected under this range of labour legislation.

Equally troublesome was the fact that the government planned to deny equality before the law even to those workers who complied with the proposed legislation. The Bill expressly declared that sex workers and business owners would have neither normal protection under administrative law nor access to natural justice under the new legal framework. The proposed Prostitution Control Board would not be accountable to any agency, authority or Minister and would exclude any sex industry representation. At the same time, the board would perform the contradictory functions of 'deterring' the sex industry while regulating it. Finally, the Bill gave police broad powers of search and seizure, and reversed the onus of proof for anyone arrested on suspicion of prostitution-related activities.

In its response to the Bill, the Women's Electoral Lobby (WEL) claimed that these 'guilty until proved innocent' provisions amounted to a gross breach of human rights. In its submission to the Police Minister, WEL argued that the government had given the board a similar legal status to that of the Supreme Court—in terms of protection, immunity and the absence of a review/appeals process—while denying people who worked in the sex industry basic rights that had long been anticipated under law reform. WEL also noted that Police Minister Michelle Roberts had vehemently opposed a similar regulation model put forward by the Court government on the very basis that it lacked accountability, quoting Ms Roberts's comments in State Parliament in May 1999:

> The PCB [Prostitution Control Board] will have sweeping powers which will allow it to act in any manner it determines, and will not be subject to review. Such totally unfettered power is inappropriate. All government Boards need to be accountable. This proposed Board should be accountable to the Ombudsman or some other appropriate authority.[20]

Having virtually elevated the industry's regulators above the law, while sidelining the civil rights and concerns of sex workers, there is little doubt that the Gallop government's proposed law reform would have caused further marginalisation and stigmatisation of this already vulnerable group of workers.

Just days following the high-profile release of this draft legislation, police in Perth dropped a bombshell when they charged Mary-Anne Kenworthy and Langtrees manager Warren George with keeping premises for the purpose of prostitution. *The West Australian* reported that two female vice detectives had initially paid a visit to Langtrees in Perth to interview workers about a man they wanted for questioning. Mary-Anne had taken offence at what she described as the detectives' 'high-handed and intimidating' manner and gave them 'a bit of lip...I said, "Don't come in here with that attitude unless you've got a search warrant"'.[21] The following morning, the officers returned with a warrant and raided the premises.

When questioned about the charges, Assistant Police Commissioner (Crime) Mel Hay explained that Mary-Anne was a high-profile madam who had always been famously frank about her illegal business and had been quite upfront with the two Vice Squad officers; she would thus be prosecuted accordingly.[22] It is meanwhile worth noting that, under the draft Bill, Mary-Anne would need a licence to operate within the new legal framework; police sources told *The West Australian* that they would almost certainly oppose her application if she were convicted on the charge of keeping premises for the purpose of prostitution.[23]

When Mary-Anne's charges under the *Criminal Code* were dropped in the District Court, police authorities responded by bringing new charges under the *Police Act 1892* in order to have the case heard in the Perth Magistrates' Court (Warren George had initially been charged under the Police Act and was still awaiting trial). This pursuit continued until January 2004 (more than a year after the initial charges were laid), when Police Commissioner Barry Matthews announced that police would not offer evidence in the forthcoming case, adding that the case had become 'bigger than Ben Hur'.[24] He conceded that Mary-Anne Kenworthy and Warren George continued to break the law; however, the high costs and resources required to pursue the case had rendered it unviable. He called on the Western Australian Government to introduce legislation to regulate the sex industry in a 'sensible way':

> Prostitution has been going on for thousands of years, this business of prohibiting it is just a nonsense and all it means is tying up police resources when we do get involved in this.

What this case clearly demonstrates is that no worker or business owner in the Western Australian sex industry can be considered immune from the threat of arrest and loss of livelihood. While business owners such as Mary-Anne Kenworthy face potentially substantial losses on their investments, any criminal conviction for a sex worker means long-term dependence on sex work, because the criminal record in itself presents a major barrier to more 'mainstream' employment opportunities. This is particularly devastating for workers with short-term economic imperatives and otherwise promising career prospects.

Thus, sex workers in the new millennium do not appear to be much better off than their predecessors in the eyes of the law. Despite the significant uncertainties and hardships associated with the current lack of regulation, law reform does not seem likely in the foreseeable future. The Prostitution Control Bill 2002 was defeated in State Parliament, owing not only to lack of support from the Western Australian Greens, but also in no small part to the political influence of a bloc of Liberal backbenchers who have long opposed any measure of sex industry decriminalisation or regulation.[25] As this book goes to press in mid-2004, there has been no further progress on the issue of law reform.

Nevertheless, workers in the sex industry are increasingly finding ways to speak out through the media and the industrial relations system. Since the late 1980s, sex workers in Western Australia have demonstrated strong initiative in terms of improving their working conditions, challenging their legal status and demanding fairer terms of employment. The two brothel workers who successfully sued their former madams for unfair dismissal were Hay Street women.

There is no doubt that the most dramatic improvement in workers' health and safety occurred in 1987, when the Health Department of Western Australia issued a recommendation for compulsory condom use. This practice was immediately voluntarily adopted by workers, despite initial resistance from some clients and madams. Since then, the Health Department and its Commonwealth counterpart have jointly funded a series of community-based outreach organisations in Western Australia (SIERA, 1987–99; Phoenix, 1999–2003; Magenta, 2003 – present) to provide sexual health information, workshops and support for sex workers. A significant improvement on the historical Containment rule that workers undergo weekly health examinations, the Health Department's support for workers' enforcement of compulsory condom use actually helped these workers to reduce their rate of STDs to lower than that of the general population.

In the absence of industrial unions or professional organisations, sex workers have also regarded these health agencies as welcoming environments where they can drop in for an informal chat to get support, advice and referral on a range of issues, including the implications of proposed law reform. During the public consultation period from November 2002 to February 2003, Phoenix publicly campaigned against the Prostitution Control Bill on the basis that it discriminated against sex workers and placed their health at risk. Then in June 2003, Phoenix's funding was withdrawn by Western Australian Health Minister Bob Kucera amid protests that the organisation was being punished for its vocal opposition to the Bill. The Minister countered that he had been outraged to discover that Phoenix had recently published material in its magazine *Working for a Living* that encouraged prostitution (a list of 'tips' for workers trying to build a regular clientele), which he considered an inappropriate use of taxpayers' funds.

Despite the occasional turmoil that rages in Perth from time to time, the future of the Hay Street red-light district appears fairly secure. Kalgoorlie remains the goldmining capital of Australia, creating a pool of well-paid and isolated men, and women continue to arrive for work in Kalgoorlie's infamous brothels. This is hardly surprising, since the social and economic conditions that have historically given rise to prostitution in Kalgoorlie remain: there is still a substantial concentration of men with unmet sexual needs who are willing to pay in order to have sex, and there are still women in economic need who are prepared to have sex in order to get paid for it.

Given the growing divide between society's 'haves' and 'have-nots'[26], women will not be finding it any easier to break the cycle of poverty. Although it is acknowledged that a number of factors may be operating at the individual level, this history confirms that the primary reason that women actually take up sex work is to meet economic needs. Many women start sex work to finance their way through university, and the Howard government's all-clear for Australian universities to increase their fees by up to 25 per cent[27] will only increase the financial pressure on these women. Even women who have gained higher professional qualifications continue to tolerate less pay than men for equal work performed[28], which increases their risk of encountering financial problems and turning to sex work as a solution. It is safe to say that as long as society has the capacity to create economic crisis, women will continue to resort to prostitution.

The resolution of economic crisis through sex work continues to come at a substantial personal cost: women who work in the sex industry still find that they suffer extreme stigmatisation. This is supported and reinforced by the industry's illegal status, and the lack of progress on law reform means that all sex workers and business owners in Western Australia continue to tolerate laws that deny them basic rights that others take for granted in their workplaces. While the Containment Policy has often been lauded as a 'commonsense' system of quasi-legal regulation, the policy has never regulated workplace practices, nor has it protected sex workers against exploitation or discrimination. At the same time, sex workers and business owners have never had the right to appeal against police decisions regarding their 'right' to operate within Containment.

It is fair to say that even Kalgoorlie's relatively pragmatic Containment Policy historically relied on the social and geographical marginalisation of the Hay Street women. Shunned by the community and confined by police to the brothels, it was not until 1995 that the women were allowed to live in private accommodation and socialise in pubs and restaurants in Kalgoorlie-Boulder. Local outrage over these Containment changes settled only after several months, when it became clear that the women's freedom would not destroy residential amenity or the character of Hay Street. The survival of the Kalgoorlie brothels through this particularly turbulent period served to further consolidate the status of the Hay Street red-light district as an important local social institution and a popular tourist attraction (see Figure 33).

The history of prostitution in Kalgoorlie certainly lends itself to the timeless adage first spoken by Alphonse Karr: 'The more things change, the more they remain the same'. One hundred years after the local council quietly gazetted the red-light district, the brothels still co-exist on the same street as the local police station, the district courthouse and the Catholic church—separated only by a partial change in street name. And in the new millennium the 'pretty ladies under the lights' continue to boldly and beautifully tame the otherwise barren territory known as Hay Street, Kalgoorlie.

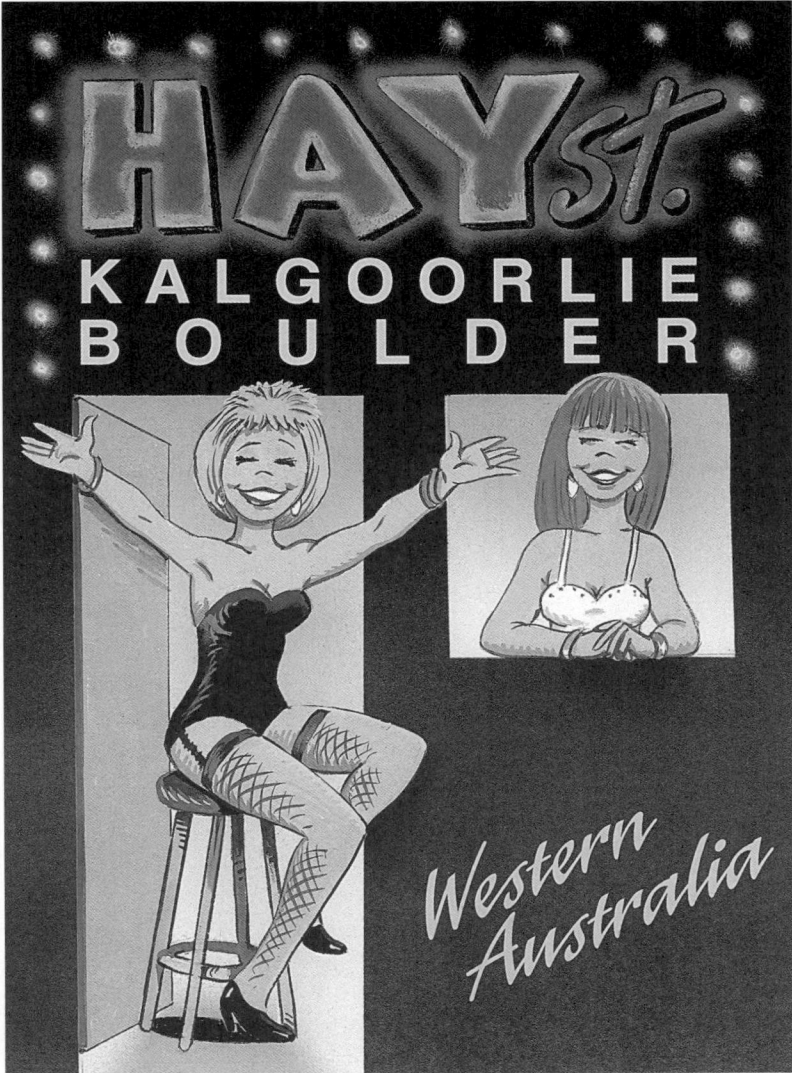

Figure 33 *Postcard featuring the Hay Street brothels, sold in local tourism shops on the goldfields.* Courtesy Nucolorvue Productions

Notes

CHAPTER 1—SCARLET WOMEN ON THE EARLY GOLDFIELDS

1   *The Illustrated London News*, 28 September 1895.
2   R. May, *The Goldrushes: From California to the Klondike*, W. Luscombe, London, 1977, p. 6.
3   Mrs A. H. Garnsey, *Scarlet Pillows: An Australian Nurse's Tales from Long Ago*, Hesperian Press, Carlisle, 1984, p. 61.
4   A. Reid, *Those Were the Days*, Hesperian Press, Carlisle, 1986, p. 27.
5   Kalgoorlie Auxiliary of the Australian Institute of Mining and Metallurgy, *Staking Our Claim: One Hundred Years of Women on the Goldfields*, Kalgoorlie, 1992.
6   Reid, *Those Were the Days*, p. 27.
7   May, *The Goldrushes*, p. 59.
8   V. Whittington, *Gold and Typhoid: Two Fevers*, University of Western Australia Press, Nedlands, 1988, p. 194.
9   M. Best (ed.), *A Lost Glitter: Letters between South Australia and the WA Goldfields 1895–97*, Wakefield Press, Adelaide, 1986, pp. 78–9.
10   Mrs M. Cowles, *Diary of Mrs Mary Cowles, 1896–1897*, J. S. Battye Library, Perth.
11   ibid.
12   ibid.
13   Garnsey, *Scarlet Pillows*, p. 54.
14   ibid.
15   May, *The Goldrushes*, p. 33.
16   Garnsey, *Scarlet Pillows*, p. 135.
17   Best, *A Lost Glitter*, pp. 141–2.
18   K. Daniels (ed.), *So Much Hard Work*, Fontana/Collins, Sydney, 1984, pp. 2–3.
19   R. Davidson, 'Dealing with the "social evil": Prostitution and the police in Perth and on the Eastern Goldfields', in Daniels, *So Much Hard Work*, pp. 163–5.
20   For example, Garnsey, *Scarlet Pillows*, p. 64; *The Sunday Times*, 8 May 1904, p. 5, 15 May 1904, p. 3.

21   *The Sunday Times*, 24 August 1902.

22   Kalgoorlie Roads Board, minute book, vol. 1, 14 January 1898 – 1 December 1899, pp. 82–3.

23   Kalgoorlie Municipal Council, minute book, vol. 10, 15 April 1901 – 18 August 1902, p. 8.

24   *The Sun*, 8, 15, 22, 29 April 1900; *The Sunday Times*, 17 March 1901.

25   *The Sun*, 16 October 1898.

26   ibid.

27   *The Sun*, 18 October 1903.

28   *The T'othersider*, 10 April 1897.

CHAPTER 2—OF VICE AND MEN: FOREIGN DEVILS AND JAPANESE FLOWERS

1   D. C. S. Sissons, 'Karayuki-San: Japanese prostitutes in Australia, 1887–1916', *Historical Studies*, vol. 17, nos 68, 69, Australian National University, Canberra, 1977; *The Sun*, 8 April 1900; *The Sunday Times*, 24 March 1901; *The Sun*, 8 April 1900.

2   *The Kalgoorlie Miner*, 20 March 1903; *The Sun*, 8 April 1903.

3   *The Sun*, 16 October 1898.

4   Certificate of Title vol. 170/fol. 98, Department of Land Information (DLI), Midland.

5   Certificates of Title vol. 1230/fol. 161, vol. 516/fol. 44, vol. 1235/fol. 245, vol. 170/fol. 98, vol. 664/fol. 125, DLI, Midland.

6   Certificates of Title vol. 516/fol. 44, vol. 391/fol. 184, DLI, Midland.

7   *The Sun*, 29 April 1900.

8   *The West Australian*, 19 April 1900.

9   *The Sunday Times*, 2 September 1900.

10   *The Sun*, 29 April 1900.

11   Kalgoorlie Police Court minute book, 1895–1922, J. S. Battye Library, Perth.

12   Mrs A. H. Garnsey, *Scarlet Pillows: An Australian Nurse's Tales from Long Ago*, Hesperian Press, Carlisle, 1984, pp. 77–81.

13   R. Davidson, 'Prostitution in Perth and Fremantle and on the Eastern Goldfields, 1895–1939', Masters thesis, The University of Western Australia, Nedlands, 1981, pp. 25–6.

14   *The Sunday Times*, 3 September 1899.

15   *The Kalgoorlie Miner*, 20 March 1903.

16   ibid.

17   N. King, *Daughters of Midas*, Hesperian Press, Carlisle, 1988, pp. 87–90.

18   ibid., p. 90.

19   ibid., pp. 75–6; *The Sun*, 24 July 1903.

20   *The Kalgoorlie Miner*, 28 March 1994, p. 1.

21   G. Casey & T. Mayman, *The Mile that Midas Touched*, Rigby, Adelaide, 1968, p. 142.

22   *The Sun*, 19 February 1899.

23   Letters of E. Cam Deland, typescript in Battye Library, Perth, p. 6.

24   *The Sun*, 8 April 1900, p. 3.

25   *The Sunday Times*, 12 November 1905, p. 12.

26   *The Sun*, 15, 29 April 1900.

27   ibid., 16 July 1904.

28   ibid., 29 April 1900.

29   ibid., 20 May 1900, p. 1.

30   ibid., 31 March 1907; *The Sunday Times*, 31 March 1907.

31   See M. Henry, *Prisoner of History: Aspasia of Miletus and her Biographical Tradition*, Oxford University Press, 1995; and S. Pomeroy, *Goddesses, Whores, Wives and Slaves: Women in Classical Antiquity*, Pimlico, London, 1994.

32   *The Sunday Times*, 31 March 1907.

33   A. Atkinson, *Asian Immigrants to Western Australia, 1829–1901*, University of Western Australia Press, Nedlands, 1988.

34   *The Mirror*, 9 April 1949, p. 1.

35   Town Clerk's Correspondence Files with the Central Board of Health (9/37–12/50) and Semi-private Correspondence (12/44–12/49); also Perth City Council Health Committee minutes, meeting 7 December 1951, p. 368.

36   *The Mirror*, 9 April 1949, p. 1.

37   *The Sunday Times*, 17 March 1901.

38   R. Pascoe & F. Thomson, *In Old Kalgoorlie*, Western Australian Museum, Perth, 1989, pp. 197–8.

39   Garnsey, *Scarlet Pillows*, p. 65.

40   *The Kalgoorlie Miner*, 4 August 1896.

41   *The West Australian*, 1 September 1898.

42   *The Sun*, 9 July 1899.

43   *The Sunday Times*, 8 May 1904, p. 5.

44   *The West Australian*, 1, 9 September 1898.

45   King, *Daughters*, pp. 81–2.

CHAPTER 3—CONTAINING THE 'SOCIAL EVIL' IN KALGOORLIE

1   Mrs A. H. Garnsey, *Scarlet Pillows: An Australian Nurse's Tales from Long Ago*, Hesperian Press, Carlisle, 1984, p. 65.

2   Kalgoorlie Municipal Council minute book, vol. 10, 15 April 1901 – 18 August 1902, pp. 165–6.

3   ibid., pp. 173–5.

4   Certificate of Title for 181 Hay Street, DLI, Midland.

5   Department of Land Surveys, *Townsite of Kalgoorlie*, 16 July 1897, J. S. Battye Library, Perth.

6   Kalgoorlie Municipal Council minute book, vol. 13, 22 May 1905 – 30 May 1906, pp. 7–8.

7   R. Davidson, 'Prostitution in Perth and Fremantle and on the Eastern Goldfields, 1895–1939', Masters thesis, The University of Western Australia, Nedlands, 1981.

8   Kalgoorlie Municipal Council minute book, vol. 14, 5 June 1906 – 17 June 1907, p. 36.

9   ibid., p. 45.

10   ibid., p. 144.

11   Kalgoorlie Municipal Council, minute book, vol. 15, 1 July 1907 – 22 December 1908, p. 103.

12   Davidson, 'Prostitution'.

13   *The Sunday Times*, 26 September 1909, p. 12.

14   Western Australian Parliamentary Debates, 1897, vol. 2, p. 1853, cited in Davidson, 'Prostitution'.

15   Davidson, 'Prostitution', pp. 67, 72.

16   ibid., p. 44.

17   Author's interview with Lorna Mitchell, 28 February 1995.

18   Author's interview with Olga Dawes, 28 February 1995.

19   Author's interview with Joy Kenneally, 2 March 1995.

20   Author's interview with Mary Lardi, 3 March 1995.

21   Author's interview with Spud, 10 November 1995.

22   Author's interview with Johnno, 20 November 1995.

23   ibid.

24   Author's interview with Frank Stevens, 29 November 1995.

25   Perth City Council Health Committee meeting minutes, 7 December 1951, p. 368; 18 January 1952, p. 377.

26   Perth City Council city building surveyor's memo to the acting town clerk dated 13 May 1952.

27   *The Mirror*, 10 May 1952.

28   Frank Stevens, 29 November 1995.

29   M. McKernon, *All In! Australia during the Second World War*, Nelson, Melbourne, 1983, p. 186.

30   Author's interview with the Red Dean, 11 November 1995.

31   McKernon, *All In!*, pp. 187–8.

32   ibid., p. 162.

33   ibid., pp. 192, 254.

34   The Red Dean, 11 November 1995.

35   Author's interview with Shirley and Norm Green, 12 May 2001.

CHAPTER 4—HAY STREET AND THE LONG ARM OF THE LAW

1   Drawn from J. Norris, *Final Report of the Royal Commission into Matters Surrounding the Administration of the Law Relating to Prostitution*, WA Government Press, Perth, 1976.

2   Author's interview with Val, 23 February 1995.

3   Author's interview with Judy, 17 November 1995.

4   Author's interview with Rita, 13 November 1995.

5   ibid.

6   Author's interview with Irene, 18 March 1997.

7   Val, 23 February 1995.

8   Author's interview with Elma, 11 October 1999.

9   ibid.

10   Val, 23 February 1995.

11 Author's interview with Rose, 23 October 1999.
12 Author's interview with Leslie, 29 March 1995.
13 Author's interview with John Bowler, 7 December 1995.
14 Val, 23 February 1995.
15 P. Blyth, *Gold Fever and Other Diseases: The Life and Rhymes of a Ten Quid Immigrant*, self-published, Salmon Gums, 1993.
16 Rose, 23 October 1999.
17 ibid.
18 Val, 23 February 1995.
19 Judy, 17 November 1995.
20 Blyth, *Gold Fever*.
21 Rita, 13 November 1995.
22 ibid.
23 Judy, 17 November 1995.
24 Val, 23 February 1995.
25 Judy, 17 November 1995.
26 Rita, 13 November 1995.
27 Judy, 17 November 1995.
28 ibid.
29 ibid.
30 ibid.
31 Author's interview with Johnno, 20 November 1995.
32 Val, 23 February 1995.
33 Rita, 13 November 1995.
34 ibid.
35 ibid.
36 ibid.
37 Elma, 11 October 1999.
38 Val, 23 February 1995.
39 Certificate of Title vol. 664/fol. 125, DLI, Midland.
40 Val, 23 February 1995.
41 Certificate of Title vol. 664/fol. 125, DLI.
42 Elma, 11 October 1999.
43 ibid.
44 ibid.
45 ibid.
46 Certificate of Title vol. 1235/fol. 245, DLI.
47 Elma, 11 October 1999.
48 Rita, 13 November 1995.
49 Judy, 17 November 1995.
50 Author's interview with George Williams, 14 May 2004.
51 *Claremont-Nedlands Post*, 16 November 1993, p. 3.
52 Rita, 13 November 1995.
53 ibid.
54 *Claremont-Nedlands Post*, 30 November 1993, p. 7.
55 Certificate of Title vol. 1235/fol. 245, caveat no. A337676, 22 October 1970, DLI.

56 Certificate of Title vol. 1036/fol. 277, DLI.

57 Elma, 11 October 1999.

58 Val, 23 February 1995.

59 Rita, 13 November 1995.

60 *Love in Limbo*, 1991, Palm Beach Pictures (WA Pty Ltd) and the Australian Film Finance Corporation, written by John Cundill, produced by David Elfick & Nina Stevenson.

61 Judy, 17 November 1995.

62 Author's interview with Allan Young, 17 November 1995.

63 ibid.

64 ibid.

65 Val, 23 February 1995.

66 Judy, 17 November 1995.

67 Author's interview with Ray Delbridge, 11 November 1995.

68 Allan Young, 17 November 1995.

69 A. N. Bingley, *On the Game*, self-published, Doubleview, 1992, p. 85.

70 Certificate of Title vol. 664/fol. 125, DLI, Midland.

71 Author's interview with Dan Collins, (former) Manager, Policy and Standards, DLI.

72 Bingley, *Game*, pp. 87–8.

73 Johnno, 20 November 1995.

74 The Royal Commission into Matters Surrounding the Administration of the Law Relating to Prostitution, transcript kindly made available by Dorrie and Kim Flatman, p. 2194.

75 Jack Hocking, oral history interview, conducted by Chris Jeffery, June 1976, J. S. Battye Library, Perth.

76 M. Winter, *Prostitution in Australia: A Sociological Study Prepared by a Qualified Research Team under the Supervision of Marcel Winter*, Purtaboi Publishing, Balgowlah, 1976, pp. 20–3.

77 ibid., p. 24.

78 Transcript of the Royal Commission, p. 2200.

79 Rita, 13 November 1995; Judy, 17 November 1995; Irene, 18 March 1997.

80 Rita, 13 November 1995.

81 Irene, 18 March 1997.

82 ibid.

83 *The West Australian*, 4 May 1978, p. 3; 5 May 1978, p. 4.

84 ibid., 16 July 1978, p. 4.

CHAPTER 5—BUSINESS AS USUAL: MADAMS' STORIES

1 Author's interview with Irene, 18 March 1997.

2 ibid.

3 ibid.

4 ibid.

5 ibid.

6 ibid.

7   ibid.
8   ibid.
9   ibid.
10   ibid.
11   ibid.
12   *The West Australian*, 24 June 1975.
13   ibid., 24 July 1975.
14   J. Norris, *Final Report of the Royal Commission into Matters Surrounding the Administration of the Law Relating to Prostitution*, WA Government Press, Perth, 1976.
15   J. Edwards, *Prostitution and Human Rights: A WA Case Study*, Human Rights Commission, Canberra, 1986.
16   Irene, 18 March 1997.
17   *The Kalgoorlie Miner*, 3 July 1984, p. 1.
18   Irene, 18 March 1997.
19   Author's interview with Rose, 23 October 1999.
20   Author's interview with John Bowler, 7 December 1995.
21   *The Kalgoorlie Miner*, 3 July 1984, p. 1.
22   ibid., 5 July 1984, p. 1.
23   Irene, 18 March 1997.
24   *The West Australian*, 9 August 1984, p. 15.
25   Author's interview with Abbey, 4 April 1995.
26   ibid.
27   ibid.
28   ibid.
29   ibid.
30   ibid.
31   ibid.
32   ibid.
33   ibid.
34   ibid.
35   Author's interview with Mary-Anne Kenworthy, 22 March 1997.
36   ibid.; confirmed in Certificate of Title vol. 11/fol. 201A, caveat E002041, DLI, Midland.
37   Mary-Anne Kenworthy, 22 March 1997.
38   ibid.
39   ibid.
40   ibid.
41   Abbey, 4 April 1995.
42   Mary-Anne Kenworthy, 22 March 1997.
43   ibid.
44   ibid.
45   Abbey, 4 April 1995.
46   Mary-Anne Kenworthy, 22 March 1997.
47   ibid.
48   Irene, 18 March 1997.
49   *The Kalgoorlie Miner*, 7 September 1991, p. 9.

50   ibid., 20 February 1992, p. 3.
51   ibid., 7 September 1991, p. 9.
52   ibid., 20 February 1992, p. 3.
53   ibid., 27 August 1991, p. 3.
54   ibid.
55   ibid., 19 July 1991, p. 3.
56   Community Panel on Prostitution, *Final Report of the Community Panel on Prostitution*, WA Government Press, Perth, 1990.
57   City of Kalgoorlie-Boulder submission (copy made available to the author).
58   ibid.
59   *The Kalgoorlie Miner*, 17 November 1990.
60   Mary-Anne Kenworthy, 22 March 1997.
61   Author's interview with Taylor, 30 November 1995.
62   Author's interview with Leigh Varis-Beswick, 21 November 1995.
63   ibid.
64   ibid.
65   ibid.
66   Mary-Anne Kenworthy, 22 March 1997.
67   Taylor, 30 November 1995.
68   Leigh Varis-Beswick, 21 November 1995.
69   ibid.
70   ibid.
71   *The Kalgoorlie Miner*, 29 June 1992.
72   ibid., 7 April 1992.

CHAPTER 6—FORESHADOWING THE END OF AN ERA

1   C. Smith (playwright), *The Starting Stalls*, Effie Crump Theatre, 1994.
2   *The West Australian*, 4 February 1994.
3   SIERA, *Working for a Living*, West Perth, 1994.
4   Performance of *The Starting Stalls* by Effie Crump Theatre, Perth, 9 February 1994.
5   *The Sunday Times*, 30 January 1994, p. 9.
6   ibid.
7   *The West Australian Weekend Magazine*, 29 January 1994.
8   *The Kalgoorlie Miner*, 5 February 1994.
9   ibid.
10   ibid.
11   ibid., 26 October 1994, p. 3.
12   *The West Australian*, 8 June 1994, p. 3.
13   ibid., 12 January 1994.
14   ibid., 8 June 1994, p. 3.
15   Stella Strong, submission to the City of Kalgoorlie-Boulder, July 1994.
16   ibid.
17   ibid.
18   Author's interview with April, 31 March 1995.

19   ibid.
20   ibid.
21   ibid.
22   ibid.
23   ibid.
24   ibid.
25   ibid.
26   ibid.
27   *The Kalgoorlie Miner*, 4 April 1992.
28   Author's on-site observations, February–April 1995.
29   Confirmed in the author's interviews with Taylor, 30 November 1995, and Mary at Questa Casa, 1 April 1995.
30   Taylor, 30 November 1995.
31   ibid.
32   ibid.
33   Mary, 1 April 1995.
34   Author's interview with Phillipa, 1 April 1995.

Chapter 7—The stormy demise of traditional Containment

1   Author's interview with Detective Sergeant Brian Cunningham, 3 March 1995.
2   ibid.
3   Author's interview with Phillipa, 1 April 1995.
4   Author's interview with Nigel Tapp, 1 March 1995.
5   *The Kalgoorlie Miner*, 25 January 1995.
6   ibid., p. 1.
7   Author's interview with (former) mayor, Ron Yuryevich, 3 April 1995.
8   ibid.
9   *The Kalgoorlie Miner*, 26 January 1995.
10   City of Kalgoorlie-Boulder, council meeting minutes, 30 January 1995.
11   ibid.
12   *The Kalgoorlie Miner*, 31 January 1995, p. 1; Phillipa, 1 April 1995.
13   *The West Australian*, 1 February 1995, p. 10.
14   ibid.
15   Nigel Tapp, 1 March 1995.
16   *The Kalgoorlie Miner*, 31 January 1995, p. 6.
17   ibid., 28 July 1995, p. 6.
18   ibid., 30 January 1995, p. 4.
19   ibid., 15 February 1995, p. 6.
20   ibid., 18 February 1995, p. 3.
21   ibid.
22   Author's interviews with madams and sex workers in Perth, 1992–97.
23   *The Kalgoorlie Miner*, 18 February 1995, p. 3.
24   Board of management meetings at SIERA, 1994–95.
25   ibid.
26   *The Kalgoorlie Miner*, 18 February 1995.

27   Author's interview with Tarna Bulman of SIERA, 17 March 1997.
28   *The Australian*, 23 February 1995, p. 11.
29   ibid.
30   ibid.
31   Author's interview with April, 31 March 1995.
32   Author's interview with Leigh Varis-Beswick, 21 November 1995.
33   April, 31 March 1995.
34   *The Kalgoorlie Miner*, 3 March 1995.
35   *The Sunday Times*, 5 March 1995.
36   ibid.
37   ibid.
38   *The Kalgoorlie Miner*, 6 March 1995, p. 3.
39   Ron Yuryevich, 3 April 1995.
40   *The Kalgoorlie Miner*, 28 March 1995.
41   *The West Australian*, 8 April 1995.
42   ibid.
43   *The Kalgoorlie Miner*, 20 July 1995, p. 1.
44   Author's interview with Robert Hicks, 30 November 1995.
45   *The Kalgoorlie Miner*, 20 July 1995.
46   City of Kalgoorlie-Boulder, council meeting minutes, 24 July 1995, p. 312.
47   Author's interviews with Val, 23 February 1995; Judy, 17 November 1995;
      Rita, 13 November 1995; Abbey, 4 April 1995; Leigh, 21 November 1995;
      Mary-Anne Kenworthy, 22 March 1997; Spud, 10 November 1995; Ray
      Delbridge, 11 November 1995.
48   ibid.
49   *The Kalgoorlie Miner*, 26 July 1995, p. 1.
50   City of Kalgoorlie-Boulder, council meeting minutes, 24 July 1995.
51   Council submission including public survey results, made available by WA Police
      Minister Kevin Prince, Perth.

CHAPTER 8—THE POLITICS OF NEW CONTAINMENT

1   Author's survey of workers employed at 181 Hay Street, November 1995.
2   Author's interview with Natassia, 14 November 1995.
3   ibid.
4   Author's interview with Taylor, 30 November 1995.
5   Author's interview with Robbie, 11 October 1999.
6   ibid.
7   Author's interview with Andy, 18 November 1995.
8   ibid.
9   ibid.
10   *The Kalgoorlie Miner*, 14 November 1995, p. 1.
11   Australian Labor Party, *Decriminalising Prostitution* (discussion paper), Australian
      Labor Party (WA Branch), November 1995.
12   E. McKewon, *Certificate of Professional Compliance Proposal*, self-published, Perth,
      1995.

13 *The Kalgoorlie Miner*, 14 November 1995, p. 1.
14 ibid., 16 November 1995, p. 5.
15 Author's observations, public debate on prostitution law reform in Western Australia, November 1995.
16 *The Kalgoorlie Miner*, 30 November 1995, p. 1; *The West Australian*, 30 November 1995, p. 28.
17 *The Kalgoorlie Miner*, 30 November 1995, pp. 1, 3.
18 Author's observations at 181 Hay Street, Kalgoorlie, 1995.
19 *The Kalgoorlie Miner*, 11 September 1996, p. 1.
20 Industrial Relations Court of Australia, *Western Australia District Registry's Minute of Orders, WI 2523*, 1996.
21 ibid.
22 ibid.
23 ibid.
24 ibid.
25 Drawn from ibid.
26 ibid.
27 ibid.
28 ibid.
29 ibid.
30 ibid.
31 ibid.
32 *The Kalgoorlie Miner*, 11 September 1996, p. 1.
33 Author's interview with Mary-Anne Kenworthy, 22 March 1997.
34 *The West Australian*, 16 December 1995, 31 May 1996.
35 ibid., 1 June 1996, p. 2.
36 Author's enquiries at local bus tour companies in Kalgoorlie-Boulder.
37 Author's observations, Goldrush Tours bus tour, Kalgoorlie, 30 November 1995.
38 Author's interview with Madison, 28 November 1995.
39 Taylor, 30 November 1995.

CHAPTER 9—SCARLET WOMEN IN THE NEW MILLENNIUM

1 E. McKewon, 'Historical overview', *Proceedings of Public Forum on Prostitution Law Reform* (held at the University of Western Australia in October 1995), self-published, Perth, 1995.
2 West Poll, *The West Australian*, 29 June 1999, p. 7.
3 *The West Australian*, 14 April 2000, p. 5.
4 *The Kalgoorlie Miner*, 25 October 1999.
5 ibid., 7 December 1999.
6 *The West Australian*, 19 November 1999.
7 ibid., 9 November 1999.
8 ibid., 4 December 1999.
9 *The Kalgoorlie Miner*, 4 December 1999.
10 ibid., 6 December 1999.
11 *The West Australian*, 8 December 1999.

12   ibid., 26 November 1999.
13   ibid., 30 November 1999.
14   ibid., 27 November 2001, p. 9.
15   Western Australian Industrial Relations Commission, case 04215, 2001.
16   *The West Australian*, 22 November 2002, p. 12.
17   ibid., 23 November 2002, p. 42.
18   ibid.
19   ibid., 27 November 2002, p. 4.
20   Michelle Roberts, *Hansard*, 12 May 1999, p. 8238.
21   *The West Australian*, 30 November 2002, pp. 1, 7.
22   ibid., 30 November 2002, p. 7.
23   ibid., pp. 1, 7.
24   ibid., 24 January 2004, p. 14.
25   ibid.
26   See, for example, *The Sunday Times*, 1 June 2003, p. 15; and *The West Australian*, 28 July 2003, p. 14.
27   See, for example, *The Australian*, 10 December 2003, Higher Education supplement, p. 29.
28   *The West Australian*, 22 October 1999, 28 March 2001.

Bibliography

BOOKS, JOURNAL ARTICLES

Atkinson, A., *Asian Immigrants to Western Australia, 1829–1901*, University of Western Australia Press, Nedlands, 1988.

Best, M. (ed.), *A Lost Glitter: Letters between South Australia and the WA Goldfields 1895–97*, Wakefield Press, Adelaide, 1986.

Bingley, A. N., *On the Game*, self-published, Doubleview, Western Australia, 1992.

Blainey, G., *The Golden Mile*, Allen & Unwin, Sydney, 1993.

Blyth, P., *Gold Fever and Other Diseases: The Life and Rhymes of a Ten Quid Immigrant*, self-published, Salmon Gums, Western Australia, 1993.

Casey, G. & Mayman, T., *The Mile that Midas Touched*, Rigby, Adelaide, 1968.

Daniels, K. (ed.), *So Much Hard Work*, Fontana/Collins, Sydney, 1984.

Davidson, Raelene, 'Dealing with the "social evil": Prostitution and the police in Perth and on the Eastern Goldfields, 1895–1924', in Daniels, K., *So Much Hard Work*, Fontana/Collins, Sydney, 1984.

Davidson, Ron, *High Jinks at the Hot Pool*, Fremantle Arts Centre Press, Fremantle, Western Australia, 1994.

Frances, R. & Scates, B., *Women at Work in Australia from the Gold Rushes to World War II*, Cambridge University Press, Cambridge, 1993.

Garnsey, A. H., *Scarlet Pillows: An Australian Nurse's Tales from Long Ago*, Hesperian Press, Carlisle, Western Australia, 1984.

Kalgoorlie Auxiliary of the Australasian Institute of Mining and Metallurgy, *Staking Our Claim: One Hundred Years of Women on the Goldfields*, Kalgoorlie, 1992.

King, N., *Colourful Tales of the Western Australian Goldfields*, Rigby, Adelaide, 1980.

—— *Daughters of Midas*, Hesperian Press, Carlisle, Western Australia, 1988.

May, R., *The Goldrushes: From California to the Klondike*, W. Luscombe, London, 1977.

McKernon, M., *All In! Australia during the Second World War*, Nelson, Melbourne, 1983.

Otis, L., *Prostitution in Medieval Society: The History of an Urban Institution in Languedoc*, University of Chicago Press, Chicago, 1985.

Pascoe, R. & Thomson, F., *In Old Kalgoorlie*, Western Australian Museum, Perth, 1989.

Raeside, J., *Golden Days*, Colour Type Press, Perth, 1929.

Reid, A., *Those Were the Days*, Hesperian Press, Carlisle, Western Australia, 1986.

Sissons, D. C. S., 'Karayuki-San: Japanese prostitutes in Australia, 1887–1916', *Historical Studies*, vol. 17, nos 68, 69, Australian National University, Canberra, 1977.

Stannage, C. T., *A New History of Western Australia*, University of Western Australia Press, Nedlands, 1981.

Whittington, V., *Gold and Typhoid: Two Fevers*, University of Western Australia Press, Nedlands, 1988.

REPORTS, STUDIES, THESES

Community Panel on Prostitution, *Final Report of the Community Panel on Prostitution*, WA Government Press, Perth, 1990.

Davidson, Raelene, 'Prostitution in Perth and Fremantle and on the Eastern Goldfields: 1895–1939', unpublished Masters thesis, The University of Western Australia, 1981.

Edwards, J., *Prostitution and Human Rights: A WA Case Study*, Human Rights Commission, Canberra, 1986.

Norris, J., *Final Report of the Royal Commission into Matters Surrounding the Administration of the Law Relating to Prostitution*, WA Government Press, Perth, 1976.

Winter, M., *Prostitution in Australia: A Sociological Study Prepared by a Qualified Research Team under the Supervision of Marcel Winter*, Purtaboi Publishing, Balgowlah, New South Wales, 1976.

Personal accounts

Cowles, M., *Diary of Mrs Mary Cowles, 1896–1897*, J. S. Battye Library, Perth.

Deland, E. Cam, letters, typescript, J. S. Battye Library, Perth.

Hocking, J., oral history interview conducted by Chris Jeffery, June 1976, Library Board of Western Australia, J. S. Battye Library, Perth

Archives

City of Kalgoorlie-Boulder, minutes of council meetings held on 30 January 1995 (p. 4300), 13 March 1995 (p. 5384), 24 July 1995 (pp. 311, 472–4).

Kalgoorlie Roads Board, minute book, vol. 1 (14 January 1898 – 1 December 1899).

Kalgoorlie Municipal Council, minute books, vol. 10 (15 April 1901 – 18 August 1902), vol. 11 (1 September 1902 – 14 March 1904), vol. 12 (28 March 1904 – 8 May 1905), vol. 13 (22 May 1905 – 30 May 1906), vol. 14 (5 June 1906 – 17 June 1907), vol. 15 (1 July 1907 – 22 December 1908).

Western Australian Directory, 'Towns—Kalgoorlie', 1903, 1910.

Western Australian Police File, 'Brothels in Perth and Kalgoorlie—General File', c. 1950–75, Archive File 2180/58, J. S. Battye Library, Perth.

Newspapers, magazines, newsletters

The Australian.

Claremont-Nedlands Post.

The Coolgardie Pioneer.

Daily News.

Goldfields Magazine (City of Kalgoorlie-Boulder).

The Illustrated London News.

The Kalgoorlie Miner.

The Mirror.

Nation.

New Statesman and Society.

Subiaco Post.

The Sun.

The Sunday Times.

The T'othersider.

The West Australian.

The West Australian Weekend Magazine.

Working for a Living (newsletter, SIERA).

Your City (newsletter, City of Kalgoorlie-Boulder).

Index